LINDLEY J. STILES
Professor of Education for Interdisciplinary Studies
Northwestern University
ADVISORY EDITOR TO DODD, MEAD & COMPANY

EDUCATION AND THE NEW TEACHER

EDUCATION

&

THE NEW TEACHER

B. J. CHANDLER
Northwestern University
DANIEL POWELL
University of Illinois at Chicago Circle
WILLIAM R. HAZARD
Northwestern University

DODD, MEAD & COMPANY
NEW YORK   TORONTO   1971

EDITOR'S INTRODUCTION

Education and the New Teacher offers a reliable, comprehensive, and sensitive introduction to education as a professional field—and as an area of social concern as well as of intellectual interest. In a stimulating and easily readable style it provides an overview of the processes and performance of teaching and of some of the institutions—in this case, elementary and secondary schools—in which teachers practice their profession. In-depth analyses are made of the personal characteristics and professional skills that one needs to be successful in the various roles that modern teachers assume. In addition, to learn about education, to choose teaching or other kinds of educational work as a professional field, the authors believe, requires a penetrating examination of the environmental ingredients that shape education as a social, economic, and political force. How one responds to the issues and controversies that are constantly interacting with teachers and schools is seen as a vital element in developing interest in the field and preparing for teaching as a career.

Keyed to conditions as they are and, also, to the changes that are taking place in schools, this book about and for the new teacher is fresh and up-to-date. It brings relevance to the study of education in a number of significant ways. First of all, it presents a candid analysis of the modern day professional life of teachers in a society in ferment. It pulls no punches: it does not gloss over problems of professional practice, nor does it hesitate to highlight the deep satisfactions and personal rewards that work in the field of education can bring. The assumption is that the reader will want the facts—both positive and negative. In a scholarly manner the authors have brought historical perspective to bear on the conditions that currently exist in elementary and secondary schools and have presented sound interpretations of the impact that contemporary social forces are having on institutional traditions. The effect is an exciting invitation to study about and to prepare for work in the field of education—for anyone sensitive to social needs and dedicated to professional service that can make a difference in the lives of young people.

The senior author of *Education and the New Teacher,* Dean B. J. Chandler of Northwestern's School of Education, is nationally known for his creative ideas concerning the preparation of new teachers. He is the author of a number of books, including a forerunner of this volume, *Education and the Teacher,* and editor of a key pioneering book, *Education in Urban Society.* Daniel Powell, of the University of Illinois at Chicago Circle, has the distinction of being the first clinical professor in the nation, in which position he pioneered the techniques of teaching teachers to teach while teaching high school students to learn. He has been associated with a number of textbooks in the field of history as author, contributor, and critic reader. Dr. William R. Hazard brings a unique background to the field of teacher education. He is an artist; he is trained as a lawyer and has practiced law; finally, he holds a Ph.D. degree in educational administration and teaches courses in this field. Dr. Hazard is nationally known for his leadership in innovative teacher-training programs, including the Clinical and Tutorial Plan and the Training of Teachers of Teachers Project at Northwestern University. He, too, has written extensively about the preparation of teachers.

LINDLEY J. STILES

PREFACE

THE world of the new teacher of the 1970's is drastically different from the world familiar to most of us who have helped to educate them. Teachers for this decade will deal with problems unfamiliar to their mentors and, indeed, to thousands of established members of the profession operating outside areas of tension and conflict. The social revolution which has overtaken so many urban communities has affected curriculum, school organization, community relations—the very nature of the teaching-learning process itself. Thus, as decentralization, community control, identification and diversification of roles, and greater accountability increase, old ground rules become obsolete.

The preparation of teachers, however, is still a key factor in the survival of American public schools. But it can no longer be exclusively entrusted to colleges and universities which have perpetuated simplistic and traditional approaches to teacher education. Time-honored autonomies serving as barriers to change must give way to partnerships involving schools, interested and concerned citizens, and government. To be prepared for teaching in the 1970's the new teacher needs more than the college of education faculty can offer him. Knowledge, wisdom, and expertise must be elicited from any and all quarters.

This volume attempts to *explore* the major issues in teacher education at an early point in the student's academic life. Few ready-made solutions, therefore, will be found in these pages. Believing that factual statements rarely resolve educational debates, we have tried to maintain open inquiry through a questioning posture and unclosed discussions. The relationships, judgments, and interpretations of multifaceted issues require human sensitivity and compromise beyond the bare facts.

We have attempted to approach teacher problems honestly and forthrightly. In our judgment, little is gained by presenting an unreal world to prospective teachers. Many of them will work and perhaps live in racially tense communities. They will confront militant students, critical community leaders, and indifferent colleagues. They will struggle to translate the world's store of knowledge into relevant learning for apathetic students. They may be involved in teacher-board conflicts and professional hassles concerning very mundane questions. Their world will change rapidly; these new teachers must also be ready to change with the times.

Our hope is that this book will trigger thought and discussion. If the material in it encourages education students to dig further and think constructively about the issues we have raised, the authors will have succeeded in their prime objective. A book is, of course, only a point of departure for personal curiosity and investigation. Perhaps our readers will be led to discover more important truths than we, ourselves, have learned. Teachers of the 1970's must deal effectively with complex, interrelated social forces. Whether we find the structures and processes to accommodate these powerful forces may well decide the continued existence of public education.

B. J. CHANDLER
DANIEL POWELL
WILLIAM R. HAZARD

CONTENTS

TABLES

CONTENTS

xi

FIGURES

EDUCATION AND THE NEW TEACHER

INTRODUCTION

EDUCATION AND SOCIETY IN CRISIS

IN NO other period of American history has education assumed a more important role than at the present; in no other period of American history have the schools been subjected to closer examination. However, since to a great extent the schools in the United States reflect the society in which they exist, it should not be surprising that they suffer from the same problems as society at large.

After World War II, for example, when problems of demobilization, conversion to peacetime industry, mushrooming and transient populations, insufficient housing, and shortage of goods were among the nation's many concerns, the educational system felt the impact of postwar shock as much as any other American institution. Characteristic of the inevitable lag between societal needs and institutional response, the schools fell behind in their ability to serve a greatly increased and diverse clientele.

By 1958 the pressure of the post-World War II baby boom was apparent. School enrollments continued to skyrocket, but there was no parallel growth in the supply of teachers and necessary facilities. By 1968, as seen in Figure 1, more than 98 percent of the children eligible to enroll were attending elementary and secondary schools.

FIGURE 1. 1968 SCHOOL ENROLLMENT

The Bureau of the Census, through its Current Population Survey on school enrollment conducted annually in October, reports that 57.5 million persons 5 to 34 years old were enrolled in school in the United States in the fall of 1968. This enrollment by level of school was as follows: kindergarten, 2.8 million; elementary school (grades 1 to 8), 33.8 million; high school (grades 9 to 12), 14.1 million; and college, 6.8 million.

Compared with the Census survey conducted in October 1960, the total school enrollment by 1968 increased 11.2 million, or 24.3 percent, during the eight-year period. The population increase of persons 5 to 34 years of age for this period was 13.8 million, or 16.8 percent. The tabulation below shows the population, the number enrolled, and the percent enrolled by age groups between 5 and 34 years for 1960 and 1968, as well as the percent of increase in population and in the number enrolled in school for the eight-year period 1960 to 1968. The chart shows the percent of the population enrolled by age groups.

—Neva A. Carlson, specialist in educational statistics.

PERCENT OF THE POPULATION 5 TO 34 YEARS OLD ENROLLED IN SCHOOL,
BY AGE: UNITED STATES, OCTOBER 1960 AND 1968

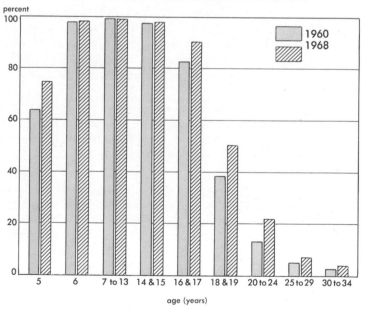

From U.S. Department of Commerce, Bureau of the Census, Current Population Reports, Series P-20, Nos. 110 and 179; and unpublished data.

FIGURE 1. 1968 SCHOOL ENROLLMENT (CONTINUED)

Age	1960			1968			Percent of increase, 1960 to 1968, in—	
	Population	Number enrolled	Percent enrolled	Population	Number enrolled	Percent enrolled	Population	Number enrolled
5 years	4,023,000	2,561,000	63.7	4,095,000	3,067,000	74.9	1.8	19.8
6 years	3,956,000	3,877,000	98.0	4,168,000	4,097,000	98.3	5.4	5.7
7 to 13 years	25,744,000	25,621,000	99.5	28,876,000	28,620,000	99.1	12.2	11.7
14 and 15 years	5,768,000	5,641,000	97.8	7,719,000	7,564,000	98.0	33.8	34.1
16 and 17 years	5,573,000	4,601,000	82.6	7,265,000	6,554,000	90.2	30.4	42.4
18 and 19 years	4,733,000	1,817,000	38.4	6,585,000	3,317,000	50.4	39.1	82.6
20 to 24 years	10,330,000	1,350,000	13.1	13,974,000	2,988,000	21.4	35.3	121.3
25 to 29 years	10,423,000	514,000	4.9	12,391,000	863,000	7.0	18.9	67.9
30 to 34 years	11,499,000	278,000	2.4	10,726,000	417,000	3.9	−6.7	50.0
Total 5 to 34 years	82,049,000	46,259,000	56.4 (ave.)	95,799,000	57,487,000	60.0 (ave.)	16.8	24.3

NOTE: Because of rounding, detail may not add to totals.
From *American Education*, (U.S. Department of Health, Education, and Welfare, Office of Education) V, No. 8 (October 1969), p. 28 and back cover.

Accentuating the school crisis was the launching of Sputnik in 1957 by the Soviet Union. Justifiably or not, Americans immediately began to draw invidious comparisons between Soviet and American educational accomplishments, especially in science and mathematics. Criticism by important scholars led to a mood of national introspection. What was wrong with the schools and what should be done? Organization for change began at all levels, but especially significant was the role of the national government during the 1960's in providing funds for construction, creation of studies, and launching of new programs. Despite the traditional reluctance of Americans to invite federal intervention in education, the inability of local and state governments to handle their school problems seemed to demand unusual alternatives. The importance of maintaining an excellent school system was an overriding concern of Americans, who responded to leadership at all levels regarding this issue.

In January 1963, the late President John F. Kennedy reflected the sentiments of millions of his countrymen when in his special message to Congress on education he said: [1]

Education is the keystone in the arch of freedom and progress. Nothing has contributed more to the enlargement of this Nation's strength and opportunities than our traditional system of free, universal elementary and secondary education, coupled with widespread availability of college education.

For the individual, the doors to the schoolhouse, to the library and to the college lead to the richest treasures of our open society: to the power of knowledge—to the training and skills necessary for productive employment—to the wisdom, the ideals, and the culture which enrich life—and to the creative, self-disciplined understanding of society needed for good citizenship in today's changing and challenging world.

For the Nation, increasing the quality and availability of education is vital to both our national security and our domestic well-being. A free nation can rise no higher than the standards of excellence set in its schools and colleges.

The "standards of excellence" referred to by Kennedy in the early 1960's were indeed threatened by a number of develop-

[1] "Special Message to the Congress on Education," Document 43, January 29, 1963, *Public Papers* (1963), pp. 105–116.

ments. The problem of accommodating increased enrollments in the city and in the burgeoning suburbs became a primary concern. However, financing of building programs in the newer communities proceeded with greater ease than in the crowded cities. In the hope of furnishing their children with a better education, younger and more affluent citizens outside of the urban centers showed greater willingness to shoulder the bill. Thousands fled the cities, leaving a void which was often filled by migrants who were least able and least interested in underwriting good education. Thus, in the swelling inner-city ghettos the deterioration of educational standards was most evident.

Combined with the lack of physical facilities was the problem of school staffing. A critical teacher shortage developed extending from preschool through college. No amount of physical equipment, no program of curricular reform could compensate for insufficient and inadequate teachers. A sharp focus of attention was directed at this problem, which was translated into attempts to retain experienced teachers and recruit able newcomers. Teacher salaries and conditions of work became subjects of examination and change. Teacher education received a kind of critical appraisal heretofore unknown.

The teaching profession is still in the process of ferment. Nevertheless, tremendous strides have been made toward improvement of education. Prospective teachers today will find a career alive with exciting possibilities for immediate satisfaction and future fulfillment. Teaching is no longer a second choice or alternative. Only career-minded, seriously oriented individuals should become involved in a profession that has assumed top priority in our nation's program for progress. Former President Lyndon B. Johnson's request to Congress for passage of the historic Elementary and Secondary Education Act of 1965 is a dramatic indication of the new spirit. "If we are learning anything from our experience, we are learning that it is time for us to go to work, and the first work of these times and the first work of our society is education." [2]

No less emphasis on education has been displayed by Johnson's

[2] From speech made July 28, 1964. Cited in *American Education*, I (April 1965), 14.

successor, Richard M. Nixon. In his special message to the 91st Congress on education reform he said:

A new reality in American education can mark the beginning of an era of reform and progress for those who teach and those who learn. Our schools have served us nobly for centuries; to carry that tradition forward, the decade of the 1970's calls for thoughtful redirection to improve our ability to make up for the environmental deficiencies among the poor; for long-range provisions for financial support of schools; for more efficient use of the dollars spent on education; for structural reforms to accommodate new discoveries; and for enhancement of learning before and beyond the school.[3]

Finally, from James E. Allen, Jr., President Nixon's former Commissioner of Education, comes this statement of goals for the 1970's: [4]

To raise the level of American education throughout the country in order to prepare our children adequately for a more complex and demanding world than we have ever known; and

To make sure that *all* our children—poor as well as rich, black as well as white, slow learners as well as gifted students—receive the best education we can possibly give them.

Most important, a renewed respect for education and the teacher is evident everywhere. The "necessary revolution" to adapt education to a changing America—long called for by former Commissioner of Education Francis Keppel and others—is now under way.

These views of education help to explain why it has become the major business in the United States if judged by the number of individuals actively engaged in it. Moreover, the system is expanding rapidly as Figure 2 shows.

The need for drastic change in education, noted by prominent statesmen and eminent educators, has also been voiced by the great American public. For the first time in the history of the schools education has become a problem to which millions of American people have energetically addressed themselves: Witness the spirited contests taking place all over the country for election to school boards. Note the intervention of minority groups in

[3] Quoted in *New York Times,* March 4, 1970, p. 28.
[4] "Looking Forward to the Seventies," *Childhood Education,* XLVI, No. 1 (September–October 1969), 3.

FIGURE 2. OUR RAPIDLY EXPANDING EDUCATIONAL SYSTEM

Enrollment in educational institutions, by level: United States, 1959–60, 1969–70, and 1979–80

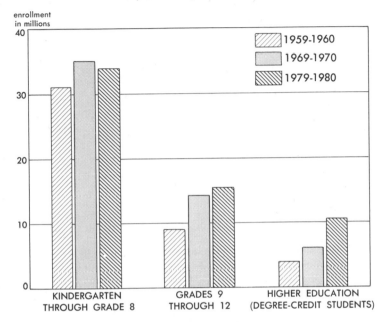

NOTE: Data are for the fall term of the school year.

SOURCE: Office of Education surveys; and estimates and projections of the Reference, Estimates, and Projections Branch, National Center for Educational Statistics, Office of Education.

From *American Education,* V, No. 8 (October, 1969), 24.

the affairs of inner-city school systems. Reflect on the extensive coverage given to such a question as school desegregation in the communications media. Undoubtedly, the education of the nation's youth is a central concern in the arena of American public affairs.

This volume is meant, first, for the teacher as an essential component in the educative process—that is, as a trained professional. A number of chapters are directed toward the teacher's personal development. It is meant, also, for the teacher as an informed, alert, and active citizen who appreciates the complexities of education beyond the particular concerns of pedagogy. Within these pages the new teacher of the 1970's will meet large and critical questions concerned with authority and governance in school systems, financing and administering education, and many other problems which extend beyond the classroom but inevitably help to shape the processes of teaching and learning.

SUGGESTED READINGS

Bell, Terrel H., *A Philosophy of Education for the Space Age*. New York: Exposition Press, 1962.

Blanshard, Brand, ed., *Education in the Age of Science*. New York: Basic Books, Inc., 1959.

Brameld, Theodore, *Education for the Emerging Age*. New York: Harper and Row, Publishers, 1965, Chaps. 1–3.

Conant, James B., *Shaping Educational Policy*. New York: McGraw-Hill Book Co., Inc., 1964.

Cremin, Lawrence A., *The Transformation of the School*. New York: Vintage Books, 1961, Chap. 9.

Elam, Stanley and William P. McLure, eds., *Educational Requirements for the 1970's*. Published for *Phi Delta Kappan*. New York: Frederick A. Praeger, Publishers, 1967.

Eurich, Alvin C., *Reforming American Education*. New York: Harper and Row, Publishers, 1969.

Goodman, Paul, *Compulsory Miseducation*. New York: Horizon Press, 1964.

Keppel, Francis, *The Necessary Revolution in America*. New York: Harper and Row, Publishers, 1966.

Meyer, Adolph E., *An Educational History of the American People*. New York: McGraw-Hill Book Co., 1967, Chap. 22.

O'Hara, William T., ed., *John F. Kennedy on Education*. New York: Teachers College Press, 1966.

Rippa, S. Alexander, *Education in a Free Society*. New York: David McKay Co., Inc., 1967, pp. 283–98.

Smith, Mortimer, ed., *A Decade of Comment on Education, 1955–1966*. Washington, D.C.: Council for Basic Education, 1966.

Thayer, V. T. and Martin Levit, *The Role of the School in American Society*, 2d ed. New York: Dodd, Mead & Co., 1966, Chap. 16.

1.

THE FEDERAL ROLE
IN EDUCATION

THE relationship between states and the federal government has been debated from the time the United States was founded. Education as a function of government has furnished some of the fuel for controversy inasmuch as the Constitution does not state which jurisdiction should control this vital area of American life. The Constitution, in Amendment 10, however, reserves to the states those "powers not delegated to the United States." It has been this provision which has furnished the basis for state support of education.

Though the states have jealously guarded this apparent autonomy, the national government has always kept a foot in the doorway, ready to chide, coerce, hearten, or nurture. The federal government assured itself of this not-too-clearly-bounded right in the Constitution (Article 1, Section 8, Clause 1): "The Congress shall have power to . . . provide for the . . . general welfare of the United States."

THE NORTHWEST ORDINANCES

Although the Founding Fathers included no specific reference to education in the Constitution written in 1787, the national government under the Articles of Confederation (1781–89) already was playing an active role in educational policy. The Northwest Ordinances passed by the Continental Congress in 1785 and 1787 provided for reserving portions of the public land for the benefit of schools. In each of the new states, provisions were made for setting aside acreage as well as for donating proceeds from the sale of public land as a source of funds for state universities. This land-grant policy was put into effect in 1802 when Ohio was admitted as a state. In 1806 the educational provisions of the Northwest Ordinance of 1787 were applied to the new state of Tennessee and later throughout the South and West, making educational land grants for new states a national policy. The grants of sections in townships for educational purposes were continued as new states were admitted, and to them were added additional funds or percentages of monies received from the sale of public lands in the states. These grants became a significant endowment for support of public schools and by 1960 totaled approximately one billion dollars. In 1962 alone, land-grant colleges and universities [1] received $678 million in federal funds, up 25 percent from fiscal 1961.

In this early period of federal activity from about 1792 to 1862, government policy followed a practice of attempting to promote general enlightenment by fostering elementary schools, academies, colleges, and universities. Until the mid-nineteenth century, the federal government placed no restrictions on the use of educational funds realized from land grants and other sources. In general, the schools developed systems based on the traditional academic curriculum—the three R's and the humanistic subjects. Little was offered in the practical trades or study of the sciences for application in industry and agriculture.

THE MORRILL ACT

This neglect of practical and scientific studies changed with the Morrill Act of 1862. As the country became a world leader in industrial and agricultural production, Congress saw a need for more practical, technical, and scientific studies to meet manpower needs. The Morrill Act channeled funds from the sale of public lands to a specific project: the founding of agricultural and mechanical arts colleges. By its provisions the federal government

[1] George Lind, *Statistics of Land-Grant Colleges and Universities* (Washington, D.C.: U.S. Dept. of Health, Education and Welfare, 1964), p. 10.

gave each state 30,000 acres for each of its representatives in Congress as an endowment fund. The importance of the Morrill Act was not only that it established a fund primarily for training of a vocational type, but it also made education available to a wider range of individuals, many of whom were not attracted to less pragmatic programs of collegiate education. The establishment of sixty-nine land-grant colleges throughout the country also helped provide outstanding institutions in areas where funds were not readily available for private endowment of comparable facilities.

With the Northwest Ordinance and the Morrill Act, the foundation of American national policy in education was set. Unlike its European counterparts in the nineteenth century, Congress exerted a conscious effort to minimize its influence on educational policy. All curricular matters, as well as supervision of the use of the land grants, were left to the states. However, the Morrill Acts of 1862 and 1890 did involve expenditures for stated purposes and required accounting for the money spent.

POST-CIVIL WAR TO SPUTNIK

The end of the Civil War marked the beginning of a new era of increasing demands for federal activity in education. Disruptive conditions in the postwar South, the increasing influx of immigrants, and the growing pains of the transition to an urban and industrial society brought repeated efforts from Congress to promote programs at the elementary and secondary levels. The Congress was not prepared in the 1880's, however, to pass legislation for reduction of illiteracy, although a number of bills were proposed. Yet during this period another program to aid the farm community, the Hatch Act, was passed in 1887, providing for agricultural experiment stations connected with the land-grant colleges. Economists have attributed the rising agricultural productivity of the United States in large measure to federal interest through such programs as the Morrill and Hatch Acts.[2]

[2] Theodore W. Schultz, "Agriculture and the Application of Knowledge," in *Look to the Future* (Battle Creek, Mich.: W. K. Kellogg Foundation, 1956), pp. 54–78.

Another important post-Civil War development in American education was the establishment of the Department of Education, forerunner of the present Office of Education. Created in 1867, this agency became the United States Bureau of Education in 1870 and was located in the Department of the Interior. In 1929, the Bureau became the United States Office of Education. In 1939, the Office of Education was transferred to the Federal Security Agency. Finally, in 1953, it was incorporated as one of the three major divisions of the Department of Health, Education, and Welfare, whose Secretary is a member of the President's Cabinet. A Commissioner of Education heads the Office of Education. Starting as merely a statistic-gathering agency, this federal office now provides vital national leadership in various fields of education. Among its important functions are the handling of educational funds appropriated by Congress and sponsoring of educational research conducted by universities.

During World War I the need for skilled workers prompted Congress to pass the Smith-Hughes Act (1917) to provide funds for secondary school courses in agriculture, home economics, and industrial education. A Federal Board for Vocational Education administered the act, which included the preparation of teachers in vocational subjects and grants-in-aid to be matched by the states. The Smith-Hughes Act provided for the greatest degree of federal control over use of funds up to that time.[3]

The Great Depression which began in 1929 brought a near collapse of public education as the states found themselves without funds. At that point, the federal government stepped in with outright grants which did not require matching funds. Two of the most significant programs of this era relating to education were the Civilian Conservation Corps (CCC) and the National Youth Administration (NYA).

The Civilian Conservation Corps, authorized by Congress in 1933, embraced the dual purpose of providing employment and vocational training for unemployed youth, as well as conserving and developing natural resources. Camps under the administration

[3] Hollis P. Allen, *The Federal Government and Education* (New York: McGraw-Hill Book Company, 1950), p. 73.

of the Army were organized for these purposes in the western United States mainly. The National Youth Administration involved an extensive student aid program principally in secondary schools and colleges. Thousands of students received direct federal grants-in-aid for work done in the institutions which they attended.[4]

Through the Works Progress Administration, during the depression period, the federal government improved educational opportunities by furnishing millions in funds for construction of school buildings. It also began a school lunch program which became a continuing feature of cooperation with local school districts.

The coming of World War II renewed and intensified federal interest in education. Responding to the need for training wartime workers, the Office of Education helped to prepare vast numbers of Americans, including rural youth, for industry. The Lanham Act of 1941 provided buildings and services in impacted plant areas unable to support greatly increased school populations. In this and in other legislation following the war the federal government appropriated large sums to areas affected by activities of the national government.[5] In the Servicemen's Readjustment Act, better known as the "G.I. Bill," billions were spent to provide assistance to veterans for continuing educational preparation. This legislation also had the important effect of helping institutions of higher learning expand as a result of greatly increased enrollments.

The Cold War and the unsettled international situation served to keep the federal government in active partnership with state and local school districts. The 1957 Sputnik launching, the first orbital flight in outer space, was a significant turning point in American education. Until this time there had been little support for long-range assistance by the federal government to increase the quality of education at all levels. Then, as Francis Keppel, former

[4] *Civilian Conservation Corps, the National Youth Administration and the Public Schools Educational Policies Commission* (Washington, D.C.: National Education Association, 1941).

[5] For an excellent treatment of this subject see I. M. Labovitz, *Aid for Federally Affected Schools* (Syracuse, N.Y.: Syracuse University Press, 1963).

Commissioner of Education, noted, Americans began to think of education as an investment rather than as consumption.[6]

THE POST-SPUTNIK REAPPRAISAL

The sense of national urgency that followed the Soviet space achievements played a decisive role in the passage of the 1958 National Defense Education Act (NDEA).[7] The major purpose of the act was to improve instruction in mathematics, science, engineering, and modern language on both the secondary and college levels. In addition, loans and fellowships were provided for college students. The most important outcome of the Sputnik "crisis," however, was the basic reevaluation of American education, especially on the elementary and secondary levels. Growing support arose for a comprehensive program to assist in the upgrading of instruction in all subjects. The Soviet challenge brought to light many serious problems confronting American education at mid-century.

First, the extension of universal public education to high school —and later to college—had made adequate financing by state and local governments extremely difficult. The "revolution" that began to take place at the turn of the century in the progressive era continued to sweep into contemporary America.[8] (High school enrollment from 1890 to 1940 doubled every decade, foreshadowing the predicament of the colleges today.) In addition, the effects of the stepped-up post-World War II birth rate were beginning to show and threatened to swamp the schools.

Second, there were wide regional differences in the quality and amount of education received. (See Table 1.) Inadequate education, reflected in school dropout rates, limitations on career

[6] Francis Keppel, *The Necessary Revolution in Education* (New York: Harper & Row, 1966).

[7] Sidney C. Sufrin, *Administering the National Defense Education Act* (Syracuse: Syracuse University Press, 1963).

[8] Good sources on the high school at the turn of the century are Lawrence A. Cremin, *Transformation of the School* (New York: Alfred A. Knopf, 1961) and Theodore R. Sizer, *Secondary Schools at the Turn of the Century* (New Haven: Yale University Press, 1964).

choices, and general economic and social malaise, was felt to be a luxury no state or country could afford.

Third, state tax resources were so unequal that poorer states could not provide funds to finance adequate educational programs. State appropriations per student were directly tied to individual income, and without federal assistance, many argued, there was little hope of raising the quality of education. (See Table 2.) It is interesting to note that Mississippi contributed a greater *percentage* of its personal income to education than many of the substantially wealthier states.

ELEMENTARY AND SECONDARY EDUCATION ACT

By the mid 1960's there was strong support for federal assistance to meet these problems. In 1965 Congress passed the Elementary and Secondary Education Act (ESEA) to begin a new era in American education. When President Johnson approved this legislation, he put into effect the most comprehensive program for education in American history. For the first year, Congress allotted $1.3 billion to meet a variety of specific educational needs.

The principal aim of the Act has been, under Title I, to upgrade the education of children in low income areas. The Southern rural states, long handicapped by inadequate tax resources, were to be major recipients of assistance. The criterion for aid has been the number of school-age children in each district from families with annual income of less than $2,000. The state departments of education receive funds from the Office of Education based on this formula for use, district by district, according to eligibility. Thus, needed funds are made available for urban slum schools in "wealthy" states. Each local education agency must propose its own plan for the use of the funds and must submit it to the state for approval.

The financial impact of the ESEA legislation was dramatic. For fiscal 1965 (year ending June 30, 1965), the year ESEA was enacted, $478 million went for elementary and secondary education; the next year, $1,646 million was spent from federal sources for

17

TABLE 1. ESTIMATED PUBLIC SCHOOL EXPENDITURES, 1969, AND
PERSONAL INCOME, 1967, BY STATES

(In millions of dollars, except as indicated. School data for year ending June 30)

STATE	CURRENT EXPENDITURES					Capital outlay	PER CAPITA		
	Total expenditures	Elementary and secondary schools	Other programs[1]	Average per pupil in average daily attendance: Total (dollars)	Rank		School expenditures[2] (dollars)	Personal income[3]: Amount (dollars)	Rank
U.S.	[4] 35,511	28,645	1,197	696	(X)	4,654	178	3,159	(X)
N.E.	1,908	1,652	22	747	(X)	198	167	3,503	(X)
Maine	143	122	4	567	36	14	147	2,657	34
N.H.	107	84	1	624	32	19	152	3,053	25
Vt.	82	63	(Z)	677	18	18	193	2,825	29
Mass.	885	778	11	748	12	88	162	3,541	9
R.I.	159	135	1	840	4	19	174	3,328	14
Conn.	532	470	6	826	5	40	180	3,969	1
M.A.	7,577	6,251	247	952	(X)	825	205	3,562	(X)
N.Y.	4,216	3,527	174	1,140	1	400	233	3,759	2
N.J.	1,352	1,119	15	852	3	175	191	3,668	5
Pa.	2,009	1,606	58	743	14	250	171	3,187	17
E.N.C.	7,032	5,645	162	687	(X)	1,018	178	3,395	(X)
Ohio	1,704	1,425	25	634	30	200	161	3,213	15
Ind.	965	718	14	635	29	225	191	3,196	16
Ill.	1,893	1,526	68	755	11	243	172	3,750	3
Mich.	1,647	1,300	43	665	[5] 21	240	188	3,396	12
Wis.[6]	823	676	13	787	7	110	195	3,156	18
W.N.C.	2,855	2,308	62	673	(X)	405	178	3,021	(X)
Minn.	812	656	9	767	9	114	223	3,116	20
Iowa	532	450	2	723	16	70	192	3,109	21
Mo.[6]	705	562	30	645	28	98	152	2,993	27
N. Dak.	103	83	1	585	35	16	164	2,487	40
S. Dak.	109	91	—	589	34	17	166	2,590	37
Nebr.	205	159	10	510	44	31	142	3,081	22
Kans.[6]	388	308	10	647	[5] 26	60	169	3,060	24
S.A.	4,782	3,853	110	597	(X)	715	159	2,759	(X)
Del.	118	87	(Z)	745	13	25	221	3,642	7
Md.	850	624	27	775	8	171	226	3,421	11
D.C.	172	123	13	920	(X)	36	213	4,123	(X)
Va.	738	590		609					

18

W. Va.	233	200	3	321	42	27	129	2,334	46
N.C.	676	565	27	505	45	72	132	2,439	43
S.C.	340	289	10	478	48	35	128	2,213	47
Ga.	618	537	9	530	39	57	135	2,541	39
Fla.	1,037	837	1	647	5 26	182	169	2,853	28
E.S.C.	1,577	1,352	34	482	(X)	149	120	2,248	(X)
Ky.	381	345	4	538	38	22	118	2,426	44
Tenn.	499	417	11	498	46	56	126	2,394	45
Ala.	407	341	2	432	50	53	114	2,163	48
Miss.	290	249	18	462	49	18	124	1,896	50
W.S.C.	2,780	2,258	16	541	(X)	418	145	2,608	(X)
Ark.	248	202	—	486	47	40	125	2,099	49
La.	610	505	1	632	31	85	164	2,456	42
Okla.	341	291	3	516	43	43	135	2,643	35
Tex.	1,582	1,260	12	526	41	250	144	2,744	32
Mt.	1,485	1,241	16	642	(X)	194	188	2,830	(X)
Mont.	142	123	4	761	10	12	205	2,765	31
Idaho	108	95	(Z)	559	37	11	154	2,575	38
Wyo.	68	59	—	715	17	8	216	3,002	26
Colo.	374	322	1	662	23	40	183	3,135	19
N. Mex.	210	173	2	676	19	32	209	2,477	41
Ariz.	285	247	2	648	5 24	29	171	2,720	33
Utah	202	150	5	527	40	42	195	2,604	36
Nev.	97	71	1	648	5 24	19	216	3,583	8
Pac.	5,515	4,084	528	681	(X)	733	215	3,589	(X)
Wash.	653	510	40	673	20	82	199	3,521	10
Oreg.	435	347	21	793	6	60	217	3,063	23
Calif.	4,189	3,041	461	665	5 21	550	217	3,665	6
Alaska	94	69	(Z)	987	2	22	343	3,738	4
Hawaii	144	118	5	724	15	19	185	3,331	13

— Represents zero.   X Not applicable.   Z Less than $500,000.

1 Includes expenditures for summer schools, adult education, community services, and community colleges and technical institutes under the jurisdiction of local boards of education.

2 Based on Bureau of the Census estimated resident population as of July 11, 1968. Source: Current Population Reports, Series P-25, No. 414.

3 Source: Office of Business Economics; Survey of Current Business, August 1968.

4 Includes interest on school debt, not shown separately.

5 The following States share the same rank: Calif. and Mich., 21; Ariz. and Nev., 24; Fla. and Kans., 26. In order to have the lowest rank equal to the number of States presented, the numbers 22, 25, and 27 are omitted.

6 School data exclude vocational schools not operated as part of the regular school system.

SOURCE: Dept. of Health, Education, and Welfare, Office of Education (except as noted); Fall 1968 Statistics of Public Schools. From U.S. Bureau of the Census, Statistical Abstract of the United States: 1969 (90th edition) (Washington, D.C., 1969), p. 116.

TABLE 2. PERSONAL INCOME, 1967, RELATED TO ESTIMATED EXPENDITURES FOR PUBLIC ELEMENTARY AND SECONDARY EDUCATION, BY STATE: 1967–68

State	Personal income		Total expenditures for public elementary and secondary education		Current expenditures for public elementary and secondary day schools	
	Total (in millions)	Per capita	Amount (in thousands)[1]	As a percent of personal income	Amount (in thousands)	As a percent of personal income
1	2	3	4	5	6	7
United States	$620,568	$3,137	[2] $31,511,051	5.08	[2] $25,361,193	4.09
Alabama	7,668	2,166	395,000	5.15	319,000	4.16
Alaska	987	3,629	83,000	8.41	60,000	6.08
Arizona	4,381	2,681	252,450	5.76	228,000	5.20
Arkansas	4,113	2,090	227,558	5.53	182,212	4.43
California	70,097	3,660	4,008,000	5.72	2,865,000	4.09
Colorado	6,094	3,086	361,973	5.94	296,473	4.86
Connecticut	11,306	3,865	458,350	4.05	400,000	3.54
Delaware	1,935	3,700	100,200	5.18	73,000	3.77
District of Columbia	3,453	4,268	[3]	[3]	[3]	[3]
Florida	16,765	2,796	944,532	5.63	680,355	4.06
Georgia	11,330	2,513	592,047	5.23	508,047	4.48
Hawaii	2,411	3,326	133,808	5.55	105,669	4.38
Idaho	1,823	2,608	101,409	5.56	86,809	4.76
Illinois	40,575	3,725	1,456,059	3.59	1,226,500	3.02
Indiana	16,205	3,241	860,200	5.31	665,000	4.10
Iowa	8,516	3,093	419,000	4.92	350,000	4.11
Kansas	6,846	3,009	326,000	4.76	275,500	4.02
Kentucky	7,612	2,387	350,975	4.61	302,000	3.97
Louisiana	8,954	2,445	589,400	6.58	482,000	5.38
Maine	2,549	2,620	128,500	5.04	105,500	4.14
Maryland	12,644	3,434	721,970	5.71	534,827	4.23
Massachusetts	18,909	3,488	761,640	4.03	676,000	3.58

Minnesota	11,144	3,111	720,033	6.32	532,401	3.23
Mississippi	4,449	1,895	236,900	5.32	187,000	4.20
Missouri	13,775	2,993	585,650	4.25	488,150	3.54
Montana	1,934	2,759	120,350	6.22	107,850	5.58
Nebraska	4,216	2,938	198,096	4.70	151,794	3.60
Nevada	1,610	3,626	87,138	5.41	66,338	4.12
New Hampshire	2,071	3,019	96,519	4.66	73,729	3.56
New Jersey	25,377	3,624	1,207,000	4.76	1,020,000	4.02
New Mexico	2,469	2,462	200,338	8.11	165,494	6.70
New York	68,315	3,726	3,494,000	5.11	2,974,000	4.35
North Carolina	12,049	2,396	628,997	5.22	513,890	4.27
North Dakota	1,588	2,485	98,115	6.18	77,615	4.89
Ohio	33,590	3,212	1,540,000	4.58	1,300,000	3.87
Oklahoma	6,545	2,623	347,800	5.31	303,600	4.64
Oregon	6,106	3,055	344,000	5.63	283,000	4.63
Pennsylvania	36,624	3,149	1,792,870	4.90	1,384,067	3.78
Rhode Island	2,914	3,238	124,862	4.28	106,482	3.65
South Carolina	5,631	2,167	297,642	5.29	256,142	4.55
South Dakota	1,719	2,550	105,225	6.12	90,000	5.24
Tennessee	9,222	2,369	461,200	5.00	383,700	4.16
Texas	29,385	2,704	1,414,991	4.82	1,133,270	3.86
Utah	2,680	2,617	195,100	7.28	143,700	5.36
Vermont	1,157	2,775	66,585	5.75	54,900	4.75
Virginia	12,592	2,776	665,000	5.28	525,000	4.17
Washington	10,746	3,481	561,000	5.22	453,000	4.22
West Virginia	4,210	2,341	218,800	5.20	188,000	4.47
Wisconsin	13,208	3,153	706,133	5.35	574,878	4.35
Wyoming	944	2,997	63,050	6.68	56,150	5.95

[1] Includes current expenditures, capital outlay, and interest.
[2] Includes estimate for the District of Columbia.
[3] Data not available.

SOURCES: U.S. Department of Health, Education, and Welfare, Office of Education, "Fall 1967 Statistics of Public Schools";
U.S. Department of Commerce, Office of Business Economics, "Survey of Current Business," April 1968.
From Kenneth A. Simon and W. Vance Grant, *Digest of Educational Statistics*, 1968 edition (Washington, D.C., 1968), p. 60.

the same purposes.[9] Although most of the ESEA funds ($1.3 out of a total $1.5 billion ESEA allocation projected for fiscal 1971) [10] go to programs for children from low-income families, Titles II and III of the Act, providing for library resources and supplementary education centers, have had no specific poverty criteria for their use. In addition, private and parochial schools could participate as long as the funds are not used for sectarian instruction or religious worship. By leaving actual disbursement of the funds to the state, Congress was able to avoid the constitutional issue. (A pragmatic solution to this has been sought for some time since Catholic schools in the large cities, especially, have helped to ease the crisis in public school enrollments. In 1968, for example, of the 50,900,000 pupils enrolled in grades K–12, 6,000,000 were in nonpublic elementary and high schools.)

Although broad in scope, the Act was not a radical departure from previous federal legislation, as, for instance the aid given to schools which were subject to unusual demands from nearby defense projects or other nearby government installations. Nor has Congress attempted to assume new legal authority over education. Section 604 of the Act is clear on this point: "Nothing contained in this Act shall be construed to authorize any department, agency, officer, or employee of the United States to exercise any direction, supervision, or control over the curriculum, program of instruction, administration, or personnel of any educational institution or school system, or over the selection of library resources, textbooks, or other printed or published instructional materials by any education institution or school system."

The ESEA broadly defined the critical needs in education—special programs for educationally deprived children, library facilities, books and instructional devices, health services, and stronger state education leadership. Title I of the act, for example (supporting special programs for low-income, handicapped, neglected, and delinquent children), reached 9.2 million children in 16,000

[9] *The Budget in Brief, Fiscal Year, 1970.* Executive Office of the President, Bureau of the Budget, p. 67.

[10] The Budget of the United States Government—Appendix. Fiscal Year 1971, p. 423.

school districts during the 1967–68 school year.[11] The funds allocated under ESEA generally flow to the states and regions of greatest financial need. In 1966–67, $915 million were granted to the states for ESEA programs. The regional distribution was:

North Atlantic	$122.7 million	
Great Lakes and Plains	256.5 million	Totals
Southeast	313.5 million	$915.1 million
West and Southwest	222.4 million	

This act could be regarded as a political masterpiece, apart from any educational assessment. The consensus politics of the Johnson administration stand out clearly as the diverse and politically appealing provisions of the act are reviewed. The appeal to the poor, the forgotten, and the neglected in a time of national economic affluence is powerful medicine. The ESEA's "war-on-ignorance" approach parallels other governmental wars—on poverty, hunger, crime.

State and local funds remain the basic source of revenue for elementary and secondary education, with less than 8 percent coming from the federal government (4 percent until the 1965 Act). Federal aid to colleges is considerably higher (approximately 20 percent), but the federal government remains a minor partner in the total picture. It is interesting to note that, despite the impressive increase in funds for education from all sources since the end of World War II, the percentage in relation to the gross national product has remained quite modest. (See Table 3.)

THE POWER BALANCE IN EDUCATION

Without question the influence of the federal government has increased considerably in recent years. The spectacular increase in expenditures and the numerous new laws (25 alone by the 88th Congress and the first session of the 89th) make clear the intention of Congress to continue to play an active role. What have these

[11] *Bureau of Elementary and Secondary Education Programs* (Washington, D.C.: U.S. Office of Education, March 1969).

TABLE 3. GROSS NATIONAL PRODUCT RELATED TO TOTAL EXPENDITURES [1]
FOR EDUCATION: UNITED STATES, SELECTED YEARS
FROM 1929 TO 1968

| | | | Expenditures for education | |
Calendar year	Gross national product	School year	Total	As a percent of gross national product
1929	$103,095,000,000	1929–30	$3,233,601,000	3.1
1931	75,820,000,000	1931–32	2,966,464,000	3.9
1933	55,601,000,000	1933–34	2,294,896,000	4.1
1935	72,247,000,000	1935–36	2,649,914,000	3.7
1937	90,446,000,000	1937–38	3,014,074,000	3.3
1939	90,494,000,000	1939–40	3,199,593,000	3.5
1941	124,540,000,000	1941–42	3,203,548,000	2.6
1943	191,592,000,000	1943–44	3,522,007,000	1.8
1945	212,010,000,000	1945–46	4,167,597,000	2.0
1947	231,323,000,000	1947–48	6,574,379,000	2.8
1949	256,484,000,000	1949–50	8,795,635,000	3.4
1951	328,404,000,000	1951–52	11,312,446,000	3.4
1953	364,593,000,000	1953–54	13,949,876,000	3.8
1955	397,960,000,000	1955–56	16,811,651,000	4.2
1957	441,134,000,000	1957–58	21,119,565,000	4.8
1959	483,650,000,000	1959–60	24,722,464,000	5.1
1961	520,109,000,000	1961–62	29,366,305,000	5.6
1963	590,503,000,000	1963–64	36,010,210,000	6.1
1965	684,900,000,000	1965–66	45,500,000,000	6.6
1966	747,600,000,000	1966–67	49,100,000,000	6.5
1967	789,700,000,000	1967–68	54,600,000,000	6.8
1968	860,600,000,000	1968–69	[2] 58,500,000,000	6.8

[1] Includes expenditures of public and nonpublic schools at all levels of education (elementary, secondary, and higher education).

[2] Estimated.

NOTE: Beginning with 1959–60 school year, includes Alaska and Hawaii.

SOURCE: U.S. Department of Health, Education, and Welfare, Office of Education, *Biennial Survey of Education in the United States; Statistics of State School Systems; Financial Statistics of Institutions of Higher Education;* and unpublished data, U.S. Department of Commerce, Office of Business Economics, Survey of Current Business, August, 1963. For 1965–68, *Statistical Abstract of the United States, Digest of Educational Statistics.*

developments done to the traditional federal-state-local relationships in the area of education?

At first glance it is clear that the real power remains in the hands of the states and local districts, as it always has. Since the early nineteenth century, Congress has worked to strengthen state supervision of education and reaffirmed this policy by Title V of the 1965 act, which turned over $25 million to state departments of education for research and projects to increase their effectiveness. In the words of Harold Howe II, then federal Commissioner of Education, "State departments of education must be strong if education is to meet effectively the challenges and responsibilities of today." [12]

The local districts, of course, wield enormous influence on personnel and instructional policies as they manage the schools on a day-to-day basis, but from teacher certification to the length of the school year and the quality of the lunches, they take their orders from the state. Meaningful local control today is "folklore," as Lawrence Cremin phrases it.[13]

One would err seriously to conceptualize the "power division" in education as simply a governmental parceling out of decisions to local, state, or federal agencies. In fact, the shape and direction of elementary and secondary school courses, programs, and operations reflect a number of nongovernmental forces. These include textbook publishers, college admission requirements, national testing programs (College Entrance Examination Board is an excellent example), teacher-board negotiations, and the American dream that all boys and girls should prepare for college (whether they go there—and stay there—or not). These developments have little or nothing to do directly with school boards or educational bureaucrats; their presence, however, is felt in many school decisions at all levels. Collectively, these and similar considerations shape our thousands of schools into ever-increasing uniformity. The recent interest in a national assessment of education supports this drift toward the nationalization of education.

[12] Quoted in *School and Society,* 94 (Summer 1966) 260.
[13] His views on current education are presented in a brief and interesting book, *The Genius of American Education* (Pittsburgh: The University of Pittsburgh Press, 1966).

In general, then, it is safe to say that in the complex power relations in education, the federal government comes out a distant third to the state and local agencies. However, the situation is changing. While once no significant influence was in the hands of the federal government, now a realistic "balance of power" relationship is emerging which Francis Keppel in particular feels will be as healthy and productive as it has been in politics.

THE SUPREME COURT AND FEDERAL POWER IN EDUCATION

The most dramatic factor in increasing the influence of the federal government has been, of course, the Supreme Court, in the words of Lawrence Cremin, "the federal agency which has shaped most powerfully educational policy since World War II." The Brown decision [14] of May 1954 which made compulsory segregation in public schools illegal gave the federal government not only moral responsibility but, what is more important, a constitutional mandate in educational policy. (Congress has always been uneasy about not having any educational responsibilities included in the Constitution. The omission is especially surprising in view of the fact that the 1787 Northwest Ordinance—giving Congress considerable duties and fully supported by the Founding Fathers—was passed in the same year that the Constitution was written. See Figure 3 on the Supreme Court.)

In implementing national goals, however, the Office of Education perhaps would rank as the most influential federal agency on a daily basis. As supervisor of the 1965 act, for example, the office is in a close working relationship with the states and indirectly plays an important role in civil rights enforcement. It can withhold funds in cases of discrimination, but the Office of Education has relied on the persuasive power of threatened termination of funds to encourage local and state compliance with civil rights legislation concerning schools.

In higher education the recent rise of federal influence has been

---

[14] *Brown* v. *Board of Education of Topeka,* 347 U.S. 483.

FIGURE 3. HOW THE SUPREME COURT MAY AFFECT EDUCATION

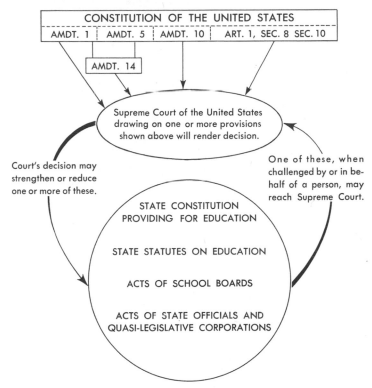

From Clark Spurlock, *Education and the Supreme Court* (Urbana, Ill.: University of Illinois Press, 1955), p. 14.

striking. Grants from numerous noneducational federal agencies directly support education through research and development projects, most of them in universities. Table 4 shows the relative amounts of federal aid distributed through four of the many federal agencies supporting education. No one can forecast the long-term effects of the defense contracts, or the great sums being made available for building construction; however, one must conclude that the federal government is most certainly a power in higher education today.

TABLE 4. FEDERAL FUNDS FOR EDUCATION, BY AGENCY: FISCAL YEARS
1967 TO 1969 (IN $1,000)

	Expenditures		
Agency	1967	1968	1969 (est.)
Dept. of Health, Education, and Welfare	3,206,830	3,754,989	3,917,578
Dept. of Defense	1,473,784	1,654,183	1,719,405
Office of Economic Opportunity (OEO)	790,121	1,045,475	1,258,854
National Science Foundation	180,965	191,900	197,100

SOURCE: Data adapted from Office of Education, U.S. Department of Health, Education, and Welfare, *Digest of Educational Statistics* (1968), p. 110.

Yet, this does not mean that all Americans accept this greatly increased role. Federal involvement in education was a hotly debated subject during the 1950's. Following are some conclusions advanced by Americans on both sides of the argument:

ARGUMENTS FOR FEDERAL PARTICIPATION IN
SUPPORT OF PUBLIC SCHOOLS

1. A population explosion since World War II has placed an educational burden on communities and states which they do not have the financial capacity to carry.

2. The geographical mobility of people today is such that living and educational standards in some of the wealthier states are lowered by in-migration to them by people from poor states; therefore, wealthy states should share in financing schools in the poorer states.

3. The ideal of equalization of educational opportunity demands that wealth be taxed where it is and distributed to the states and localities in proportion to their educational need, financial ability, and effort to support schools.

4. Draft rejections in World War II were in direct proportion to the educational standards of the states; therefore, in order to remain militarily strong, federal support of schools is necessary.

5. The forms of wealth have become so diversified that only tax machinery on the national level can tap these forms of wealth in a fair manner.

6. To train a jet pilot costs ten times the amount needed to educate a physician, engineer, teacher, or scientist, and yet such professional people are as vital to national defense as military personnel; therefore, the federal government should help to finance their preparation.

ARGUMENTS AGAINST FEDERAL PARTICIPATION IN SUPPORT OF PUBLIC SCHOOLS

1. Increasing federal aid would "produce the sickening cadence of the goose step," some contend. In other words, centralization of power, sometimes a prelude to totalitarianism, would be encouraged by federal support of public schools.

2. If federal funds were given the public schools for growth, private education would be interfered with, according to some religious authorities.

3. Too much of the money that is collected by taxes from states by the federal treasury goes to overhead costs.

4. Federal support of schools would constitute a serious encroachment upon states' rights.

5. States do not need assistance; they can pay for their own schools. Rich states should not be taxed to support schools in poor states.

Many of the arguments about federal aid are actually based on struggles and controversies in which the fiscal and educational considerations are of secondary importance. For example, an issue of increasing importance, though technically in the church-state field, comes into focus in the federal-aid controversy. The issue is: "Shall tax funds be used to support private and parochial schools?" Public policy throughout the history of the United States has been that tax money shall not be used to support nonpublic schools. Tremendous pressure is building up to reverse that policy. As we have seen, federal funds for Catholic children have already become available for certain purposes. Some states have made tuition grants available to children whose parents want them to attend an "all-white" school.

Some religious groups, notably the Roman Catholics, are opposed to federal aid unless it would help parochial as well as public schools. Today about 15 percent of the children in the United States attend a nonpublic school. Of these, 90 percent are in parochial schools conducted by the Roman Catholic Church. In writing about the problem, R. Freeman Butts expressed the difficulty this way:

In recent decades, the arguments for diverting public funds to private schools have changed. It is now argued that the states should aid all parents to send their children to the kind of school they wish. This would not aid *schools;* it would aid parents to exercise their freedom of educational choice. So if parents want their children to go to religious schools, they should receive their fair share of tax funds. If they want their children to go to all-white schools, they should receive tax funds to help them do this. Obviously, the whole idea of a common school is now under severe attack.[15]

Already, these arguments against federal aid seem quaintly old-fashioned and totally irrelevant. The issue in 1970 is not *whether* federal funds will go to education but rather, *how much* aid, for what purposes, and how best to distribute the funds. The traditional barriers to general aid are under attack. However, to require the Congress to specify the uses of federal support funds may encourage competitive educational lobbying. Categorical aid seems to reward novel proposals and extravagant rhetoric— commodities and skills not usually found in the poor districts with the greatest need for federal support.

There is little doubt that education is a national and state responsibility; whether or not the piper's financier calls the tune is another question. Undeniably, the state and national tax-gathering machinery is vastly superior to local tax schemes. The state and national tax bases are more equitable and balanced than local districts forever caught in the rich district-poor district struggle.

[15] R. Freeman Butts, "Search for Freedom—The Story of American Education," *NEA Journal,* XLIX, No. 3 (March 1960), 43.

Short of an economic miracle at the school-district level, there seems to be no alternative to radically increased financial participation in education by state and federal governments.

Those who are interested in the federal aid to education controversy will need to keep under close scrutiny developments bearing on the religious issue, the race issue, the economy issue, and state-federal relationships. Coalitions of power groups are likely to arrive at compromises which will lead to legislation and fiscal policy. Such compromises may or may not be in the public interest. Only an informed, intelligent, and politically active citizenry can assure a fiscal policy that is for the common good.

SUMMARY

Public education in America is generally regarded as a function of state government. Despite the constitutional silence about education, the Congress has taken an active role in shaping and influencing the state school systems. The land-grant legislation, allocating land and the proceeds of its sale to public education, goes back as far as the federal Constitution itself. The Morrill Act of 1862, establishing land-grant colleges in the states, is but one example of Congressional support of public education. Subsequent legislation granted substantial federal monies to support specific training, research, and building programs directly benefiting public schools. Support for colleges and universities typically comes directly from a federal agency; public elementary and secondary school support usually is channeled through the state education agency.

Since World War II, and particularly since Sputnik I, federal support to education has focused on national goals. The improvement of the basic and applied sciences, research facilities, and later, support of the humanities, were considered important to the national interest and funded accordingly. The nation's priorities may best be reflected in the national budget. Obviously, defense, social programs in health, housing, etc., and roadbuilding take national priority over education, but the annual infusion of $7 to $9 billion into education indicates substantial federal interest.

State support of public schools varies widely; gross inequality of educational opportunity among and within the states is an inescapable conclusion. The Elementary and Secondary Education Act of 1965 sought to correct the grosser dimensions of this inequality. The poor, the disadvantaged, and the undereducated were the primary beneficiaries of the act.

The federal influence on education is disproportionate to its financial support. Local tax dollars constitute the greatest source of school funds in most states. State and federal funds are a poor second and third, in that order. National goals and interests are powerful factors, however, in the making of local school curriculum. Through programs for teacher training and retraining, the federal influence extends to the school staffs. The curriculum reforms in mathematics and the laboratory sciences, supported by the National Science Foundation, extend the federal role into the classrooms of the great majority of secondary schools.

The great debate over federal aid to education appears to be history now; unless revived by some as yet unforeseen issue, the question is not *whether* federal aid, but *how much*. Balance among local, state, and federal influence on education likely will not be achieved in a dynamic society. The social ferment, the extremely volatile problems of urban education, and the unpredictable national and international future in the decade ahead all militate against stable relationships. In education, as in other social enterprises, the pendulum swings of educational ideas, institutions, and practices build in their countervailing forces. About the only safe prediction for the federal role in education is that it will persist, change its form to meet political shifts, and, to some extent, reflect the national priorities.

SUGGESTED READINGS

Brademas, John, "The National Politics of Education." *The Unfinished Journey—Issues in American Education.* New York: Van Rees Press, 1968, pp. 33–52.

Cressman, George R., and Harold W. Benda, *Public Education in America.* New York: Appleton-Century-Crofts, 1966, pp. 81–99.

Garber, Lee O., and E. Edmund Reutter, Jr., *The Yearbook of School*

Law, 1969. Danville, Illinois: The Interstate Printers and Publishers, Inc., 1969, pp. 1–14, and 151–172.

Mushkin, Selma J., and Eugene P. McLoone, *Local School Expenditures: 1970 Projections.* Chicago, Illinois: Council of State Governments, 1965, pp. 5–10.

Simons, Joseph H., *Problems of the American University.* Boston: The Christopher Publishing House, 1967, pp. 13–26.

CHAPTER
2.

STATE RESPONSIBILITY
FOR EDUCATION

THE United States Constitution makes no provision for the control of education; consequently, under the Tenth Amendment, this authority legally is vested in state governments. In practice though, the tradition of local autonomy, fostered by political and economic, as well as geographical factors, shaped the development of the early schools. To a remarkable extent, each community or school district, with substantial restrictions or prescriptions from the state, is free to develop and maintain the kind of educational program it prefers.[1]

In spite of the degree of local control that has prevailed over the years, the state government has always played an important role in the administration of the public schools. Moreover, in the past decades the state has been an increasingly active partner with the local systems in the effort to improve the quality of education.

In many ways the educational revolution of the 1960's brought new responsibilities to the state: the traditional roles of the major

[1] However, many have been calling for a basic revision of this view. W. W. Wayson, for example, has argued that "there never has been local control of education, especially in recent decades. Numerous laws, universal American values, cultural ideas, nationwide competitiveness, mass media, state and national policies, and all sorts of pressures—both explicit and covert—dictate local educational practices and policies. Local control not only is a mythology but to the degree that it predominates in policy decisions, it has depressed the resources made available to the schools. It is time to dispel the myths of localism so that localities can indeed become full partners in shaping educational policy." "Political Revolution in Education, 1965," *Phi Delta Kappan,* XLXVII (March 1966), 337. See also Roald F. Campbell, "Folklore of Local Control," *The School Review,* LXVII (Spring 1959), 1–16.

policy-making agencies of the state—the legislature, the state department of education, and the board of education—are now taking on new importance. The former governor of North Carolina, Terry Sanford, a leader in interstate educational planning, sees the current situation in these decisive terms: "The future of the states will rest on the pivotal question of whether or not they will be able to make the sacrifices and meet the demands of the American people for educational excellence, as well as the commands of the age for educational innovation." [2]

It should be noted that education is a self-imposed responsibility of the people in the various states. Most of the state constitutions include clauses for the establishment and maintenance of a system of free public schools. State responsibility for public education has been further established by court decisions, of which a case in the state of Kentucky is typical. The court ruled: "Under our system, every common school in the state, whether located in a city or in the country, is a state institution, protected, controlled, and regulated by the state." [3] The establishment of local school districts represents the state's way of providing for the administration of its system of free public schools. Regardless of the degree of local autonomy provided or permitted, the state is the agency responsible for the maintenance of public education, subject of course, to the will of the people expressed through representative government.

ROLE OF THE STATE LEGISLATURE

The state legislature is a major influence in education. Although the control varies from state to state, similarities do exist in the general operation of educational programs.

1. All school laws are enacted by the state legislature in the same way that other laws are passed and put into effect.

2. The state, in all cases, accepts some degree of responsibility for the support of public schools.

[2] "The States—The Revitalized Senior Partners in Education," *Bulletin of the Secondary School Principals Association,* XLIX (April 1966), 41.

[3] *Board of Education of Jefferson County v. Board of Education of Louisville,* 206 S.W., 869 (Ky., 1918).

3. The state establishes standards for certification of teachers and other educational personnel and awards certificates, thus controlling admission to the practice of teaching.

4. Compulsory school attendance laws which specify the ages during which children must be in school are maintained by the state.

5. Certain content in the school curriculum is made mandatory by legislative enactments—for example, state and American history, health and physical education, alchohol and narcotics information, and in some cases the minimum general. requirements in elementary and secondary schools.

6. The state sets standards of state financial aid to local school districts and determines by budgetary appropriations the amount of support available each year.

7. Most states have established minimum salaries for teachers depending upon amount of training.

8. Certain school services, such as provision of free textbooks and transportation, are authorized by state law.

9. Some states provide for the approval of textbooks to be used in schools by establishing "adopted lists" from which books may be selected.

10. The states have established teacher welfare programs like retirement pension plans.

In addition to specific legislation, the state legislature may enact supplementary regulations to the provisions of the state constitution relative to the responsibilities of the state board of education. Forty-eight states maintain such a board; the others delegate administrative powers to the state superintendent of instruction.

THE STATE BOARD OF EDUCATION

State board of education members are selected in a variety of ways. Thirty states provide for board members to be appointed by the governor. The New York State legislature elects members of its state board, which is called the Board of Regents. In the remaining seventeen states which maintain state boards of education, members are elected, either in general elections or through school boards conventions.

The function of the state board of education typically is that of policy approval and the general administration of state education laws. The power of state boards varies from state to state. In some, the board is little more than a figurehead body whose authority is restricted to advising the state superintendent of public instruction. In most cases, however, the state board is delegated substantial control of the state's system of education. Such authority is commonly discharged through administrative officials who usually are appointed by the board. In a few states, the chief state officer, the superintendent of schools, is an elected official who works with an appointed state board. In others, the elected state board appoints the state superintendent. The governor actually appoints both the state board and the superintendent in Virginia and New Jersey. In states which do not maintain a state board, the superintendent of public instruction is responsible both to the people who elect him and to the legislature, which approves the budget for the state department of education and authorizes specific administrative procedures in the educational program.

THE STATE DEPARTMENT OF EDUCATION

All states, whether or not they maintain state boards of education, provide for departments of public instruction to administer the state system of public schools. The state department is typically headed by a state superintendent of public instruction or an officer with a similar title, such as commissioner of education. This office is filled by (1) popular election, (2) appointment by a state board, or (3) appointment by the governor. Appointment by the board is considered the most desirable means of selecting the state superintendent.

The state department of education is staffed with specialists in various phases of education. Typically, the state department of education renders four major types of services:

    1. Leadership and advisory services—for example, state department personnel—encourage school improvement by preparing publications, sponsoring educational conferences and workshops, and consulting with local school people.

2. Supervisory and regulatory services—for example, state department personnel—make certain that state laws and state board regulations are observed, accredit secondary schools, and issue teaching or administrative certificates to qualified applicants.

3. Fact-gathering and research services—for example, state department personnel—compile fiscal data, keep official school records, and issue reports on educational matters.

4. Public relations services—for example, state department personnel—are usually consulted by the legislature when it comes time to appropriate state tax funds to the schools.

Recent federal legislation has taken major strides toward strengthening the state departments of education. As already noted, the historic Elementary and Secondary Education Act of 1965 allocated $25 million to improve the effectiveness of their operation. Long handicapped by lack of adequate funds, the state departments now have available resources for needed programs and projects such as educational research and publication, improvement of teacher preparation, development of curriculum materials, and training individuals for state and local educational agencies.

The 1965 act was a landmark in American education. The Title V section of the legislation, "to stimulate and assist States in strengthening leadership resources," was the first federal law aimed specifically at assisting state departments of education in their general operation. By the provisions of Title V, the federal government made clear its intention to preserve the American tradition of federal-state-local cooperation in education. Federally-funded support programs reinforce this three-way relation: "State leadership and authority coupled with local control, and both backed by federal assistance, provide the soundest basis for fulfilling the national interest in obtaining strong educational opportunities for all." [4]

[4] Robert L. Hopper, "Strength Where it Counts," *American Education,* II (June 1966), 21.

THE CHANGING VIEW OF
STATE RESPONSIBILITY

The major changes in American education in the 1960's brought a reexamination of the aims of the state as a partner in the field. The regulatory powers of the legislature, for example, are now seen as effective tools to upgrade the minimum standards in the schools. Higher standards for certification of teachers is another method states are using to improve the general quality of the schools. And the new view of responsibility is most clearly seen in the state department of education. The emphasis is on leadership for innovative change, a definite trend away from accounting and inspection chores as chief responsibilities.[5]

STATE AND LOCAL RELATIONS
IN EDUCATION

The local districts are the basic administrative unit in American education. Under their supervision the actual day-to-day instruction takes place. Despite the increasing activity on the federal and state level, the tradition of local autonomy remains unchanged. In fact, both the state and federal agencies are working to strengthen the local districts in helping to provide the best educational opportunities for their students. In the first year of operation of Title V of the 1965 Elementary and Secondary Education Act, for example, 83 percent of the projects begun by the state departments of education included programs for leadership training for local school districts and educational agencies.[6] Some understanding of the operation of local districts is necessary to see how they function in partnership with the state.

[5] Truman M. Pierce, *Federal, State, and Local Government in Education* (Washington, D.C.: The Center for Applied Research in Education, 1964), p. 48.
[6] *School and Society,* LI (Summer 1966), 260.

ORGANIZATION OF SCHOOLS
BELOW STATE LEVEL

Variations in patterns of local organization range from highly centralized control at the state level in Alaska and Hawaii, to a middle practice of rather positive state control in some Southern states, to the other extreme of practically no centralized control in certain states in New England and the Midwest. Despite these differences, it is common practice for local control to be vested in an administrative type of unit called a school district. Some states also maintain intermediate units, often synonymous with the political county units, to function as a coordinating body between local districts and the state board or department of education.

THE INTERMEDIATE DISTRICT

The intermediate district typically includes a number of local school districts representing either towns, cities, or rural areas. It may, depending upon the population to be served, represent only a portion of the political county unit; or if the population is sparse, it may include more than one county. Its function is to keep official records on school populations, distribute state funds, and generally to supervise the operation of schools under its jurisdiction. Often, larger local school districts which represent sizable towns or cities are excluded by law from the jurisdiction of the intermediate, or county, unit. In such instances, the excluded local school district serves as its own intermediate district in relationships with the state. When large school districts are not under the jurisdiction of the intermediate unit, as is the case in most states, the county system of schools gives leadership to, and exercises legal control over, the smaller districts, most of which exist in rural areas.

The intermediate unit should not be confused with the county school units which function as local school districts. Some states have established the county as an inclusive local school district, similar in function and authority to large city school districts which operate directly under state jurisdiction. The three basic patterns of legal relationships between the local school district, intermediate districts, and the state are shown in Figure 4.

FIGURE 4. BASIC PATTERNS OF LEGAL RELATIONSHIPS BETWEEN LOCAL, INTERMEDIATE, AND STATE EDUCATIONAL UNITS

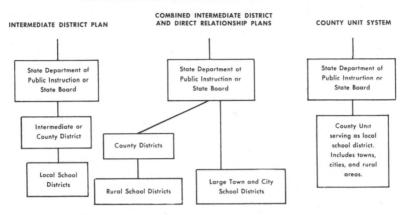

The intermediate, or county, district has not been a strong unit in the state system of education. The county superintendent of schools typically has been a political officer, elected by popular vote every two or four years, and frequently poorly qualified for the post. Authority and responsibility assigned to the intermediate unit have been minimal. Yet this organizational agency has been the only source of control and assistance for the schools of the thinly populated rural areas of the nation.

As the character of life in the United States has changed from rural to urban, with the consequent reduction in number of local school districts, the intermediate unit has become a source of controversy in a number of states. The opposing positions regarding its future usefulness in the structure of the state school system are these. (1) The intermediate unit should be defined and established, with relatively uniform size in terms of the pupil population served, and should be given authority and state support to provide vital school services. (2) Economies can be achieved by organizing schools on the county unit system. The intermediate unit has served its usefulness and should be discontinued, thus permitting every local district to relate itself directly with the central state structure. (3) The dual or combined plans are still essential to the nature of urban and rural life in many states; consequently, they

41

should be maintained to assure that rural areas are not neglected educationally. Proponents of this position often differ regarding the amount of authority and control that should be vested in the intermediate unit.

LOCAL SCHOOL DISTRICTS

Local school districts are the major agencies for the control and operation of schools. They are official governmental units which have been established by action of the state legislature as legal, corporate entities of the state, similar to municipalities. The state has the authority to establish local districts, to reorganize them, and to abolish them individually or on a statewide basis.

Substantial diversity in type, size, and name of local school districts prevails from state to state. Hawaii, for example, has one district; South Dakota has 2,388 (of which 1,258 are one-teacher elementary schools). Two common bases are employed for determining the nature and designation of a district.

AREA INCLUDED. The standard way of designating a school district is by the area included within its boundaries. The district may incorporate all the territory and the people residing therein within a town or township, a city, or a county. School district lines are not always coterminous with political subdivisions. In fact, many suburban school districts include all or parts of several towns or villages. The title "community district" may indicate that two or more towns, or a town and adjoining village and perhaps rural areas, have been organized into a single local school district.

In districts defined by the area included, the school board has responsibility for providing a total educational program from either kindergarten or first grade through high school—and in some states through the junior college—for all children and youth of school age residing within the district. In accordance with legal statutes to provide funds for the support of schools and the construction of school buildings, the school board may levy taxes or may recommend the levying of taxes and sell school bonds.

SCHOOL SERVICES PROVIDED. Another way to designate school districts is by the types of services provided to particular segments of the population of an area. For example, a district that operates only an elementary school is called an elementary school district. Similarly, those which are restricted to operating secondary schools are called high school districts. Both may overlap each other in terms of the area included. Other types of districts of this kind are the junior college district, which may serve a number of local school districts cooperating to provide the junior college services; the unified school district, which typically designates some form of cooperation or consolidation between other types of districts or may only indicate that for certain services unification has been achieved; and the contracting district, which does not itself maintain schools but instead contracts with other districts for the education of its school age population.

Districts designated by the services provided also have geographical boundary lines which define their taxable property and the population to be served. They concentrate, however, on the school programs within their legal responsibilities, while maintaining usually only informal cooperative relationships with other districts serving the same area. Citizens served by two or more of such school districts vote separately for school board members for each and are assessed separate tax rates for each district.

As Table 5 shows, most school districts serve more than 300 and less than 10,000 pupils. The national trend toward urbanization will undoubtedly change this picture over the next few years. As population centers grow, big school districts will get bigger and pressure may build to carve the large districts into smaller units.

LOCAL SCHOOL BOARDS

The local district, no matter how large or how small, is governed by a school board or board of education. Such boards represent the local people, but they also represent the state legislature that created them and delegated to them certain authority. Of course, many powers are reasonably implied from specifically delegated authority, and consequently boards of education are more powerful than a literal interpretation of state statutes would indi-

TABLE 5. DISTRIBUTION OF OPERATING LOCAL PUBLIC SCHOOL SYSTEMS
AND NUMBER OF PUPILS, BY SIZE OF SYSTEM, FOR THE UNITED STATES:
FALL 1968

Size of system	Public school systems		Public school pupils	
	Number	Percent	Number [1]	Percent
Total operating systems	19,977	100.00	43,105,101	100.00
Systems with 300 pupils or more	11,750	58.82	42,405,583	98.38
25,000 or more	168	0.84	12,318,363	28.58
10,000 to 24,999	516	2.58	7,570,468	17.56
5,000 to 9,999	1,068	5.35	7,398,119	17.16
2,500 to 4,999	1,952	9.77	6,783,897	15.74
1,000 to 2,499	3,498	17.51	5,666,626	13.15
600 to 999	2,008	10.05	1,561,286	3.62
300 to 599	2,540	12.72	1,106,824	2.57
Systems with less than 300 pupils	8,227	41.18	699,518	1.62

[1] These figures represent the sums of the reported "enrollment" figures, which are not comparable from State to State. The official Office of Education Fall 1968 elementary-secondary enrollment figure is reported in the publication *Fall 1968 Statistics of Public School Systems*.

From *Education Directory*, 1968–69, Part 2, National Center for Educational Statistics, p. 5.

cate. In general, states have been quite generous in conveying powers to the local boards.

About 95 percent of the board members in the United States are elected by popular vote, usually on a nonpartisan ballot. The other 5 percent are appointed, usually by the mayor, city council, or county board of supervisors. In only one state, Virginia, are all school board members appointed. Most school boards in the United States have five or seven members.

THE STATE AND FINANCIAL AID

The major responsibility of the state is to assist the local districts in adequate financing of their school programs. In this aspect the state has been especially important as a partner in the educational enterprise. The median support in recent years has been about 39 percent of the local district budget. Although federal assistance (channeled through the state department of education) has been increasing on the local level, it accounts for only a small percentage of the total budget. (See Figure 5 and Table 6.)

FIGURE 5. REVENUE RECEIPTS (EST.) FOR PUBLIC ELEMENTARY AND SECONDARY SCHOOLS, BY SOURCE: UNITED STATES, 1967–68

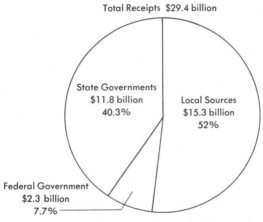

Total Receipts $29.4 billion

State Governments
$11.8 billion
40.3%

Local Sources
$15.3 billion
52%

Federal Government
$2.3 billion
7.7%

NOTE: Because of rounding, detail may not add to totals.
SOURCE: Office of Education, U.S. Department of Health, Education, and Welfare, *Digest of Educational Statistics* (1968) table 65.

In most states the method of distribution of funds is based on a foundation concept—the establishment of a minimum level of financial support per pupil below which no district should be permitted to fall. The basic idea of the foundation is to help provide equality of educational opportunity. The amount of aid given to each district by the state to meet the minimum, or foundation, depends on the financial resources of the individual districts. The funds are raised mainly by statewide income or sales taxes. The most common plan used by the states is to provide a fixed grant to

TABLE 6. PUBLIC ELEMENTARY AND SECONDARY SCHOOL REVENUE
RECEIPTS FROM FEDERAL, STATE, AND LOCAL SOURCES:
UNITED STATES, 1919–20 TO 1965–66

School year	Total	Federal	State	Local (including intermediate)[1]	School year	Total	Federal	State	Local (including intermediate)[1]
1	2	3	4	5	1	2	3	4	5
	AMOUNT IN THOUSANDS OF DOLLARS					PERCENTAGE DISTRIBUTION			
1919–20	$970,120	$2,475	$160,085	$807,561	1919–20	100.0	0.3	16.5	83.2
1929–30	2,088,557	7,334	353,670	1,727,553	1929–30	100.0	0.4	16.9	82.7
1939–40	2,260,527	39,810	684,354	1,536,363	1939–40	100.0	1.8	30.3	68.0
1941–42	2,416,580	34,305	759,993	1,622,281	1941–42	100.0	1.4	31.5	67.1
1943–44	2,604,322	35,886	859,183	1,709,253	1943–44	100.0	1.4	33.0	65.6
1945–46	3,059,845	41,378	1,062,057	1,956,409	1945–46	100.0	1.4	34.7	63.8
1947–48	4,311,534	120,270	1,676,362	2,514,902	1947–48	100.0	2.8	38.9	58.3
1949–50	5,437,044	155,848	2,165,689	3,115,507	1949–50	100.0	2.9	39.8	57.3
1951–52	6,423,816	227,711	2,478,596	3,717,507	1951–52	100.0	3.5	38.6	57.8
1953–54	7,866,852	355,237	2,944,103	4,567,512	1953–54	100.0	4.5	37.4	58.1
1955–56	9,686,677	441,442	3,828,886	5,416,350	1955–56	100.0	4.6	39.5	55.9
1957–58	12,181,513	486,484	4,800,368	6,894,661	1957–58	100.0	4.0	39.4	56.6
1959–60	14,746,618	651,639	5,768,047	8,326,932	1959–60	100.0	4.4	39.1	56.5
1961–62	17,527,707	760,975	6,789,190	9,977,542	1961–62	100.0	4.3	38.7	56.9
1963–64	20,544,182	896,956	8,078,014	11,569,213	1963–64	100.0	4.4	39.3	56.3
1965–66	25,356,858	1,996,954	9,920,219	13,439,686	1965–66	100.0	7.9	39.1	53.0

[1] Includes a relatively minor amount from other sources (gifts and tuition and transportation fees from patrons), which accounted for 0.5 percent of total revenue receipts in 1965–66.

NOTE: Beginning in 1959–60, includes Alaska and Hawaii. Because of rounding, detail may not add to totals.

SOURCE: U.S. Department of Health, Education, and Welfare, Office of Education, "Statistics of State School Systems." From Kenneth A. Simon and W. Vance Grant, *Digest of Educational Statistics* (1968 edition), p. 56.

all districts and to supplement that amount in districts without adequate tax resources to meet the foundation minimum.[7]

In recent years the states have faced increasing problems in providing adequate aid to school districts. The situation is especially severe in those states without a broad industrial base as an added source of tax revenue. Although Mississippi, for example, ranked 49th in per-pupil public expenditures for education in the country in 1969, it ranked 50th in per capita income. California ranked 6th in per capita income but was 21st in per-pupil expenditure. On the basis of comparative economics, California made less effort than Mississippi.[8] In general, the amount of funds made available for education, on both a state and local level, are closely related to the per capita income of the state (see Table 2, pp. 20–21). A basic feature of the Elementary and Secondary Education Act of 1965 provides a partial solution to this problem by granting larger allocations to the poorer states—in other words, applying the "foundation" concept on a national basis.

The disparity in size of school districts has always presented a problem to states, rich and poor alike, in legislative decisions on appropriations. Local school districts range in size from those which maintain only one rural school to the other extreme, New York City School District, which serves over a million pupils. In a geographical sense, districts range from two or three to 17,000 square miles.

Over the years, there has been a steady trend toward eliminating, through consolidation and reorganization, the small school districts which are expensive to operate and whose educational services are usually not up to standard. Since 1948, for example, the total number of school districts has been reduced from almost 100,000 to fewer than 22,000 in 1970. As Table 5 indicates, however, very small districts still comprise over half of the na-

[7] Office of Education, *Profiles in School Support* (Washington, D.C.: Dept. of Health, Education, and Welfare, Misc. Bulletin, No. 47, 1965), p. 87; Office of Education, *State Programs for Public School Support* (Washington, D.C.: Dept. of Health, Education, and Welfare, Misc. Bulletin, No. 52, 1965), pp. 1–8.

[8] *Statistical Abstract of the United States 1969* (Washington, D.C.: Government Printing Office, 1969), p. 116.

tion's districts. The U.S. Supreme Court ruling in the 1962 *Baker v. Carr* case in Tennessee marked an important turning point. By the Court's decision stating that states were obligated to reapportion their legislatures on a "one man, one vote" basis, the metropolitan areas are increasing their representation. Thus the state legislatures are becoming more responsive to the problems of the rapidly growing urban and suburban school enrollments.

Finally, in any discussion of state financial assistance, it is important to remember that the state's responsibility extends beyond the elementary and secondary schools to higher education. Most state institutions of higher learning lack the local tax support of the lower schools and are largely dependent on the state legislature for their operating funds. The great increase in the demands for higher education has made increasingly difficult the state's ability to finance an adequate educational program at all levels. Table 7 illustrates the rapid increase in expenditures for *public* higher education. State funds constitute the major source for these expenditures.

SUMMARY

The state legislatures and agencies across the country are filling roles of increased responsibility in education. Always recognized as legally responsible for public schools by the Tenth Amendment of the Constitution, the states are providing renewed leadership in planning, curriculum, and teacher education to raise educational standards.

The state works in partnership with the federal government and the local school districts. But basic control of the schools is in the hands of the citizens at the local level.

Local school districts constitute the basic unit in the organizational pattern of schools. The state creates school districts as administrative units in order to preserve the practice of local autonomy. Consolidation to eliminate small school districts has proceeded at a rapid pace in recent years. About 20,000 districts exist today as compared with about 100,000 a decade ago. Educational authorities are in general agreement that in spite of the

TABLE 7. TOTAL CURRENT EXPENDITURES BY PUBLIC INSTITUTIONS OF
HIGHER LEARNING, 1956–57 TO 1976–77 *
(Amounts in billions of 1966–1967 Dollars)

YEAR	AMOUNT
1956–57	2.6
1957–58	2.8
1958–59	3.1
1959–60	3.3
1960–61	3.6
1961–62	4.1
1962–63	4.6
1963–64	5.2
1964–65	5.7
1965–66	6.7
1966–67	7.5
1967–68	8.3
1968–69	9.0
1969–70	9.5
1970–71	10.1
1971–72	10.9
1972–73	11.6
1973–74	12.3
1974–75	13.1
1975–76	13.9
1976–77	14.6

* Projections for 1967–68 and thereafter.
SOURCE: U.S. Office of Education, *Projections of Educational Statistics to 1976–77* (1967).

trend toward reducing the number of small school districts, too many small districts still operate.

Another serious problem facing the state is its growing inability to provide adequate financial assistance in meeting its commitments on all levels of education. Responsible for the public schools and state universities, the state must find new sources of revenue in the future as enrollments continue to grow.

SUGGESTED READINGS

Ashby, Lloyd W., "Man In The Middle?" *The Superintendent of Schools*. Danville, Illinois: The Interstate Printers and Publishers, Inc., 1968, pp. 25–66.

Garber, Lee O., and E. Edmund Reutter, Jr., *The Yearbook of School Law 1969*. Danville, Illinois: The Interstate Printers and Publishers, Inc., 1969, pp. 1–14 and 151–172.

Gauerke, Warren E., and Jack R. Childress, *The Theory and Practice of School Finance*. Chicago: Rand McNally & Co., 1967, pp. 122–178.

Stone, James C., and Frederick W. Schneider, *Foundations of Education*. New York: Thomas Y. Crowell Co., 1965, pp. 240–267.

Westby-Gibson, Dorothy, *Social Foundations of Education*. New York: The Free Press, 1967, pp. 211–214 and 217–219.

Zimmer, Basil G., and Amos H. Hawley, *Metropolitan Area Schools, Resistance to District Reorganization*. Beverly Hills, California: Sage Publications, Inc., 1968, pp. 155–186.

3.

FORCES AFFECTING THE SCHOOLS

MODERN society may be thought of as an enormously complex machine made up of various separate parts, each performing essential functions. All of the parts are interrelated and influenced by the total pattern. If the economic function of society is impaired, for example, through a severe depression such as that of the 1930's, school construction and educational innovation often slow down. When new advances are made in science and technology, they, too, exert great influence on both the educational curriculum and teaching methods.

A great variety of forces are constant influences on the schools. The schools must and do adjust themselves to changing conditions. New elements are injected into society from time to time, creating, in some instances, serious imbalances. Consequently, a major role of the schools is to prepare students to understand and deal effectively with the factors impinging on individual and group life.

As historian Henry Steele Commager has stated: "Schools reflect the society they serve." Clues as to how major values come to be accepted may be found in a study of contemporary social, political, and economic forces that affect schools.

IDEALS OF SOCIETY

Foremost among the forces that affect schools are the ideals that chart the course for the society they serve. In the United States democracy, freedom, and education for all are the guiding tenets for the nature and structure of education. Because education must serve the goals of society, it must maintain in its program appropriate instruction to guarantee that the ideals to which people pay allegiance are transmitted to future generations. The force of societal ideals, more than any other, shapes a nation's system of education.

Changes in these ideals can have a great effect on the schools. For example, free education has always been a basic ideal in the United States, but for a long time this "birthright" was limited to an elementary education. As late as 1900 less than 12 percent of the nation's teen-agers received further education in the relatively small number of tax-supported public high schools then in existence. By the turn of the century, however, Americans realized the need for more education to meet new demands as the United States grew into a complex industrial society. The ideal of American education was extended to include a high school education for all. Today over 94 percent of American teen-agers attend secondary schools. (See Table 8).

In the years ahead it is clear that the American ideal of education will include opportunity for a college education for all. Throughout the United States, tax-supported colleges and universities are undergoing great growth. The rise in college enrollments and particularly the increased ratio of enrollment to college-age population in recent years reflect the increased educational opportunities that are being provided (See Table 9.)

The Supreme Court's historic decision in 1954 making compulsory segregation in public schools illegal is another example of the influence of changing ideals on the schools. Despite the resistance to the mandate for desegregation in that decision, the elimination of *de jure* school segregation is a powerful force for change. The educational inequalities of segregated schools have been recognized, and a racially integrated school system is now felt to be the best way to implement the long-cherished American aim of equality of educational opportunity for every citizen.

TABLE 8. ENROLLMENT IN GRADES 9–12 OF PUBLIC AND NONPUBLIC
SCHOOLS COMPARED WITH POPULATION 14–17 YEARS OF AGE:
UNITED STATES, 1889–90 TO 1967–68

[Beginning in 1959–60, includes Alaska and Hawaii]

School year	Enrollment, grades 9–12 and postgraduate [1]			Population 14–17 years of age [2]	Total number enrolled per 100 persons 14–17 years of age
	All schools	Public schools	Nonpublic schools		
1889–90	359,949	202,963 [3]	94,931 [3]	5,354,653	6.7
1899–1900	699,403	519,251 [3]	110,797 [3]	6,152,231	11.4
1909–10	1,115,398	915,061 [3]	117,400 [3]	7,220,298	15.4
1919–20	2,500,176	2,200,389 [3]	213,920 [3]	7,735,841	32.3
1929–30	4,804,255	4,399,422 [3]	341,158 [3][4]	9,341,221	51.4
1939–40	7,123,009	6,635,337	487,672	9,720,419	73.3
1949–50	6,453,009	5,757,810	695,199	8,404,768	76.8
1951–52	6,596,351	5,917,384	678,967	8,516,000 [5]	77.5
1953–54	7,108,973	6,330,565	778,408	8,861,000 [5]	80.2
1955–56	7,774,975	6,917,790	857,185	9,207,000 [5]	84.4
1957–58	8,869,186	7,905,469	963,717	10,139,000 [5]	87.5
1959–60	9,599,810	8,531,454	1,068,356	11,154,879	86.1
1961–62	10,768,972	9,616,755	1,152,217	12,006,000 [5]	89.7
Fall 1963	12,255,496	10,935,536	1,319,960	13,499,000 [5]	90.8
Fall 1965 [6]	13,010,000	11,670,000	1,340,000	14,110,000 [5]	92.2
Fall 1967 [6]	13,750,000	12,310,000	1,440,000	14,605,000 [5]	94.1

[1] Unless indicated, includes enrollment in subcollegiate departments of institutions of higher education and in residential schools for exceptional children. Beginning in 1949–50, also includes Federal schools.

[2] Includes all persons residing in the United States, but excludes Armed Forces overseas. Data shown are actual figures from the decennial censuses of population unless otherwise indicated.

[3] Excludes enrollment in subcollegiate departments of institutions of higher education and in residential schools for exceptional children.

[4] Data for 1927–28.

[5] Estimated by the Bureau of the Census as of July 1 preceding the opening of the school year.

[6] Preliminary data.

SOURCE: U.S. Office of Education, *Progress of Public Education in the United States of America 1967–1968.* From Kenneth A. Simon and W. Vance Grant, *Digest of Educational Statistics* (1968 edition), p. 30.

TABLE 9. ENROLLMENT IN INSTITUTIONS OF HIGHER EDUCATION
COMPARED WITH POPULATION AGED 18–21: UNITED STATES,
FALL 1946 TO FALL 1967

Year	Population 18–21 years of age [1]	Enrollment	Number enrolled per 100 persons 18–21 years of age
1	2	3	4
1946	9,403,000	[2] 2,078,095	22.1
1947	9,276,000	2,338,226	25.2
1948	9,144,000	2,403,396	26.3
1949	8,990,000	2,444,900	27.2
1950	8,945,000	2,281,298	25.5
1951	8,742,000	2,101,962	24.0
1952	8,542,000	2,134,242	25.0
1953	8,441,000	2,231,054	26.4
1954	8,437,000	2,446,693	29.0
1955	8,508,000	2,653,034	31.2
1956	8,701,000	2,918,212	33.5
1957	8,844,000	3,036,938	34.3
1958	8,959,000	3,226,038	36.0
1959	9,182,000	3,364,861	36.6
1960	9,550,000	3,582,726	37.5
1961	10,252,000	3,860,643	37.7
1962	10,761,000	4,174,936	38.8
1963	11,154,000	4,494,626	40.3
1964	11,319,000	4,950,173	43.7
1965	12,127,000	5,526,325	45.6
1966	12,888,000	[2] 5,885,000	45.7
1967	13,632,000	[2] 6,348,000	46.6

[1] These Bureau of the Census estimates are as of July 1 preceding the opening of the academic year. They include Armed Forces overseas.

[2] Estimated.

NOTE: Beginning in 1960, data are for 50 States and the District of Columbia; data for earlier years are for 48 States and the District of Columbia. Beginning in 1953, enrollment figures include resident and extension degree-credit students; data for earlier years exclude extension students.

SOURCES: U.S. Department of Health, Education, and Welfare, Office of Education, circulars on "Opening Fall Enrollment in Higher Education"; and U.S. Department of Commerce, Bureau of the Census, "Current Population Reports," Series P-25.

From Kenneth A. Simon and W. Vance Grant, *Digest of Educational Statistics* (1968 edition), p. 68.

INFLUENCE OF RELIGIOUS SECTS

Religion, long a vital force in American life, has great influence on education. The diversity of faiths in a school district often produces crosscurrents of interests that make difficult the efforts of teachers and school officials to maintain schools which, while stressing commonly recognized moral and spiritual values, remain neutral and separate from religious control. Despite the expressed dedication to nonsectarian public schools, subtle ways are found in some communities to employ teachers committed to particular religious faiths. Historically, teachers in some communities have been required to teach Sunday school classes in particular churches as a condition of their employment. Although this practice has generally been discontinued, the dominant religious denominations of communities, when such exist, may well influence the selection and appointment of teachers.

The insistence that because public schools do not teach religion they are godless, the efforts to introduce religious instruction into public school programs, the stressing of certain religious rituals such as reciting the Lord's Prayer and the Christian celebration of Christmas—all are evidences of efforts, subtle or direct, to achieve religious training in the public schools. Court rulings to the contrary, pressure is brought in many situations on teachers and school officials to evade the law regarding this point. In general, the more homogeneous a community with respect to religious denominations, the more likely it is to press for the inclusion of religion in its schools. Yet, certain religious groups have taken a firm stand against the teaching of religion in public schools because of their conviction that the principle of separation of church and state is the only valid course that can be taken to preserve the public schools and to assure the continuation of a nation in which freedom of religion prevails.

POPULATION FACTORS

Population changes are of obvious importance. In the past half century—when great numbers of new students were attending high schools and colleges as a result of new attitudes of society toward education—the total population of the United States increased dramatically, from approximately 76 million in 1900 to over 200 million today. This spiraling population results in a demand for several thousand new teachers and classrooms each year.

Demographic changes—for instance, the movement of Americans within the country—also are of great significance. Today about two out of every three people in the United States live in urban areas—a major reversal from population distribution earlier in the century, as Table 10 indicates. Urban residents have educational needs that differ from those of people who live in rural areas. There is less neighborhood cohesiveness, and the school loses some of its community-center function as population increases in urban areas. Recent developments in urban community politics (particularly the demands by ethnic minorities for greater community control over their schools) may reverse this trend, however. Since schools are the focus of social change, urban citizens may demand more voice, more control, and more response in school affairs.

The development of great concentrations of population in certain areas of the country adds to the problems of urbanization. A complex of continuous urban areas over a great distance (called a

TABLE 10. URBAN AND RURAL POPULATION OF THE UNITED STATES: SELECTED YEARS, 1910–68

Census Year	Total Population (Thousands)	Urban Population		Rural Population	
		Total (Thousands)	Percent of Total	Total (Thousands)	Percent of Total
1910	91,972	41,999	45.7	49,473	54.3
1920	105,711	54,158	51.2	51,553	48.8
1930	122,775	68,955	56.2	53,820	43.8
1940	131,669	74,424	56.5	57,246	43.5
1950	150,697	88,927	59.6	61,770	40.4
1960	180,100	113,056	63.0	65,267	37.0
1968	198,200	127,477	64.3	70,754	35.7

Revised chart data from U.S. Dept. of Commerce, Bureau of Census, *Statistical Abstracts of the United States* (Washington: Dept. of Commerce, 1966), p. 15.

"megalopolis" by city planners) already exists along the eastern seaboard from Boston to Washington, D.C. Other megalopoli "belts" are developing between New York and Chicago and on the west coast between San Francisco and San Diego. Administrators and schools must adjust to increased coordination as these dense population areas grow.

SOCIOECONOMIC CONDITIONS

A related factor of great importance is the movement of people within the metropolitan areas. These changing patterns of population are creating serious racial and economic imbalances in many communities and directly affect the schools. In recent years, the white middle-class residents of the inner city have been moving to the suburbs as rural newcomers—many of them nonwhites— migrated to the cities. A study of Chicago in the mid 1960's revealed that between 1940 and 1965 the white population of the city decreased from 3.1 million to 2.5 million, while nonwhites increased from 282,000 to 980,000. In the suburbs during the same period, the white population rose from 1.1 million to 2.9 million, while the nonwhite population increased from 25,000 to 113,000.[1] However, Bureau of the Census figures released early in 1970 indicate that Negroes and other minorities too have begun fleeing the inner cities, with a 9 percent decline of such families shown from 1960 to March 1968.[2]

These socioeconomic changes, of course, have a decisive influence on education. The schools must be ready to adapt to new community conditions. In general, school curricula reflect the needs of their communities. The suburban town, the rural village, and a metropolis like Chicago obviously differ in their socioeconomic structure. Thus, the functions of the schools in these different settings vary as well. A high school in a wealthy suburb, for example, where most of the children go to college, will concen-

[1] Robert J. Havighurst, *The Public Schools of Chicago* (Chicago: Board of Education, 1964), p. 24.
[2] "Negroes, Too, Found Quitting City Slum Areas," New York *Times*, January 6, 1970.

trate on an academic, college-oriented curriculum. In contrast, a large city school with few students preparing for college faces a different set of problems. Indeed, the schools' failure to provide relevant, appropriate education is the chief complaint by urban citizens. Empty rhetoric and education jargon is rejected by increasing numbers of dissatisfied pupils and parents.

LEGAL AND POLITICAL INFLUENCES

Public schools are created and controlled by state legislative enactments. They are also regulated by local school board policies. Any biennial or annual session of the legislature or any monthly meeting of a school board may produce additional statutes and policies which determine the direction of school programs or influence in one way or another the professional work of teachers. Similarly, a decision by a state board of education or court on an educational issue gives direction to the course of education.

Politicized school issues characterize the past decade. Sex education, racial integration, student dress, grooming, and conduct, and a variety of curriculum decisions spurred political controversy in school districts across the country. Board members were defeated, superintendents ousted, and communities polarized by decisions affecting school management and operation. Student unrest, teacher militancy, strikes, boycotts, and demands for community control pressed schools into difficult positions during the 1960's. It has become apparent, therefore, that the politics of education can no longer be confined to the legislature: the pressures and fire-power of parents and citizens are aimed directly at school boards and school administrators. Hopefully the influence of these events will be felt in the coming decade through more responsive school policies, a more flexible curriculum, and increased participation by teachers, parents, and students in the control of schools and schooling.

EXPECTATIONS OF PARENTS

Because schools in the United States are subject to local control, citizens in most communities are able to elect the school board members, who in turn select administrative officials and teachers. Consequently, the attitudes and expectations of parents are an important influence on schools and the work of teachers. Not only do some parents endeavor to keep the schools as they were in the "good old days" of their youth, many of them demand that schools serve their children as the elevators to social status, college admission, and financial success, regardless of the abilities of particular students.

The impact of parental expectations on school programs is clearly evident in the expansion of curricular offerings that has taken place in secondary schools during the past half-century. Demands of parents for particular types of courses to prepare their children for a variety of vocations have resulted in the addition of technical studies to the school program. Similarly, parents' interests in recreational, sports, and aesthetic opportunities for young people have played an important part in bringing many extracurricular activities—such as music, art, dramatics, sports, and journalism—into the regular school offerings.

Often the demands of parents are highly individualistic. Most frequently, however, parental expectations operate as forces that influence the school through the organized efforts of parent groups such as the PTA, citizens' council, or school advisory committee. However the influence may come, teachers find that it is persistent, often forceful, and beneficial as well as detrimental. The greater the interest in education in given communities, the more likely are parents to organize to make their desires known to school boards and to school authorities. The better the school, the more welcome such expressions of parental attitudes are likely to be.

ORGANIZED GROUPS

America has been aptly described as a nation of joiners. This tendency toward use of organizations to promote causes or change conditions was noted early in American history by Alexis de Tocqueville, the Frenchman whose description of American society in the 1830's was incorporated in his well-known volume, *Democracy in America*. De Tocqueville said:

59

Americans of all ages, all conditions, and all dispositions, constantly form associations to give entertainment, to found establishments for education, to build inns, to construct churches, to diffuse books, to send missionaries to the Antipodes; and in this manner they found hospitals, prisons, and schools.[3]

The inclination to form or to join an organized group has produced in the United States more than 200,000 voluntary organizations, with membership approaching 100 million people. Many of these groups center their interest on, or become involved with, the schools, bringing pressure on educators and school officials to accomplish goals endorsed by their members.

Several nationwide bodies have education as their primary reason for existence. For example, the widely known National Congress of Parents and Teachers (more commonly, the PTA) attempts to promote mutual understanding between those who are most directly concerned with the process of education—parents and teachers. In addition, this organization works to unite the efforts of citizens to improve schools throughout the nation. With its approximately 47,000 local chapters and a membership hovering around 12,000,000, the National Congress of Parents and Teachers has exerted influence in promoting legislation involving child welfare, as well as educational policy. For the most part, the influence of PTA's locally has been more marked in the elementary schools than in secondary schools.

Teacher organizations, including the National Education Association (NEA), the American Federation of Teachers (AFT), and the organizations of teachers in the various subject fields, also give support to the improvement of schools, particularly to those aspects that relate to the welfare of teachers. The National Education Association is, by far, the largest teacher organization in the country and with its numerous departments, state and local affiliates, wields considerable influence in educational matters. The American Federation of Teachers, connected with the AFL-CIO, has been concerned largely with salaries and conditions of teach-

---

[3] Alexis de Tocqueville, *Democracy in America* (New York: Oxford University Press, 1947), p. 319.

ing, but in recent years has shown great interest in academic excellence in upgrading the nation's school systems.

Although the AFT long held a militant, aggressive stand toward school boards in teacher welfare matters, the NEA has moved recently (since 1965 when it affirmed the use of collective bargaining in teacher-board relations) toward an equally hard-line position on matters of salary, working conditions, and organized teacher participation in school decisions.[4] Despite a surfeit of rhetoric, there is little substantive difference between the AFT and NEA in strategy, tactics, and organized thrust in teacher–board relations.

One type of organization which is giving increased attention to the strengthening of education is represented by philanthropic foundations which support various aspects of educational developments. In recent times such giant foundations as Ford, Rockefeller, Carnegie, and Kellogg have allocated increasing amounts to education at the elementary and secondary levels. Often foundation activities have pointed the way to government involvement in similar programs.

IMPORTANCE OF FOUNDATIONS

The impact of foundations on education is unquestionable. Some concern has existed, however, regarding the role of these organizations in public education. Since tax-exempt foundations greatly influence American education, a question has arisen as to the propriety of their role.[5] The achievements of the Rockefeller funds in creating experimental schools, the Carnegie Corporation in developing testing programs and innovative programs of teacher training, the Ford Foundation in fostering fellowship programs, programmed learning, educational television, and team teaching, all attest to the helpful role foundations can play. Education

---

[4] William R. Hazard, "Collective Bargaining in Education: The Anatomy of a Problem," *Labor Law Journal*, 18, No. 7 (July 1967), pp. 412–19.

[5] "Schoolmen Give Foundations a Conditional O.K.," *Nation's Schools*, 72 (December 1963), reports results of a poll of school administrators on this question.

has come to be recognized as the key element in the continuation of self-government, free enterprise, and progress in various aspects of human endeavor. It is, therefore, understandable that a substantial number of major foundations will direct increasing amounts of their financial resources to help strengthen educational programs. However, it is well to be aware that the projects selected for support, the research conducted, and the procedures publicized by foundations are likely to bear substantial weight in directing the course of American education.

Numerous other organized groups, although they do not exist primarily to work in the interests of education, exercise influence over schools. Their impact may be direct; it may be made through pressure on school boards, through members of the state legislatures, or the national Congress; or it may be subtle, accomplished by influencing public opinion and the attitudes of school officials. Some such groups boldly attempt to exercise censorship over textbooks or to provide materials of instruction that are in accord with the points of view they desire to see inculcated into the training of the young; others oppose school expansion and improvements to protect vested interests.

Examples of these groups include taxpayers' organizations, civil rights groups, patriotic organizations of various persuasions, political clubs, and civic groups of all kinds. The influence may be exerted directly on school boards and school employees or indirectly through lobbying at the local, state, or national levels. Whatever the motive of given groups, in a democratic society each one is free to attempt to exert its influence on the school and on teachers.

INFLUENTIAL INDIVIDUALS

The impact made by influential citizens at local, state, and national levels is often overlooked when the forces which affect schools are examined. People of influence usually hold positions of importance in a community; they may head what social scientists such as C. Wright Mills have called the "power structure" and be experts in creating public consent for action on projects they favor.[6] They may also block changes that they consider undesirable. Often influential individuals hold status positions in management of political affairs, on school boards and city councils, or they are officers in major business and industrial organizations which influence large numbers of people.

The professional educator, including the classroom teacher, may well become an influential figure whose opinions and attitudes toward education exert considerable influence on the nature and quality of education in a community or wider region. The militant teacher organizations, whose demands go beyond dollars and challenge the traditional notions of power and decision-making in the schools, also see the influence and direction of their profession as a major objective. Often successful and respected teachers gain a wide following for their views on education. University scholars, alert to educational needs and concerned with conditions in the schools, have achieved leadership positions by studying problems and making recommendations which receive national recognition. Perhaps the best fairly recent example of the manner in which a professional person may individually influence education has been the impact on the secondary school of the studies and views of James Bryant Conant, often referred to as the "Inspector General" of American education. Conant's studies of American high schools, teacher education, and his penetrating analysis of schools in metropolitan areas have furnished fertile fields for discussion and innovation.

In recent years many national leaders have emerged as a sort of "new guard" in education and have exerted substantial influence.[7] Many of these leaders have worked in foundations, government posts, and commercial organizations, as well as in universities. John Gardner, Francis Keppel, and Harold Howe II offer good examples of this kind of vigorous leadership in education. Keppel and Howe, both of whom served as Commissioners of Education

[6] C. Wright Mills, *The Power Elite* (New York: Oxford University Press, 1956), pp. 269–74.

[7] See "Current Forces Shaping U.S. Education: The New Guard Emerges," *Changing Education* (journal of the American Federation of Teachers), I, No. 4 (Winter 1967), 6–18.

in the HEW Department and Gardner, Secretary of Health, Education, and Welfare from 1965 to 1968, represent academic figures who were thrust into crucial public positions with tremendous opportunities for shaping the direction of the nation's schools.

INTERNATIONAL CONDITIONS

World conditions and especially wars, both hot and cold, are bound to influence education. The exigencies of military preparedness may greatly reduce the financial resources available to strengthen schools. National emergencies place a premium on certain types of schooling and training, and the possibility of military conscription influences directly the lives of students and teachers.

At the same time, public opinion is molded by changing world events and in turn influences the school curriculum. While McCarthyism following World War II created an atmosphere which deterred objective teaching about Communism, the trend in recent years has been toward rapid increase in the opportunities for study of this competitive ideology. No doubt the success of the Russian space program has spurred the study of Soviet institutions, as has the split in the Communist world following the emergence of Red China as a power. Thus, the curricula in many American schools now include courses in Russian and Chinese language, culture, and history. The emphasis on science and mathematics, in the interests of national defense, is another example of how curriculum may be influenced by international conditions.

MASS MEDIA OF COMMUNICATION

An important part of the social milieu in which pupils live is created by television, radio, motion pictures, newspapers, and magazines. Mass media take up a great deal of young people's time. Studies indicate that American school children spend as many as 25 hours a week watching television. Children bring space-age concepts and understanding to school; too often the school fails to build on this knowledge and turns, instead, to a primitive (and deadly) "See Jane, see Dick" teaching style.

The extent to which mass media influence attitudes and concepts of young people is not known definitely. That is, no one can say that one-tenth of a person's attitudes are a result of television, radio, and newspapers. But it can be stated with a good deal of confidence that mass media represent forces that affect schools because they affect children. They also help to shape public opinion toward education. Not infrequently, school bond issues, budgets, and proposed educational programs are defeated or passed in accordance with the predilections of opinion makers in the press and on the air.

Mass media are important, too, as rapid, efficient means of communication that may change the techniques of teaching. With the developments in television teaching, for example, the very process of instruction itself is undergoing serious review. New experiments with teacher teams are endeavoring to find ways of extending, via television, the contributions of outstanding teachers to increasing numbers of students while using teachers in the classroom to give personal assistance to individual pupils.

ECONOMIC CONDITIONS

The general state of the economy—the amount of money in circulation and the ease with which it circulates—determines to some extent the amount of money that is available for the support of schools. In general, the size of a nation's gross national product is a good indication of its capacity to finance education. The increased expenditures for education in the United States parallel the growth of the gross national product, as Table 11 shows. A country like the United States, with great economic resources, should be able to spend large amounts on education without short-changing other sectors of the economy. Although Americans spent an estimated 55 billion dollars on education in 1969–70, for example, this expenditure (slightly over 6 percent of the gross national product) did not impair the nation's capacity to wage an expensive war in Viet Nam, continue roadbuilding, foreign aid, and a host of other national commitments.

TABLE 11. GROSS NATIONAL PRODUCT RELATED TO TOTAL EXPENDITURES FOR EDUCATION: UNITED STATES, 1929–30 TO 1967–68
[Beginning with 1959–60 school year, includes Alaska and Hawaii]

Calendar year	Gross national product (in millions)	School year	Expenditures for education [1] Total (in thousands)	As a percent of gross national product
1929	$103,095	1929–30	$3,233,601	3.14
1931	75,820	1931–32	2,966,464	3.91
1933	55,601	1933–34	2,294,896	4.13
1935	72,247	1935–36	2,649,914	3.67
1937	90,446	1937–38	3,014,074	3.38
1939	90,494	1939–40	3,199,593	3.54
1941	124,540	1941–42	3,203,548	2.57
1943	191,592	1943–44	3,522,007	1.84
1945	212,010	1945–46	4,167,597	1.97
1947	231,323	1947–48	6,574,379	2.84
1949	256,484	1949–50	8,795,635	3.43
1951	328,404	1951–52	11,312,446	3.44
1953	364,593	1953–54	13,949,876	3.83
1955	397,960	1955–56	16,811,651	4.22
1957	441,134	1957–58	21,119,565	4.79
1959	488,650	1959–60	24,722,464	5.11
1961	520,109	1961–62	29,366,305	5.65
1963	589,238	1963–64	36,010,210	6.11
1965	683,900	1965–66	44,800,000 [2]	6.55
1967	785,100	1967–68	52,200,000 [2]	6.65

[1] Includes expenditures of public and nonpublic schools at all levels of education (elementary, secondary, and higher education).

[2] Estimated.

SOURCE: U.S. Office of Education, *Progress of Public Education in the United States of America 1967–1968.*

From Kenneth A. Simon and W. Vance Grant, *Digest of Educational Statistics* (1968 edition), p. 21.

DEMANDS OF BUSINESS AND INDUSTRY

When the United States was an agrarian society, the skills and knowledge required of workers were simple, even primitive. As technological developments occurred, however, business and industry became more complex, requiring workers with more highly developed skills. They looked to schools and colleges for educated individuals. Consequently, demands upon the schools for trained graduates have steadily increased. People who can build and operate complex business machines, factory machines, and other types of equipment are needed, just as are highly educated professional people for executive positions. Engineers and other specialists are required in more and more industries. Secretaries and clerical personnel in general are expected to be well educated. As business and industry continue to grow in size and complexity, the educational background of personnel must increase in both breadth and depth.

TECHNOLOGICAL CHANGES

Machines are now being used to run other machines—automation is a reality. Its full implications for education are as yet impossible to visualize. Already observable is the fact that as industries turn to automatic machines, new jobs are created to produce the machines. Such new jobs require a higher level of training and skill than those replaced by automation. The educational implications, particularly in the fields of technology and the sciences, are obvious.

The process of education itself has already been affected by technological developments. Industry and the armed forces, for example, have successfully used automatic machines to provide routine instruction, thus freeing the teacher for other activities. Experiments with teaching machines at Harvard University suggest that certain types of learning may be conducted by the student with the help of a teaching instrument that poses questions and automatically evaluates responses. Computers have been used successfully in experimental teaching situations; and with increasing sophistication in programming, evaluation, and improved hardware, computerized teaching holds considerable promise for schools. Developments in the field of electronics bring to the school possibilities in the field of audiovisual resources that promise to enrich and accelerate learning.

On the other hand, a recent review [8] of the present state of technology in the schools has tempered much of the early optimism surrounding it. After examining the assertion that technology will promote individualization of instruction, the authors note:

. . . we remain at quite some distance from implementing truly individualized instruction in the classroom and begin to become aware of the difficulties of integrating technology into the school on a large scale.

These difficulties include the teachers' reluctance to change their teaching styles; the unreliability of machines and teaching devices and the resultant frustration; and the hard facts of school finance to support some expensive technology systems. To speak of a "technological breakthrough" does not guarantee an "adoption breakthrough" in the schools.

There are far-reaching implications for education in the increased leisure time made possible by technological inventions. As people are required to work less, they undoubtedly will call upon schools to help with programs of continuing education for leisure and citizenship efficiency. Yet new jobs require new skills; consequently, in education for adults, greater emphasis may need to be placed on adapting workers to the changing requirements of a technological age.

THE SOCIAL REVOLUTION

Perhaps the most explosive and pervasive influence on education in the 1970's is the radically changed social context. The traditional power structures in many school districts are under attack for their alleged failures in school, community, and national leadership. The urban schools—born in frustration and nurtured in a polluted, overcrowded, man-made environment—catch the brunt of these charges. The oppressive poverty of many in the midst of affluence is difficult to understand, and to ask for patience with a nonresponsive school system borders on insanity. There is some doubt that cities, as we have known them in the nineteenth and

[8] Anthony Oettinger and Sema Marks, "Educational Technology: New Myths and Old Realities," *Harvard Educational Review,* XXXVIII, No. 4 (Fall 1968), 697–717.

twentieth centuries, will survive; the parallel doubts about the school system are even less optimistic. Unless massive infusions of creative ideas and resources, both human and material, flow to the cities and the urban schools, the social structure may fall to the rising demands for reform.

SUMMARY

Society, like a machine, is composed of various interrelated parts. All must function smoothly or maladjustments will result. A variety of forces exists in modern society. These general forces may be social, religious, political, economic, or scientific; yet all in one way or another affect schools.

Social and political forces that affect schools are rooted initially in the ideals that give direction to the society. Population factors, the socioeconomic conditions of the community, religious issues, the efforts of organized groups, international conditions, and developments in technology are some of the social and political forces with which the schools and teachers must contend.

Economic issues and circumstances that make an impact on education are also numerous and diverse. The state of the national economy governs to some extent the amount of money that is devoted to the support of the schools. In turn, the amount of money expended for schools largely determines the quality and extent of their educational programs. Business and industry often expect the schools to equip pupils with skills and knowledge needed by productive employees. Finally, technological changes require highly educated innovators and personnel capable of adapting to new conditions.

SUGGESTED READINGS

Duker, Sam, *The Public Schools and Religion: The Legal Context.* New York: Harper & Row, Publishers, 1966, pp. 14–148.

Eurich, Alvin C., *Reforming American Education.* New York: Harper & Row, Publishers, 1969, pp. 147–158.

Full, Harold, *Controversy in American Education.* New York: The Macmillan Co., 1967, pp. 9–57.

Rudy, Willis, *Schools in an Age of Mass Culture*. Englewood Cliffs, New Jersey: Prentice-Hall, Inc., 1965, pp. 50–105.

Shannon, Robert L., "The Numbers Racket in Education." J. A. Battle and Robert L. Shannon, *The New Idea In Education*. New York: Harper & Row, Publishers, 1968, pp. 76–79.

Spaght, Monroe E., *The Bright Key*. New York: Appleton-Century-Crofts, 1965, pp. 1–12 and 30–38.

COMMUNITY OBJECTIVES
FOR EDUCATION

"WHOM, then, do I call educated?" asked Isocrates in his search for the aims of education. In answering his own question, the philosopher expressed several ideas that are acceptable to many today —Isocrates called educated those "who manage well the circumstances which they encounter day by day. . . ." and those who "are decent and honorable in their intercourse with all men, bearing easily and good-naturedly what is unpleasant and offensive in others. . . ." The most important characteristic of educated people, he thought, is that they "are not spoiled by their successes, and do not desert their true selves, but hold their ground steadfastly as wise and sober men. . . ."

Others have faced the question, "What should education accomplish?" Educators as well as citizens, individually and collectively, have attempted to devise statements of aims of education that would gain general acceptance. So far, none has met with complete success. Their failure is due to both the diversity and the change that characterize a free society. Especially in the United States, in very recent times, this pluralism and the tremendous changes in urban and suburban societies have drastically affected community objectives for education.

PROBLEMS OF ACHIEVING
EDUCATIONAL OBJECTIVES

While the transportation and communication revolutions have served to greatly reduce regional differences and helped to create broader national viewpoints, community aspirations for educating boys and girls still differ greatly. For instance, black action groups in New York City, as well as in other large urban centers, have been concerned with community emphasis and decentralization, a relatively new development of the late 1960's. The Ocean Hill-Brownsville confrontation in Brooklyn, New York—involving a local school board, white teachers, a black administrator, the United Federation of Teachers, and thousands of school children —was typical of a growing movement in deprived areas to change the educational environment for black students.[1] On the other hand, in many of the plush suburban areas around large cities such as Chicago and Detroit, the major community educational problem may very well be the struggle over propriety of sex education in elementary schools.

The achievement of common agreement on the aims of education is complicated by several factors. First, even professions of agreement relative to aims may be highly tenuous, or they may be weakened by differences in weight or priority assigned to particular aims or emphases. Second, because the language by which aims are stated often enjoys no exact meaning, differences in interpretation frequently develop. Third, the current public expectations of schools are sometimes paradoxical. Goals that the public claims for education are sometimes mutually exclusive. For example, some insist that pupils be taught to think critically; yet, the same people demand a highly chauvinistic content for history courses. A fourth obstacle to common agreement on aims of education grows out of the wide diversity that characterizes the people of the United States.

Just as all social policy is a compromise in a free society, including the Constitution of the United States, so, too, are the aims of education. Common agreements with respect to goals for schools must be recognized as only tentative guides. Operational agreements, including aims of education, will, of course, be relatively dependable; but they will always be subject to change since differences in a democracy are never completely resolved.

[1] Wallace Roberts, "The Battle for Urban Schools," *Saturday Review,* November 16, 1968, p. 97.

Another basic problem in establishing aims for education is the historic difference of opinion on the role of the schools in American society. Roald Campbell, former Dean of the Graduate School of Education at the University of Chicago, has noted the importance of this issue, especially in planning for education in today's urban communities.

[M] any school people and many civil rights people are polarized around two different views regarding the role of the school in our society. To many school people, the overriding purposes of the school are the teaching of literacy, some appreciation of the American culture, and preparation for work or for college. In this view, the assumption is made that we are a middle-class, or perhaps even better, a classless society, and that the values of that homogeneous society are to be reflected in the school. This view worked rather well over most of our history. . . .

The traditional view of the school appears to have served well a society largely dependent on agriculture, largely Anglo-Saxon in origin, and largely Protestant in religion. For a society based on industrial development with people clustered in metropolitan areas and pluralistic in religion and culture, there have been many strains. The determination of the Negro to take his full place in this new world has augmented these strains. Many people in present-day America, including civil rights groups, see the school as a powerful instrument of social policy and they insist that such power be exercised. . . .

Back of much of the strife now found in city schools is this polarization of position. Many school people wish to carry on the traditional functions of the school and they resist using the school to solve social problems. Indeed, they feel that social problems should be solved by the larger society. Many civil rights adherents think it of primary importance that schools take direct action to contribute to urban renewal, including integration of the races and stabilization of city neighborhoods. So important is the school seen by civil rights advocates in the achievement of these ends that we may get the impression that no attention is being paid to the educational function of the school. In any case, the polarization around the school as an "educational" agency and as a "social" agency is a factor of consequence in most of our cities.[2]

[2] Office of Education, *Contemporary Issues in American Education* (Washington, D.C.: U.S. Dept. of Health, Education, and Welfare, 1966), p. 148.

NEW APPROACHES IN COMMUNITY OBJECTIVES

Despite this controversy on the basic function of the schools—a question that existed long before the civil rights issue renewed public interest in the question—it is clear today that the "literacy-only" idea no longer has broad support.

Through the help of federal, state, and local agencies, communities are developing a wide variety of programs to meet specific educational needs, especially for economically and culturally deprived citizens. With Title I funds from the Elementary and Secondary Education Act of 1965, for example, Wasco, California, established a special course of study for children of migrant Mexican-American families that come there each spring. In a different setting, East Chicago, Indiana, created a Neighborhood Youth Corps and Home-School Project with federal assistance to maintain effective contact between the homes in deprived neighborhoods and the schools. The city also used its Title I funds for eliminating educational deprivation by sponsoring cultural field trips, elementary guidance, speech therapy, extension of library services, and remedial reading and arithmetic classes.

Many communities have programs to assist teen-agers who have dropped out of school. The Los Angeles school system, for example, has established a guidance center program which focuses on guidance and counseling services, individualized courses of study, involvement of parents in vocational-educational planning, and other means of improving pupil and family self-images.[3]

In another example, Minneapolis has been experimenting with a store-front junior high—a special school in one of the city's poorest neighborhoods—with individualized instruction to make education meaningful to potential seventh, eighth, and ninth grade dropouts. A new type of "high school without walls" was organized in Chicago in late 1969. Drawing students from many ethnic

[3] Office of Education, *A Chance for a Change: New School Programs for the Disadvantaged* (Washington, D.C.: U.S. Dept. of Health, Education, and Welfare, 1966), p. 16.

groups, the project, which is a combined effort of the Chicago Board of Education and university educators, has established an innovative, elastic curriculum which concentrates on correlation of classroom studies and real-life experiences in the civic, business, recreational, and other public communities. Many eminent educators have suggested "competitive" educational complexes which radically depart from the conventional "establishment" type school structures and activities.[4]

In other ways, communities are making major innovations in shaping educational objectives. More than ever, they are using the schools for instruction on subjects that were long held to be reserved by tradition for the family. The increase of sex education in the schools is an example of new community attitudes toward the educational role of the schools. Evanston, Illinois, for several years has included sex education in its elementary school curriculum, and its program has served as a model for many other communities. The Evanston curriculum in particular has received national attention for its objectivity and emphasis on instruction in the preadolescent years.

SOURCES OF OBJECTIVES

In a broad sense, the objectives of the community in education are derived from (1) society itself, including its ideals, nature, and structure; and (2) the individual, who exists within the social matrix. From these two sources come the "needs of society" and the "needs of the individual." Differences in educational objectives often are caused by the concern for the perpetuation of the group as contrasted to helping satisfy personal educational ambitions. Yet no sharp lines of demarcation may properly be drawn between society and the individual as exclusive and differentiated bases for determining the aims of education. Goals of a society, in a democratic nation at least, may be realized only by helping individual citizens achieve their personal educational objectives.

As reference points, basic categories separating the aims of so-

[4] Theodore R. Sizer, "The Case for a Free Market," *Saturday Review*, January 11, 1969, p. 34.

ciety and the individual have been established by educators and appear in Figure 6. But more than ever, educators are aware of the limited use of this type of abstract analysis in shaping constructive policy on the community level.

The wide acceptance of the close interaction of societal and individual needs—especially in the necessity of coordination and cooperation between local and national agencies—in many re-

FIGURE 6. SPECIFIC REFERENCE POINTS FOR AIMS OF EDUCATION

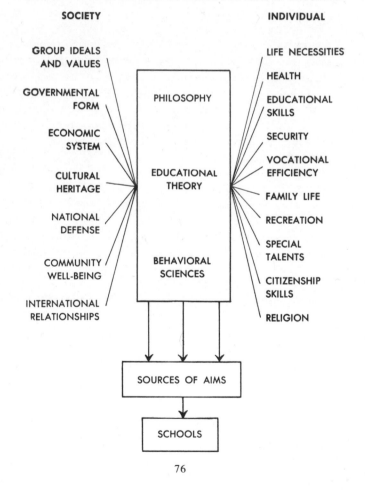

spects is a recent development. But today economists as well as educators agree that expenditures for education, for example, are sound investments in the future of the nation, the community, and the individual.

INDIVIDUAL FULFILLMENT AS A COMMUNITY OBJECTIVE

Today everyone recognizes that the continued vitality of American institutions depends to a great extent on the quality of education each citizen receives. Communities across the country are implementing imaginative programs to increase the educational opportunities for students of all ability levels. But educational planners also realize that a great deal more needs to be done in the future. As Francis Keppel, the former Commissioner of the U.S. Office of Education, has said:

Between 1965 and 1975, approximately thirty million young men and women will leave school to embark upon the adventure of looking for their first jobs. Unless current projections are changed by conscious action of federal, state, and local action, at least two million of these youngsters may never enter high school and at least another seven million may not receive a diploma. And many may, therefore, find no jobs. Skill obsolescence affects the youth most of all. A Department of Labor survey in October, 1964, found 695,000 unemployed dropouts and graduates aged sixteen to twenty-one.

Thus nearly a third of the crop of this American resource will—unless the necessary revolution occurs remarkably soon—be unprepared to make the contribution to the economy that the nation is coming to expect. Surely more important, they may well individually lead unsatisfying and drab lives confined to uninteresting jobs and inadequate wages.[5]

SUMMARY

More than ever, educational leaders are recognizing the need for sound programs for the individual as awareness grows of the reciprocal benefits society receives from quality education for all

[5] *The Necessary Revolution in American Education* (New York: Harper & Row, 1966), pp. 52–53.

its citizens. The distinctions between "community" and "national" educational objectives are also becoming increasingly blurred as a result of the communications revolution and the growth of large metropolitan areas in the United States.

Despite the trend toward greater agreement in educational policies, disputes still exist on the basic function of the schools. Although the traditional "literacy-only" view still has support, educational leaders today are taking a broader view of the school's role in community life and implementing a wide variety of innovative programs to increase educational opportunities for all students.

SUGGESTED READINGS

Cohen, S. Alan, "Local Control and the Cultural Deprivation Fallacy," *Phi Delta Kappan,* January 1969, pp. 255–59.

Fantini, Mario, and Marilyn Gittell, "The Ocean Hill–Brownsville Experiment," *Phi Delta Kappan,* April 1969, pp. 442–45.

Gibbons, Richard P., "Teacher Evaluation: Job for the Community, Administrators, or Peers?" *Changing Education,* Summer 1967, pp. 20–22.

Haskins, Kenneth W., "The Case for Local Control," *Saturday Review,* January 11, 1969, pp. 52–54.

McPherson, R. Bruce, "Administrators and the Inner-City Increase of Power," *School Review,* November 1969, pp. 105–13.

Mothner, Ira, "The War for City Schools," *Look,* May 13, 1969, pp. 43–49.

Selakovich, Daniel, *The Schools and American Society.* Waltham, Mass.: Blaisdell Publishing Co., 1967, Chap. 4.

Stoffel, Fred, "The Right Spirit All Year Long," *American Education,* December 1968, pp. 2–4.

Task Force on Urban Education, "Trying to Find the Pony: Decentralization, Community Control, Governance of the Education Profession," *Today's Education,* February 1969, pp. 58–60.

Wilcox, Preston R., "The Community-Centered School," in *The Schoolhouse in the City,* Alvin Toffler, ed. New York: Frederick A. Praeger, Publishers, 1968, Chap. 9.

5.

CURRICULUM AND INSTRUCTION

CURRICULUM and instruction are at the very heart of education. As subject fields they are extremely broad and difficult to define. One concise and useful definition brings the two together in this fashion:

. . . Curriculum is the entire body of courses offered by a school including the selected, refined and organized knowledges, understandings, attitudes, skills, values, and behavior to be transmitted to the student. In contrast, instruction is the process by which the curriculum is taught or transmitted. In this sense, curriculum is concerned with *what* is taught; instruction with *how* teaching is accomplished.[1]

Logically, the nature of the curriculum and the character of instruction have changed as a result of evolutional experiences of the past. Changes, undoubtedly, have reflected stages of American development and have not come with any degree of regularity. To cover in detail the history of how these changes have come about is not possible in this chapter, which will attempt to deal with only the broadest manifestations of this historical movement.[2]

HISTORICAL BACKGROUND

In the Colonial period of our country's history, education was dominated by theological, social, and political orthodoxies. The

[1] Lindley J. Stiles, "Instruction," in *Encyclopedia of Educational Research,* 3rd ed. (New York: The Macmillan Company, 1960), p. 710.

[2] Ryland W. Crary, *Humanizing the School: Curriculum Development and Theory* (New York: Alfred A. Knopf, 1969), is a modern and comprehensive survey of curriculum development.

goals of education were largely based on religion. Because of these religious motives, the colonists required only rudimentary education for the common folk. The study of classical languages, philosophy, and similar esoteric subjects was reserved for boys who attended exclusive schools.

Although American schools reflected the British culture, methods of instruction in the colonies differed from those in Europe. In Europe instruction was largely oral, with little emphasis on reading. Since one major purpose of early American schools was to enable men and women to study the Bible and to be able to read civil edicts, it was inevitable that reading should be emphasized.

Education in the period just preceding the Revolutionary War differed according to region. The development of schools occurred with greatest speed in the North, especially in Massachusetts and Connecticut, where preoccupation with religion promoted education as a means of studying the Word of God. Organized religion, however, restricted teaching of such subjects as art, music, secular literature, and some of the sciences. To some extent, due to the needs of trade, instruction in practical subjects such as writing, arithmetic, bookkeeping, and English grammar were offered by private tutors. Diversity of nationalities, differing social values, economic groupings, and religions characterized the Middle Colonies. These factors tended to retard development of public schools for all, and schools were part of religious institutions. In the South, the plantation system, which prevented the rise of a middle class, deterred the development of a system of free schools. The aristocratic segment developed the practice of employing private tutors for their children, and many young men were sent to England to finish their education. Education was largely a private matter to be provided by families.

While there was a decline in emphasis upon education during and immediately after the Revolution, several developments then were to have important influences on education in the years to come. Benjamin Franklin's idea of the academy had materialized in 1751 as a protest against the classical, college preparatory Latin grammar school. This academy movement was to result in a broadened curriculum including modern foreign languages, English, history, and natural sciences.

In the period from 1800 to 1860, increasing democratization and development of scientific interests created demands for an expansion of the program of studies offered in schools. A broader curriculum was necessary if pupils were to be prepared for "the ordinary duties of life." The study of geography, government, and history was endorsed on the assumption that it would prepare students for citizenship. Physical training, drawing, and natural science were accepted as necessary for the common education of all. Of course, reading, writing, and arithmetic still constituted the heart of the curriculum in the elementary schools.

Between 1860 and 1918, elementary education in the United States expanded considerably. Kindergartens were beginning to be made part of the public school systems, thereby pushing the age for school entrance downward. Morals, hygiene, drawing, natural science, physiology, music, and physical culture joined the basic subjects of grammar, literature, history, geography, and arithmetic in the elementary school curriculum.

A development of great significance for secondary education during this period involved the question of the very purpose of the high school. Some claimed that its function was to prepare people generally for life; others advocated vocational or specialized education. Because of the trend toward broadening the secondary school program and the growing popularity of the elective system, educators addressed themselves to definition of the college preparatory curriculum. The interest in practical subjects and in general preparation for citizenship forced the high school to become more comprehensive in scope and purpose.

Several general characteristics of the period from 1860 to 1918 were important to curriculum and instruction. Social, economic, and political forces were changing rapidly to keep abreast of the growing complexity of business and industrial life. At the same time, European scholars were projecting theories about learning and education that appealed to people in a new nation which was attempting to develop an educational program to serve a wide range of individual abilities. In the United States itself, educational leaders of stature were setting the stage for the development of the most universal program of education the world has ever known.

The growth of universal public education received a significant blueprint in 1918 from a report of the Secondary School Principals' Association of the National Education Association. This definition of the functions of the high school—which came to be known as the Seven Cardinal Principles of Education—gave direction to the development of a comprehensive secondary school program which would prepare for citizenship, prepare for college, develop marketable skills, and prepare for life. In addition to furnishing guidelines for high school curriculum construction, the principles applied also to the elementary school.

Compulsory attendance laws and the rapid industrialization of society, adding millions to school rolls, necessarily slowed down the momentum of adaptation and change. The massive task of physically handling all these students took priority over other matters. Meanwhile, great stress was placed on standardized tests and collection of educational statistics. Sequence—or *when* learning is best presented—became the subject of studies such as those of Hollis L. Caswell, of Teachers College, Columbia University, under whom scope and sequence studies were begun. These studies attempted to relate the needs of the child and his level of readiness for the subject matter.

Following World War I, elementary and secondary school curricula felt the effects of the growing progressive movement in education.[3] Sparked by such men as Edward J. Sheldon, Francis W. Parker, and John Dewey, the emphasis in curriculum and methods of instruction changed from preoccupation with subject matter to a more child-centered approach. Progressives objected to "treating children as statistics" and introduced the "activity movement" in elementary education, stressing active participation in

---

[3] Lawrence A. Cremin, *The Transformation of the School* (New York: Vintage Books, 1964), is a thorough study of the progressive movement in education.

learning in contrast to passive experiences through mere textbook lessons and their regurgitation.[4]

Studies of child development aided by psychology and psychiatry seemed to reinforce the ideas of progressives that the aims of education could not be tied to the intellect alone and that the whole personality of the student must be considered. More and more was becoming known concerning the learning process, indicating that the role of the teacher and the school and the nature of the curriculum had to change in accordance with the interests and needs of the children. The curriculum no longer need concentrate on preparing pupils for future life; the primary emphasis of education should be on learning through physical and social activity. Thus, subjects such as art and musical training, home economics, and manual arts were stressed and an "experience curriculum" recommended, in which the child, through enjoyable activities, learned to read, write, and spell. In the junior high school, a core curriculum cutting across subject-matter fields became the vogue.

Opposed to progressive ideas were the essentialists, a school of educators who insisted that knowledge, attitudes, and skills necessary for years to come should be the teaching and learning goals of the schools. They favored a narrower curriculum based on the three R's and the learning of traditional subjects such as grammar, mathematics, science, and history through books and diligent study.

During the depression years, many of the ideas of the progressives came under attack. Slowly the Progressive Education Association, spokesman of the movement, declined in membership, so that by 1950 the organization was in the process of dissolution. Meanwhile, following World War II, the essentialists—backed by subject-matter departments of universities and represented by such critics as Arthur E. Bestor, Jr.,[5] Admiral Hyman Rickover, Al-

[4] See George A. Beauchamp, *The Curriculum of the Elementary School* (Boston: Allyn and Bacon, 1964), pp. 41–52, for an excellent description of these developments.

[5] See *Educational Wastelands* (Urbana: University of Illinois Press, 1953).

bert Lynd, Robert M. Hutchins, and Mortimer Smith—demanded an end to emphasis on "life adjustment" and "frills" of the school program and a return to what they considered basic education and fundamental learning. The apparent lack of a solid academic background among many high school graduates, which was revealed by military testing programs, helped to reinforce this criticism. The successful launching by the Russians of Sputnik I in 1957 added to the drive for reappraising the curricula of American schools.

RECENT DEVELOPMENTS

The mid-twentieth century represents an important watershed in the history of American education. Much of the activity concerning curriculum reform and new modes of instruction began around 1950 and has continued with growing momentum since then. The purpose of the rest of the chapter will be to highlight these developments.

A great deal of the ferment over curriculum and instruction hinges on the determination (if this is possible) of the proper societal role of the school in American life. That this role has changed considerably in recent times is obvious. The massive increase in school population has brought to the fore physical problems connected with inadequate space and outmoded facilities. Beyond this the tremendous increase in school population has inevitably put millions of students with low academic interests and abilities into the high school. Add to this the ever-growing problem of maintaining an adequate professional staff and it becomes clear that curricular questions are closely tied up with many of the growing public questions of our time.

What is the function of the curriculum today? Is it different from that which it has served in the past? Understandably, a latitude of opinion exists on these questions. According to an important volume on methodology:

The curriculum consists of selected portions of the social heritage. . . . [it] is not prepared by social scientists; it must be prepared by teachers who know the limits as well as the capacities of boys and girls. The curriculum consists of reorganized, simplified, and purposive selected portions of information and experience. It is an instrument of the schools, not a storehouse of knowledge. Expectations of scholars, parents, and other adults must not determine the contents of the curriculum. The gap between society's wishes and the capacities of students can be bridged only by the teacher. The stock of culture is not the only factor in making a curriculum; it is sharply delimited by the interests, capacities, maturation and needs of the students.[6]

In contrast to this teacher-centered approach to the curriculum, many educators, including C. Glen Hass,[7] feel that the curriculum is the combined task of "interested citizens, parents, learners, and scholars [who] must work with teachers, principals and supervisors in the planning."

John Goodlad [8] sees the curricular reform beginning at the mid-century as both evolutionary and revolutionary, incorporating elements of past endeavors and significant new departures. In addition to the postwar conditions already mentioned which produced critical appraisal of the schools, he mentions the impact of swelling college populations as a result of a prosperous middle class sending more and more youngsters to college. Consequently, interest mounted in college preparatory studies undertaken in high school. At the same time the knowledge explosion made it impossible to deal with the immense accumulation of facts, so that the curriculum, in Goodlad's words, turned to "fresh infusion of content and comprehensive reorganization emphasizing the structure of the academic disciplines and man's way of knowing." A new interest grew in experimentation with children's abilities to learn and in early childhood schooling.

[6] Edgar B. Wesley and Stanley P. Wronski, *Teaching Social Studies in High Schools* (Boston: D.C. Heath and Company, 1965), pp. 24–25.

[7] C. Glen Hass, "Who Should Plan the Curriculum," *Educational Leadership,* XIX (Washington, D.C.: Association for Curriculum Development, National Education Association, October 1961), 2–4.

[8] *The Changing American School,* Sixty-Fifth Yearbook of the National Society for the Study of Education (Chicago: The University of Chicago Press, 1966), pp. 32–58.

THE NEW CURRICULA

Research in creating of new curricula and establishment of projects for their development were underwritten not by local educational agencies, but by the federal government and national foundations. Leadership was assumed mainly by subject-matter specialists in the universities, who were concerned with creation of new courses, using new methods and materials. Such innovations emphasized single disciplines and application of modern theories of learning which took notice of the structure of the discipline itself. Profound influence on curriculum and instruction was exerted by Jerome S. Bruner of Harvard University,[9] whose writings emphasize the readiness of most school children to tackle the foundations of any subject at practically any age. By discovering the structural principles of a subject, says Bruner, educators could teach it in an intellectually honest fashion to most students. Although Bruner's ideas are not accepted by many educators and academicians, they have served to arouse healthy interest in methods of arranging subject matter and creation of new approaches to teaching.[10]

The movement to create new curricula [11] had its inception and progressed most rapidly in mathematics and science. In these areas it was discovered that the great expansion of knowledge was not reflected in postwar courses. Textbooks were outmoded, and too many teachers were not abreast of modern developments.

MATHEMATICS. Early and significant programs in high school mathematics education originated at the University of Illinois in 1952.[12] Combining the efforts of scholars from liberal arts and

[9] See his *Process of Education* (Cambridge, Mass.: Harvard University Press, 1962).

[10] An excellent treatment of these developments is given in Gail Inlow, *The Emergent in Curriculum* (New York: John Wiley & Sons, 1966), pp. 12–23.

[11] *New Curricula,* a collection of readings edited by Robert W. Heath (New York: Harper & Row, 1964), offers a full picture of recent curricular innovations.

[12] Max Beberman, *An Emerging Program of Secondary School Mathematics,* Inglis Lecture for 1958 (Cambridge, Mass.: Harvard University Press, 1958).

sciences, education, and engineering, this group undertook to create new mathematics courses and to train teachers in its procedures. Basic to the philosophy of the "new math" was the goal of gaining operational understanding of mathematical concepts through student discovery emphasizing the use of precise language. Identified as the University of Illinois Committee on School Mathematics (UICSM) this group, in cooperation with teachers in the schools, has created courses and textbooks, and has constantly revised this approach as new findings emerged.

Another of the many significant projects in mathematics education is the School Mathematics Study Group (SMSG), which started its work in 1958 under the direction of E.C. Begle at Yale University and subsequently at Stanford University.[13] In an imaginative project—which enlisted university scholars and school teachers in cooperation with the College Entrance Examination Board—this group participated in summer workshops or writing sessions in which they undertook to write sample textbooks, which have ultimately influenced commercial textbook offerings. The project has addressed itself to many basic questions in mathematics education involving mathematical learning processes of children and the effect of negative attitudes toward mathematics. Many other projects in mathematics education, with support from the federal government and private foundations, have continued to work on programs designed to upgrade teaching and learning in this crucial field.[14]

SCIENCE. Almost simultaneous with curricular developments in mathematics have come innovations in science education. Millions of dollars of research funds have been channeled into projects involving science teaching by the federal government, principally through the National Science Foundation. As a result of scholarly research, summer institutes, and development of materials, a great deal has been done to close the gap between the tremendous knowledge explosion in science and up-to-date instruction in the

[13] See William Wooton, "The History and Status of the School Mathematics Study Group," Heath, *op. cit.* (above, n. 11), pp. 35–53.

[14] For a critical review of the new mathematics programs, see Morris Kline, "Intellectuals and the Schools: A Case History," *Harvard Educational Review*, XXXVI (Fall 1966), 505–511.

nation's schools. Emphasis has been placed on making scientific subject matter meaningful not only to specially oriented students who are potential engineers or scientists, but also to the broadest range of students. This is vital in an age when all Americans are so closely affected by scientific developments.

University scholars and school teachers combined again in 1956 to form—under the direction of two physics professors, Jerrold R. Zacharias and Francis L. Friedman, both of the Massachusetts Institute of Technology—the Physical Science Study Committee (PSSC).[15] The initial purpose of this group was to create a better introductory physics course than already existed in most high schools. To assure continuity in its efforts, a nonprofit corporation, Educational Services Incorporated, was created which produced textbooks, motion picture films, laboratory equipment, and student and teacher guidebooks. As is the case with all of the new curriculum projects, PSSC materials have been tested in classes, evaluated, and revised if necessary. Realizing that a one-year physics course cannot hope to give high school students anything approaching comprehensive coverage of this rapidly expanding field, the committee realistically chose as its goal to provide a good base for further learning. Emphasis was placed on basic ideas of physics and encouragement of inquiry and discovery among students through experimentation.

Two programs in creating new courses in chemistry are significant. One, the Chemical Bond Approach Project,[16] initiated around 1957, stresses atomic and molecular structure and encourages students in problem solving through experimentation and analysis on their own. The other important chemistry program was the Chemical Education Material Study (Chem Study), operating between 1960 and 1963. This project produced a one-year course designed to accommodate both terminal students or those requiring a good background for further study. The National Science Foundation underwrote both projects, which resulted in textbooks,

[15] Gilbert C. Finlay, "The Physical Science Study Committee," *The School Review,* LXX (Spring 1962), 63–81.

[16] See Inlow, *op. cit.* (above, n. 10), pp. 125–26, for a brief description of this program.

laboratory guides, teaching materials, and other learning aids.[17]

In the area of the biological sciences, the American Institute of Biological Sciences in 1959, spurred on by excellent results in the Physical Sciences Study Committee, began work on a curriculum study.[18] Again, support came from the National Science Foundation. Under direction of Arnold B. Grobman, of the University of Colorado, and Bentley Glass, of Johns Hopkins University, a committee of college and high school people attacked the problem of outmoded biology curricula in the secondary schools and determined to close the gap between tremendous advances in this field and what was being taught in the schools.

While innovative programs were changing curriculum and instruction in mathematics and science, considerable criticism was being directed at the slow progress toward change being made in foreign languages, English, and the social studies.

FOREIGN LANGUAGES. As a result of the need to quickly train military personnel in foreign languages during World War II, an important background of language-teaching techniques and materials already existed. Another, and most important, factor in promoting research in foreign language instruction has been the Modern Language Association, which began its Foreign Language Study Program in 1952. Aided by government funds, this organization has conducted experimentation in audio-lingual techniques and use of language laboratories and other technical arrangements. An interesting facet of the work in this field has been the emphasis on foreign language instruction in the elementary school.[19]

ENGLISH. No more important area of curriculum and instruction improvement exists than in the field of English. For all students, college bound and otherwise, skill in communication in one's own language has become more than a sign of education—it has be-

[17] J. A. Campbell, "CHEM Study—An Approach to Chemistry Based on Experiments," Heath, *op. cit.* (above, n. 11), pp. 82–93.

[18] Bentley Glass, "Renascent Biology: A Report on the AIBS Biological Sciences Curriculum Study," *The School Review,* LXX (Spring 1962), 16–43.

[19] For a description of recent developments in foreign language instruction, see David H. Harding, *The New Pattern of Language Teaching* (London: Longmans, Green & Co., Ltd.), 1967.

come a dollars and cents consideration in employment, conduct of business, politics, and countless other life activities. Project English, which had its start in 1961 under auspices of the U.S. Office of Education, was an effort to improve English instruction at all academic levels. Involving curriculum study centers at a number of universities, with cooperation between professors and school teachers, these projects have tackled problems dealing with linguistics, reading, literature, composition, and spelling.[20] Now known as the English Program of the U.S. Office of Education, these studies have investigated communication problems concerning the culturally deprived, delved into sentence structure of gifted students, and appraised the practicality of programmed learning in English instruction. Stress on inductive methods of teaching, encouraging students to think in depth, and to appreciate literary craftsmanship are characteristic of the program.[21]

SOCIAL STUDIES. The object of its share of post-Sputnik criticism, social studies education has undergone serious examination.[22] Of all subjects, history and the social studies as taught in elementary and high school are perhaps the most difficult to relate to everyday life and to needs of students in an ultrascientific world. Overcoming student apathy, revising course content, introducing novel teaching strategies and other curricular activities— all these considerations went into what came to be known as the "new social studies." [23] The U.S. Office of Education sponsored more than a dozen social studies curriculum centers at important universities, where professors and school teachers attempted to

[20] A good description of work in the area of English education is given in articles by Francis A. J. Ianni and Lois Josephs, "The Curriculum Research and Development Program of the U.S. Office of Education: Project English, Project Social Studies and Beyond," in Heath, op. cit. (above, n. 11), pp. 161–212.

[21] John Goodlad, The Changing School Curriculum (New York: The Fund for the Advancement of Education, 1966), pp. 72–79.

[22] Charles R. Keller, "A Revolution in the Social Studies: Still Needed?" in Revolution and Reaction: The Impact of the New Social Studies, ed. Nancy W. Bauer (Bloomfield Hills, Michigan: The Cranbrook Press, 1966), pp. 15–26.

[23] Patricia Pine, "The New Social Studies," American Education, IV (September 1968), 14–15.

create new materials and course designs. Inductive teaching and understanding of the structure of the various social science disciplines were elements of stress in the preparation of the new curriculum. To some critics of this curricular movement there has been too marked a tendency to reduce the importance of history as an anchor area in social studies education.[24]

INNOVATIONS IN INSTRUCTIONAL ARRANGEMENTS

Beyond new developments in curricular content, American schools in recent times have introduced interesting innovations in actual instructional arrangements involving manipulation of students, teachers' time, and space. As in the case of the new curricula, ideas of classroom organization which depart from traditional modes have by no means swept the country.[25]

It is too soon, moreover, to make judgments concerning the survival value of team teaching, television teaching, programmed instruction, flexible scheduling, and the ungraded school. Undoubtedly, these are significant modern developments which deserve treatment in any discussion of modern education.

Instructional teams provide for a better employment of various types and levels of teacher competence and, in addition, suggest opportunities for advancement in teaching that may become more generally available in the future. The variety of teaching assignments made possible by team teaching means a move toward a type of differentiation of personnel that has been accomplished in the field of medicine and is now being developed for engineering.

Trump and Miller have aptly described the instructional team approach as follows:

The term "team teaching" applies to an arrangement in which two or more teachers and their assistants, taking advantage of their respective

[24] Mark M. Krug in "History and the Social Sciences: The Narrowing Gap," *Social Education*, XXIX (December 1965), explores this area of controversy, 515–520.

[25] An interesting observation on extent of innovation in schools is made by Francis S. Chase in "School Change in Perspective," in *The Changing American School, op. cit.* (above, n. 8), p. 281.

competencies, plan, instruct, and evaluate in one or more subject areas a group of elementary or secondary students equivalent in size to two or more conventional classes, using a variety of technical aids to teaching and learning through large-group instruction, small-group discussion, and independent study. If one of the foregoing ingredients is missing, the result is *not* team teaching. It may be "cooperative teaching," "rotation of teaching," "utilization of teacher aides," or something else—but it is not team teaching.[26]

As stated, educators are not, as yet, convinced that team teaching can provide a major answer to problems of instructional staffing and curriculum improvements, but many observers deem it an important step in the right direction.[27]

Educational television has made much progress since 1953 when the Pittsburgh school system pioneered in experimenting with this medium. By 1965 there were at least 118 authorized educational television stations in operation in the United States, with most states having at least one and many, two or more.[28] By rules of the Federal Communications Commission, which is the regulating agency of these stations, they operate on a nonprofit basis offering programs during school hours which are pointed toward the classroom. Many of the educational television stations are licensed to institutions of higher learning, public educational institutions, and civic groups. A recent attempt at network telecasting of educational television programs is the Midwest Program on Airborne Television Instruction. Headquartered at Purdue University, this experimental undertaking transmits programs from altitudes beyond 20,000 feet to schools in six midwestern states.

Closed-circuit television systems have been introduced into many schools. When telecasts include only films, teaching arrangements are relatively simple. Live presentations, however, involve teachers in technical arrangements which require a great deal of

[26] J. Lloyd Trump and Delmas E. Miller, *Secondary School Curriculum Improvement* (Boston: Allyn and Bacon, 1968), p. 318.

[27] Francis Keppel, *The Necessary Revolution in Education* (New York: Harper & Row, 1966), pp. 97–103 and Gail Inlow, *op. cit.* (above, n. 10), pp. 287–305.

[28] *Broadcasting: The Business Weekly of Television and Radio,* LXVIII (March 22, 1965), 12.

preparation and cooperation. Team teaching situations using closed-circuit television to facilitate large group instruction is being used in many secondary schools throughout the nation.

The merits and shortcomings of television instruction are still subjects of debate among educators.[29] Many cite its practical advantages in terms of numbers reached, variety and change of pace in teaching, best utilization of personnel, and possibilities of increased receptivity. Important disadvantages include the impersonal nature of such teaching, its limitations to lecture-type situations, emphasizing memory rather than reflection, and complications involved in staffing and technological arrangements. General agreement exists that television teaching can be an important and significant adjunct to teaching, but that it cannot and will not replace the live classroom teacher in the foreseeable future.

Although the full implications of automation for education are, as yet, not possible to visualize, the learning process itself may well be affected by the impact of technological developments on instructional programs. Industry and the armed forces have utilized automatic machines with success to provide routine instruction, thus freeing teachers for other activities. Experiments with teaching machines at Harvard University under Professor B. F. Skinner suggest that certain types of learning may be conducted by the student with help of a teaching instrument that poses questions and automatically evaluates responses.

How does a program teach? [asks Susan M. Markle, a former director of programming of the Center for Programmed Instruction, Incorporated]. It teaches by age-old methods of telling the student what he should know or carefully leading him through steps of discovery. Textbooks and teachers have always done this. It teaches by fractionating the subject matter into small digestible parts, forward steps that the student can take. . . . These steps are arranged in some sort of logical order as teachers and textbooks would do. It teaches by asking the student to put his new knowledge to work immediately, to finish a sentence, do a problem, answer a question—not at the end of the chapter or the end of the unit or the end of the semester, but at the moment of acquisition. . . . Programs teach by letting the student

---

[29] Inlow, *op. cit.* (above n. 10), pp. 139–161, offers an excellent treatment of the uses, advantages, and disadvantages of educational television.

know immediately after he responds that he has been correct, or, unhappily, in error.[30]

In response to supporters of programmed learning, some writers voice the fear that this is an attempt to change teaching from a "subtle art into a precise science"—that programming discourages critical thinking, fosters only rote learning, is mechanical and monotonous, and a joyless way to learn.[31]

Despite the above strictures, the number of applications of programs to teaching has grown considerably. Teaching machines and programmed instruction have entered the areas of reading, mathematics, social studies, English, and other school subjects. Undoubtedly limited in their use to specific kinds of instruction, these innovations are certainly worthy of investigation by all teachers.

Perhaps one of the most dramatic departures from conventional school instructional organization may be seen in the idea of the ungraded school. Both on the elementary and secondary level, a small number of schools have attempted to do away with traditional grade structure and create progression from one level to another based on readiness or achievement of the educational objectives of the particular level. In the elementary school,[32] the child does not fail or skip grades, but is assigned to subgroups of instruction which include pupils moving at about the same level in that area of the curriculum. In the high school, B. Frank Brown of the Melbourne, Florida, Senior High School has been a pioneer and spirited exponent of the idea of the nongraded secondary school.[33] Aimed at adjusting the school to the individual student —since youngsters come to school with differing degrees of readiness—the Melbourne High School, a three-year institution,

---

[30] Susan M. Markle, "Inside the Teaching Machine," in *American Education Today,* ed. Paul Woodring and John Scanlon (New York: McGraw-Hill Book Company, 1963), pp. 231–232.

[31] Richard Margolis, "Programmed Instruction: Miracle or Menace?" *Redbook,* September, 1963.

[32] John Goodlad, "Meeting Children Where They Are," *Saturday Review,* March 20, 1965, pp. 57–59, describes such a situation.

[33] B. Frank Brown, *The Appropriate Placement School* (Englewood Cliffs, N.J.: Prentice-Hall, 1965). Also see his *The Non-Graded School* (Englewood Cliffs, N.J.: Prentice-Hall, 1963).

organizes the content of courses into five phases graduated according to special needs of the students.

The whole subject of educational technology is an intriguing and controversial one in the record of modern school developments.[34] Sparked by the growing public interest in creation of an educational establishment which will satisfy the stringent demands of a fast-moving, scientific society, American businessmen have entered the school market in a significant fashion. An important spur to this movement, of course, has been the availability of federal funds, which has put hitherto prohibitive materials and equipment within the reach of school boards.

Giants of industry—including publishers, electronics manufacturers, communications firms, and others—have begun to produce educational systems designed to make teaching and learning more successful. A great deal of emphasis is placed on methods of individualizing instruction and overcoming the tremendous lag in education of the disadvantaged. How much of a dent will be made in difficult areas of instruction by "educational hardware" remains to be seen. Considering the projected increases in school population and apparent continuing problems of staffing schools, technology may be one answer to the growing education crisis.

SUMMARY

At best, a very general survey of the development of curriculum and instruction has been presented in this chapter. An attempt has been made to trace the background against which schools in the United States have responded to societal needs in furnishing experiences to students which would help to prepare them for life and work. Changing curricula have reflected the differing philosophies of education that characterize important pedagogical schools of thought. Following periods of national stress and especially after World War II, educators became concerned with ways of organizing instruction and curriculum to best utilize the country's intellectual resources in order to survive in a highly

[34] *Phi Delta Kappan*, XLVIII, No. 5 (January 1967), devotes its entire issue to a discussion of this subject.

competitive world. The "new curricula" became a popular term designating reform movements which still remain controversial. Educators are engaging in continuing soul-searching aimed at discovering the best ways of educating a diverse, mass population in a democratic society.

SUGGESTED READINGS

Crary, Ryland W., *Humanizing the School: Curriculum Development and Theory.* New York: Alfred Knopf, Inc., 1969.

Cuban, Larry, *To Make a Difference: Teaching in the Inner City.* New York: The Free Press, 1970, Chap. 13.

Foshay, Arthur W., "Curriculum," in *Encyclopedia of Educational Research,* 4th ed., Robert W. Ebel, ed. New York: The Macmillan Co., 1969, pp. 275–280.

Gage, N. L., "Teaching Methods," in *Encyclopedia of Educational Research,* 4th ed., Robert W. Ebel, ed. New York: The Macmillan Co., 1969, pp. 1446–58.

Goodlad, John, *The Changing School Curriculum.* New York: The Fund for the Advancement of Education, 1966, pp. 72–79.

Gwynn, J. Minor, and John B. Chase, Jr., *Curriculum Principles and Social Trends.* New York: The Macmillan Co., 1969.

Heath, Robert, ed., *New Curricula.* New York: Harper and Row, 1964.

"High School Curriculum Survey," *School and Society,* April 1970, pp. 239–254.

Hoover, Kenneth H. and Paul M. Hollingsworth, *Learning and Teaching in the Elementary School.* Boston: Allyn and Bacon, Inc., 1970.

Howes, Virgil M., ed., *Individualization of Instruction.* New York: The Macmillan Co., 1970.

Inlow, Gail, *The Emergent in Curriculum.* New York: John Wiley and Sons, Inc., 1966, pp. 12–23.

Michaelis, John U., *New Designs for Elementary School Curriculum.* New York: McGraw-Hill Book Co., 1967.

Raths, Louis E., *Teaching for Learning.* Columbus, Ohio. Charles E. Merrill Publishing Co., 1969.

Sanders, Norris M., *Classroom Questions, What Kinds?* New York: Harper and Row, 1966.

Taba, Hilda, *Curriculum Development.* New York: Harper and Row, 1966.

Trump, J. Lloyd, and Delmas F. Miller, *Secondary School Curriculum Improvement.* Boston: Allyn and Bacon, 1968.

CHAPTER

6.

ORGANIZATION AND ADMINISTRATION OF SCHOOLS

PUBLIC schools are organized around tradition rather than logic. The current financial crises clearly indicate an irrational pattern of school support: rich districts barely stay abreast of school costs while poor districts drop further behind in programs, facilities, and resources. School districts as geographic units in fact reflect nineteenth-century rural-American thinking.

Public schools originated as grammar or elementary schools; high schools developed only in the last quarter of the nineteenth century. Elementary school districts served the political, educational, and financial needs of the citizens; high school districts serve primarily financial ends in that their separate tax powers produce school funds but may or may not enhance the learning of children. Moreover, the divisions or "breaks" in our system—elementary, junior high (more recently, the "middle school"), high school, and junior college—are obviously artificial and related to no known learning theories.

Thus, despite a substantial body of professional literature on school organization, few experts claim that the present organization is the most logical structure. Tradition, history, expediency, and resistance to structural change seem to be more crucial factors than any notions of child growth, learning patterns, or educational efficiency. This chapter describes some patterns of school organization, discusses the general nature of administrative control, and sketches some broad problems confronting school administrators in the decade of the 1970's.

SCHOOL DISTRICT ORGANIZATION

Every public school is a part of a school district. The districts, defined geographically and governed by an elected or appointed board, vary in size, population, wealth, and purpose. With some minor variations, districts can be classified as (1) elementary—grades kindergarten through 8; (2) secondary or high school—grades 9 through 12; (3) unit (also called union or consolidated)—grades kindergarten through 12; and (4) junior or community college—grades 13 and 14. Some states provide for charter districts (created by contract between the state and the citizens in the district), but most school districts are created by legislative action at the state level. Most school districts are governed by an elected or appointed board, representative of the district residents, and most have the power to tax district property to raise school revenue. A few districts are fiscally dependent upon some other governmental unit (such as the city council or other municipal or intermediate governing body). Within broad guidelines mandated by the state legislature and state education agency, the management and control of district schools are the board's responsibility.

SCHOOL ORGANIZATION

Elementary schools are usually organized around grade levels. This pattern, commonly called "graded" schools, assumes that children of a given age can meet certain academic and social expectations. The graded schools normally consist of one or more groups of classes ranging from kindergarten to grade 6. The classroom teacher is responsible for all or most of the teaching. In addition, many of the more affluent districts employ special teachers for such subjects as music, art, and physical education; specialists for social work, guidance and counseling; and teachers for the very bright and the very slow children.

Many elementary school districts provide separate units for

grades 7 through 9. These units, called junior high schools, are usually organized and administered separately from the K–6 elementary schools. The junior highs generally are organized around subjects (social studies, mathematics, science, etc.); but many group subjects into "cores," such as language arts (English, spelling, and literature), home arts (shop, art, and home economics), and other related groupings. Contrasted with the "self-contained" classroom in the elementary schools (in which one teacher teaches all subjects to the class), junior high schools are organized into departments. The pupils are assigned to a home-base room (homeroom) and go from there to subject-matter classes on a scheduled basis. Teachers in the junior high schools are identified with their teaching field (e.g., mathematics, language arts, etc.) rather than the grade level taught. With departments, department chairmen, and other professional trappings, the junior high school organization takes on many characteristics of the high schools. A recent trend in American education is the reshuffling of pupils and teachers into "middle schools." These schools, usually consisting of grades 6, 7, and 8, base their structure on social rather than intellectual arguments. The notion that children need a special school for the institutionalized rites of passage to adulthood seems to underlie both the junior high and middle school organizations.

High schools usually embrace grades 9 (or 10 in the systems with junior high schools) through 12 and are organized in a somewhat more custodial college pattern. The students enroll in specific courses and are generally obliged to account for their presence and behavior throughout the day. The range of offered subjects varies along with departmental structures, but most high schools include the basic subject departments (English, history, mathematics, etc.) plus one or more specialized areas (art, music, etc.). Administratively, high schools pattern themselves after the nineteenth-century colleges (i.e., with deans, departmental chairmen, principals, and intermediate functionaries in a district hierarchical structure).

Teachers identify themselves as specialists in "disciplines" and with some exceptions, take their academic specialties, rather than the students or their colleagues, as a primary referent group. The standard high school organization consists of school days divided into equal time segments (40 to 55 minutes), to which students apply their study on various subjects. Under the "Carnegie unit" (a system devised at the turn of the twentieth century to seek standardization in subject study), students attend each class every day of the week throughout the school year for one unit of credit. Fortunately, the lock-step structure has been altered in some schools over the past few decades. In more flexible high school programs, some classes meet with a frequency and for time periods related more to the content than to symmetrical structure. For example, many schools schedule studio art courses for double-time units and meet less frequently than might a course in mathematics. A 40-minute period may be ample for mathematics, but totally inadequate for a laboratory science.

The public junior colleges are a twentieth-century phenomenon. Organized to provide the first two years of college work (as preparation for advanced collegiate study), the junior or community colleges have expanded their purposes to include terminal education in vocational skills, community services, adult education, and academic preparation for senior college work. The typical junior college organization blends features of both the high school and the traditional four-year colleges. The faculty and academic courses are organized by departments; the personnel services are extensive; and the administration is hierarchical. There seems to be some notion that junior college faculty take their teaching responsibilities more seriously than their colleagues in four-year colleges and that junior college students get more personalized teaching than their counterparts in the four-year colleges. These claims are as yet undocumented. About all that one can safely generalize about junior colleges is that they offer opportunities for postsecondary instruction to many students who otherwise would not go on. This, in itself, echoes the American dream of education for all.

SOME ORGANIZATIONAL CHANGES AND PROBLEMS

Further organizational changes reflect new concepts of schooling. The "Schools-within-a-school" structure at Evanston

Township High School [1] is an example of one district's effort to decentralize the management of several thousand students and fight the dehumanization implicit in mass education. The larger universities have attempted similar goals through resident colleges, to which students are assigned for both instruction and social relations. Some tinkering with time schedules has borne fruit; the "modular scheduling" (the school day is carved into short segments, or "modules," and courses scheduled in multiples of a module) [2] has gained some acceptance, particularly in high schools. A few schools have experimented with the "Trump plan," [3] which provides for large-group, small-group, and individual instruction. This latter plan requires rooms of varying sizes to accommodate the groups and, unfortunately, most school buildings are not so arranged.

The problems of urban schools frequently are tied to organizational shortcomings. Curricular irrelevance; depersonalized instruction; bureaucratic red tape; intellectual, emotional, and physical abuse of pupils; alienated parents; and rotting school buildings are familiar issues in urban schools. Some alternative organization patterns are desperately needed. The urban tax base is inadequate to support the existing schools. The metropolitan school district, which would include both rich suburbs and poor inner cities, is one suggested modification to upgrade education. Community control over schools—rather than a central, autonomous, insulated board—has become both a political and an educational issue. Both pupils and parents demand curriculum reform. Schools therefore must reform both their organization and content, or face increased rejection by their alienated pupils and the citizens they seek to serve.

[1] Charles William Brubaker and Stanton Leggett, "How to Create Territory for Learning in the Secondary Schools," *Nation's Schools,* LXXXI, No. 3 (March 1968).

[2] See Donald C. Manlove and David W. Beggs III, *Flexible Scheduling* (Bloomington, Indiana: Indiana University Press, 1965), and Robert N. Bush and Dwight Allen, *A New Design For High School Education* (New York: McGraw-Hill Book Company, 1964).

[3] J. Lloyd Trump, *Images of the Future* (Urbana, Ill.: Commission on the Experimental Study of the Utilization of the Staff in the Secondary School, National Association of Secondary School Principals, 1959).

SCHOOL ADMINISTRATION

Administration is a complex process of planning, implementing, assessing, and leading school programs. Locally-controlled school systems place considerable value on effective school leadership; consequently, the administrator is generally accorded higher status, salary, and better working conditions than other school employees. In some schools, administration includes all noninstructional management and supervision activities. In others, it includes any decision-making below school board level and implies a process shared among teachers, students, and "administrators." In most schools, however, there are some activities clearly defined as administrative (e.g., scheduling classes, assigning teachers, arranging the overall school calendar of curricular and extracurricular activities). Other activities are clearly defined as instructional (e.g., planning, teaching, and evaluating classroom activities). And there are some activities in between (e.g., curriculum planning, extracurricular programs, and other nonclassroom activities sponsored by the school). For our purposes here, school administration means the management and control functions performed by specialists identified as administrators.

ADMINISTRATIVE ROLES

Schools have not always been blessed with administrators: they appeared only in the past 100 years and then not in their present roles. Not until after the Civil War did administrators show up in the common schools; indeed, there was no need for them until schools and school districts grew to a size requiring program coordination.[4] City superintendents emerged first and their duties, by modern standards, were quite limited—often to little more than a clerkship to the board. The first city school superintendent was ap-

---

[4] Raymond E. Callahan and H. Warren Button, "Historical Change in the Role of the Man in the Organization," in *Behavioral Science and Educational Administration,* the Sixty-third Yearbook of the National Society for the Study of Education, Part II (Chicago, Ill.: NSSE, 1964), p. 73.

pointed in Buffalo, New York, in 1837;[5] but the position was not widespread until the last quarter of the nineteenth century. The early superintendents dealt largely with business matters and only incidentally with instruction and educational leadership. As agents of the school board, attuned to the board concerns of the time, the pioneer superintendents focused on fiscal management and record-keeping. Subsequent developments in learning theory and organizational structures brought new demands for personnel and program leadership to the office.

DEVELOPMENT OF
THE SCHOOL SUPERINTENDENCY

As school enrollments increased[6] and school systems became more complex, particularly in cities, school administration centralized and staff roles developed. The superintendency evolved toward professionalization, with sharper distinctions drawn among administrative, staff, and instructional responsibilities. Superintendents undertook far-reaching supervisory and staff leadership functions.

Callahan and Button have distinguished four principal stages in this evolutionary process.[7] From his early beginnings as a minor functionary of the board, the school superintendent developed, in the last third of the nineteenth century, into a philosopher-educator. The notion of school leadership as an exercise of the superintendent's superior intellect developed. Then, with centralized administration, the superintendent became an unusually powerful figure in schools; authority over school matters moved down from boards and up from teachers. Finally, business-management tech-

[5] Carroll Atkinson and Eugene T. Maleska, *The Story of Education* (New York: Bantam Books, 1964), p. 235.
[6] Enrollment in grades 9–12 went from 360,000 (6.7% of the United States population, age 14–17 years) in 1889–90 to 4,804,000 (51.4% of the population) in 1929–30. See Kenneth A. Simon and W. Vance Grant, *Digest of Educational Statistics* (Washington, D.C.: U.S. Office of Education, 1967), p. 29.
[7] Callahan and Button, *op. cit.* (above n. 4), pp. 73–92.

nique and executive functions merged in the superintendency during the first two decades of the twentieth century.

The school hero had changed from the embattled, dedicated school man to the omniscient (and omnipotent) school superintendent. During the period from about 1920 through the early 1950's, the superintendent's role shifted its emphasis from the business executive to the leadership of people. The concept of democratic administration gained wide acceptance, and the human relations aspect of administrative behavior was emphasized. Responsibilities for finance, school plant management, and public relations were not ignored, but attention turned to the social responsibilities of schools and the superintendent's relations with teachers. Oddly enough, the development of teaching as a profession during this period led administrators into direct conflict with teachers, who often were regarded as silent members of the school planning process. The teachers' perceptions of their professional roles and responsibilities were at odds with the administrators' and boards' views.

Today, the superintendent seems more closely identified with the school board than with the teachers; and recent development of teacher militancy has forced the superintendent into an even closer identification with the board. Public concern about schools and education generally focuses on the chief administrator; he feels the pressures and is expected to respond on behalf of the board and the school organization. The skills needed for administrative survival in many school districts are not at all clear. Certainly the superintendent must respond effectively to the political, social, and economic demands made on schools if he is to retain support from the board, the teachers, and the community. The frequent turnover of chief school administrators in the larger districts across the country attests to the strenuous demands on the office. Frey and Getschman,[8] in describing the school administrator's role, have stated:

At this time in our nation's history, the school administrator is one of the most highly visible public servants, which makes his job one of

[8] Sherman H. Frey and Keith R. Getschman, ed., *School Administration: Selected Readings* (New York: Thomas Y. Crowell, 1968), p. v.

the most frustrating and most fascinating in the world. What society expects from someone in this crucial position, particularly in the larger cities of this country, is often so all encompassing as to exceed the capabilities of any one human being.

STAFF SPECIALISTS

With centralization of administrative responsibility, staff assistance to the superintendent became necessary. Specialists in school finance, pupil accounting, personnel, plant management, transportation, and curriculum were needed to handle the growing demands generated by large numbers of schools, teachers, and pupils. The superintendent could not personally attend to all aspects of school management and was forced to delegate many responsibilities. This required delegation introduced new demands on the superintendent, the gist of which called for leadership of large numbers of people by indirect means. Staff organizations and relations, wise recruitment procedures, and decision-making that was forced to rely on secondhand information became vital elements in administrative behavior. The need for systems of information and communication grew from the superintendent's increased insulation from the day-to-day operations in classrooms within the district. It should be noted that administrative staff specialists may work more or less independently under the chief school administrator or in various teams with the second-echelon administrators.

THE SCHOOL PRINCIPAL

Paralleling the rise of superintendent's power, the school principal's role grew less clear. Originally appointed as "principal teacher" in the small multi-teacher schools, the principal has come to be an agent or arm of the superintendent. Rather than shape the educational program in a particular school, the principal interpreted and implemented policies determined by the central administration. By and large, autonomy has fled the principal's office: his leadership is exercised essentially in directing school efforts (faculty and students) toward goals emanating from the superintendent's office. Haskew and McLendon see the principal in a many-faceted role: [9]

The principal of a school has so many roles to play that it is difficult for him to get around to all of them. In order that good teaching may take place he has to manage and coordinate the school program. . . . And since his school must be kept in gear with the entire school system, his office serves as a link between system-wide policies and individual school policies.

The school principal usually carries full responsibility for the educational program in his school, including curricular, extracurricular, and public events such as athletic events, concerts, lectures, etc. Of the major tasks commonly undertaken by principals, the one most controversial seems to be that of curriculum and instructional leadership.

The principal's role has been complicated by the pressures from students and teachers to "go to the top" (i.e., the superintendent or board) with their demands. Further role ambiguity stems from the development of instructional supervision as a central administration function of coordinators and supervisors who bypass the principal. In many school districts, the principal has what amounts to a license to hunt for whatever role he can wrest from the teachers and the superintendent. Assistant principals are frequently assigned in larger schools and generally take charge of such tasks as attendance, discipline, and other building-level problems. Principals in larger schools usually are assigned to full-time administrative roles with no teaching responsibilities. Figure 7 illustrates typical line and staff relations among school district employees. Solid lines represent lines of supervisory authority and dotted lines represent staff relations with no supervisory authority.

CHANGING ADMINISTRATIVE ROLES

Administrative roles are undergoing change. The traditional role expectations for superintendents, principals, supervisors, and other administrative personnel have changed to meet new demands

[9] Lawrence D. Haskew and Jonathan C. McLendon, *This Is Teaching,* 3rd ed. (Glenview: Scott, Foresman & Company, 1968), p. 107.

FIGURE 7. TYPICAL LINE AND STAFF RELATIONS IN SCHOOL ORGANIZATION

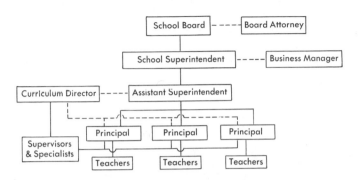

and pressures on the schools. As schools grow larger in size, the demands for improved communications with the community increases. Schools must respond to social needs in more appropriate ways. The chief administrative officer needs better lines of information back from schools, teachers, pupils, and parents in order to assist the board in shaping appropriate school policies. Bureaucratic structures do not meet the current demands for change; pressures mount for decentralized decision-making in most urban school systems. Principals are frequently caught between the demands for local school change from teachers, pupils, and the community and the monolithic authority structures of the total school system. As noted above, the principals are bypassed more and more as militant teachers and parents seek direct response from the school board.

ADMINISTRATIVE RESPONSIBILITIES

Administrators administer; we need only define the verb to get a fair notion of what they do. The literature on administration generally deals with work roles, work flow, interrelations among various administrative roles, the work setting and its manipulation (of things, ideas, feelings, etc.), and the schoolhouse consequences (i.e., what effects follow to teachers, pupils, and the adult world in general). We frequently consider the administration of schools as a process, such as problem-solving,[10] goal-setting and attainment; as a hierarchical exercise of decision-making power over given inputs [11] (money, teacher talent, knowledge, etc.); or as a social process.

Regardless of which model one studies, one common element appears: school administration clearly concerns the administrator's *responsibilities* to a variety of clients. The superintendent must be responsible to the community (through the school board), the teachers (on whom he must rely to implement any school program), the pupils (whose acceptance or rejection of the administrator's plans determines their success), and the parents. Similarly, the principal must respond both to demands from his superintendent and the teachers, pupils, and parents affiliated with the particular school. Failure of administrators to respond to these numerous demands seems to explain the contemporary public disenchantment with the schools in many communities.

ADMINISTRATORS' CLIENTELE

Administrators serve various clients: (1) the community, acting through the school board; (2) the teachers; (3) the school clients (pupils and parents); and (4) the profession.

Administrators are responsible to the school board for the total school program. This responsibility encompasses personnel problems, curriculum planning, instruction, the extracurricular program, and community-school relations. In meeting these responsibilities, the administrator must exercise good judgment both as a professional and as a person. The knowledge resources of the administrator, though important, must be coupled with some measure of human understanding. This is not to suggest that all administrators should *think* or *feel* alike, but either knowledge or wisdom alone portends disaster in the administrative role. The di-

[10] See John K. Hemphill, "Administration as Problem-Solving," *Administrative Theory in Education,* Andrew W. Halpin, ed. (New York: The Macmillan Company, 1967), pp. 89–118.

[11] See Daniel E. Griffiths, "Administration as Decision-Making," *ibid.,* pp. 119–149.

chotomous notions of scientific management in human skills administration have given way to a blend of both. As school systems grow larger, more complex, and somewhat less humane, the need for administrative skills to manage feelings as well as ideas and things becomes more urgent.

TEACHERS' ROLES
IN ADMINISTRATION

Teachers share some responsibilities with administrators. Obviously, the teachers must accept primary responsibility for instruction and much of the supervision of pupils in the school. Administrators, however, are obliged to enhance the teachers' efforts by arranging for a school environment in which the teaching-learning process can work. This obligation includes arranging class schedules to facilitate learning goals; providing adequate facilities, equipment, and support services; and, in cooperation with the teachers, developing working conditions appropriate for professional effort and performance. The basic tasks of curriculum planning (including the selection of materials) should be shared by teachers and administrators. Despite the traditional superman stature attributed to administrators in American school folklore, they rarely possess any monopoly on knowledge, wisdom, or judgment in matters of curriculum.

PERSONNEL RESPONSIBILITIES

Administrative responsibility for school personnel matters encompasses the tasks of recommending teachers, specialists, and nonprofessional employees to the board for employment; evaluating work performance; devising and implementing procedures for evaluation and assessment, promotions, and discharge. Board members have little or no opportunity to observe the teachers in their work and must rely on administrative recommendations in personnel matters. The disparity between employee perceptions and administrative evaluations of work performance prompts much of the current teacher militancy. The responsibility to develop salary schedules and working conditions has passed from administrators and school boards in many districts. With the advent of collective bargaining between teachers and boards, many of the issues surrounding salaries, schedules, work assignments, and the like are now resolved through negotiations; and administrators take only a limited roles in the process. In many districts, the administrative personnel act as the consultants to the board, rather than agents of the board, in the negotiation process.[12]

THE CHANGING
ADMINISTRATIVE ROLE

Shared decision-making in schools has changed the traditional relations among teachers, administrators, and boards of education. Teachers and students, through militant organizational behavior, demand a greater influence in school operations. Collective bargaining between teachers and boards includes many decisions once left solely to administrators. Hours of work, extra class assignments, salaries, promotions, and other working conditions are now decided collectively by teachers and boards rather than by boards or administrators. Teacher demands focus on their greater responsibility in decisions affecting their professional careers; this teacher participation in such decisions encroaches on some traditional management prerogatives. Teacher-administrator relations in some districts, as a consequence of this new stance, take on the nature of dialogue among professionals rather than the earlier top-down communication from deciders to doers.

Although the administrator's authority, and, to some extent, his responsibilities, have become less clear as a consequence of increased teacher and student participation in decision-making, the

---

[12] See Bernard E. Donovan, "Speaking For Management," in "Collective Bargaining vs. Professional Negotiation," *School Management,* IX, No. 11 (November 1965), 69–72; Alden H. Blankenship, "The Role of the Superintendent in Teacher Negotiations," *Theory Into Practice,* IV (April 1965), 70–74; and Luvern L. Cunningham, "Implications of Collective Negotiations for the Role of the Principal," in *Readings on Collective Negotiations in Public Education,* eds. Stanley Elam, Myron Lieberman, and Michael Moskow (Chicago: Rand McNally & Company, 1967), pp. 298–313.

need for administrative leadership in the schools has increased. In any organization under stress from internal or external pressures, the demands on administrative leadership increase. Schools today are not composed of dynamic leaders and quiescent followers; in many areas, the led want to lead.

Leadership in school administration seems to be a complex set of human skills appropriate to organize and move quasi-independent and diverse interests toward common goals. The professional and personal desires of teachers, the aspirations of pupils and parents, and the far-ranging demands of the community must be fused into school goals and procedures. Administrative decisions by fiat or from a power base are not appropriate in most schools today. Social unrest, political and economic forces, and confused conceptions about the aims of education threaten the continued existence of school systems in many urban centers.

The administrator must possess the skills to stand aside from the schools for perspective; the ability to understand conflicting demands from the school clients; a commitment to reconciling the demands in light of rational analysis. In a sense, the older concept of the administrator, particularly the superintendent, as a superman has been revived. The attributes needed today are not superior knowledge or intellect but superior ability to manage conflict and marshal diverse inputs to identify and solve human problems in the schools.

EMERGENT PROBLEMS IN SCHOOL ORGANIZATION AND ADMINISTRATION

Role demands on administrators grow more complex as urbanization continues. The schools undertake increasingly difficult social tasks such as racial integration, mass education of increasingly differentiated clients, and organization of the knowledge explosion into manageable educational programs. Alternatives to existing school organizations are many and varied. Sizer recently outlined four approaches [13] to school reorganization: (1) decen-

[13] Theodore R. Sizer, "The Case For a Free Market," *Saturday Review,* January 11, 1969, p. 34 ff.

tralized control, (2) publicly financed private schools for minorities, (3) contracting with private firms who compete to produce a measurable educational product, and (4) a voucher system by which public money goes directly to children to use in schools of their choice. Focusing on the voucher system, Sizer argues: [14]

Competition is the newest old panacea for the reform of American schools. The argument for it is simple. The public schools are a monopoly and monopolies offer neither variety nor high quality. As America needs both varied and excellent schools, competitive pressure is clearly required. A marketplace must be created for education, with children and their parents as the choice-making consumers. The consumers, the argument continues, will pick the better schools most of the time and, in so doing, will force the quality of all to improve.

Coupled with these external demands on schools, internal pressures from teachers and clients tend to complicate the administrative role. Administrators are expected to perform various roles, some of which appear to be contradictory. For example, we expect the administrator to speak for the school (students and faculty) to the public; but in teacher-board relations, the administrator is the board's man. The administrator often is asked to evaluate teaching performance and make decisions in areas far afield from his own area of expertise. Student demands conflict with adult expectations for schools, and the administrators frequently are caught in the squeeze. As more voices enter the administrative dialogue, the decision-making becomes less neat and requires greater patience, judgment, and, on occasion, the wisdom of Solomon. These emerging forces affect administrative roles and change the ground rules for decision-making.

Schools are not organized to respond quickly to changing needs of pupils and parents. The schools' response mechanisms to social demands are notoriously sluggish. Educational systems are much slower to change than fields such as medicine and agriculture. Carlson's research revealed three barriers to change in the public schools: (1) the absence of a change agent, (2) a weak knowledge base, and (3) the "domestication" of public schools. [15] Unlike the

[14] *Ibid.*, p. 34.

[15] Richard O. Carlson, "Barriers to Change in Public Schools," *Change Processes in the Public Schools* (University of Oregon: The Center for the Advanced Study of Educational Administration, 1965), pp. 3–8.

field of agriculture, which uses the county extension agent to promote change in forming practices, education does not have a readily identifiable change agent. The state and intermediate unit (county) school officers see their role as regulation rather than advocacy of change. Thus, to expect local school administrators to act as change agents does not appear to be reasonable. The administrator must respond to local demands for economy of operation and stability of school procedures; moreover, the organizational demands are frequently inconsistent with the high risk involved in change.[16]

To manage change, school administrators need far more knowledge about alternatives than they usually possess. Few administrators have either staff assistance to gather the data or time to analyze the needful information prior to instituting basic changes in schools programs or organization. Recent efforts to establish federally supported research and development centers for education could however, provide the knowledge base presently lacking for substantial school changes. The administrator is further limited in change options by being identified as a part of his school system. Certain choices of action may be closed to the administrator by local pressure to continue the status quo, and the administrator is vulnerable to allegations of disloyalty if he disagrees.

The third barrier to change, in Carlson's view, is the "domestication" of the public schools. Unlike most business organizations which survive only if efficient and generally viewed as useful, the schools continue regardless of their efficiency. The school clients have little choice but to use the schools, and the schools are generally obliged to accept all clients. To Carlson, the label "domesticated organization"

. . . [indicates] that this class of organization is protected and cared for in a fashion similar to that of a domesticated animal. They are not compelled to attend to all of the ordinary and usual needs of an organization. For example, they do not compete with other organizations for clients; in fact, a steady flow of clients is assured. There is no struggle for survival for this type of organization—existence is guaranteed.[17]

[16] For a helpful description of innovators, see Everett M. Rogers, "What Are Innovators Like?" *ibid.*, pp. 55–61.

[17] Carlson, *op cit.* (above, n. 15), p. 6.

So long as the administrator perceives greater threat from efforts to change than from nonchange, the chances are slight that administrators will be effective change agents.

IMPLICATIONS FOR ADMINISTRATIVE TRAINING

Programs of preparation of school administrators must recognize the changing role demands and modify the training components accordingly. Broad study in social and behavioral sciences combined with appropriate clinical training is needed to broaden the administrator's knowledge base and to give him opportunity to build newer models of behavior. The administrator is simultaneously sociologist, politician, educator, and psychologist. These and other disciplines are crucial to his understanding the complex forces operating on and in the schools. In dealing with community power groups, administrators dare not be naive but must be capable of translating diverse demands into honest reality. Teachers no longer can be regarded as well-paid hired hands; administrators must deal with them fairly and professionally in a colleague relationship—not paternally. There are few reasons to think demands on administrators will decrease; if anything, they will become more complex and more intense. The future of the role and, in some measure, the future of the schools, depends on how well the demands are met.

SUMMARY

Public school organization reflects historical development, rather than the logic and theory of learning. School districts, created in the second half of the nineteenth century, basically serve political and economic purposes, with teaching and learning as incidental by-products. Public schools are organized through elementary, junior high school, high school, and junior college districts. Under this organizational pattern, school control is in the hands of elected or appointed school boards.

Pressure to reorganize schools, curriculum, and management

procedures comes from within and without the schools. Urban schools face serious challenges from militant teachers, students, and community groups. Demands grow for local control, alternatives to public schools, increased resources, and improved teaching. Schools must find viable ways to respond to these demands and reform both the content and organization of education.

The school administrators, perhaps the most visible target of criticism, are pressed by teachers, pupils, and parents to improve the schools. There is serious doubt that substantial change can be achieved by administrators alone. The problems of school organization and administration are complex, involving finance, personnel, facilities, curriculum, and a host of accumulated grievances by the people concerned. Schools must respond to demands for change. The mechanisms for change must be built into school operation to encourage responsible participation in school decisions by teachers, pupils, and parents.

SUGGESTED READINGS

Bennis, Warren G., Kenneth D. Benne, and Robert Chin, eds., *The Planning of Change.* New York: Holt, Rinehart and Winston, 1964.

Campbell, Roald F., Luvern L. Cunningham, Roderick F. McPhee, and Ray Nystrand, *The Organization and Control of American Schools,* 2d ed. Columbus, Ohio: Charles E. Merrill Books, Inc., 1970.

Carver, Fred D., and Thomas J. Sergiovanni, *Organizations and Human Behavior: Focus on Schools.* New York: McGraw-Hill Book Company, 1969.

Franklin, Marian Pope, *School Organization: Theory and Practice.* Chicago: Rand McNally & Company, 1967.

Frey, Sherman H., and Keith R. Getschman, eds., *School Administration: Selected Readings.* New York: Thomas Y. Crowell Company, 1968.

Hencley, Stephen P., Lloyd E. McCleary, and J. H. McGrath, *The Elementary School Principalship.* New York: Dodd, Mead & Company, 1970.

Hillson, Maurie, *Change and Innovation in Elementary School Organization.* New York: Holt, Rinehart and Winston, 1965.

Knezevich, Stephen J., *Administration of Public Education.* New York: Harper & Row, 1969.

Lane, Willard R., Ronald G. Corwin, and William G. Monahan, *Foundations of Educational Administration*. New York: The Macmillan Company, 1967.

McCleary, Lloyd E., and Stephen P. Hencley, *Secondary School Administration*. New York: Dodd, Mead & Company, 1965.

FINANCING PUBLIC EDUCATION

THE public schools are big business in most American communities. Over two million teachers in nearly 19,000 school systems teach approximately fifty million elementary and secondary school pupils, at a total cost of over $40 billion. Public education goes on both in rural schools, where as few as a dozen or so pupils comprise the entire student body, and in urban school systems having as many as a half-million or more pupils.

The extent and quality of school facilities vary widely among the states and among districts within a single state. One index of this variation is the total dollar investment per pupil in public schools in each state. For the 1968–69 school year, the estimated national average total expenditure per pupil was $834, with a range of $503 (Mississippi) to $1,348 (Alaska).[1] Paralleling the state variations in per-pupil expenditures, districts within a given state spend widely varied amounts on the education of their pupils. In the Cook County, Illinois, schools, for instance, spending per pupil during 1968–69 ranged from a low of $446 to a high of $1,572. The wide range of educational expenditures among states and districts clearly indicates the serious obstacles to the ideal of equality of opportunity in public schools.

This chapter deals with the sources of school finance; the competing demands on state resources; the system of assessment, collection, and distribution of school funds; and some financial problems of public schools. Given the public demand for im-

[1] Kenneth A. Simon and W. Vance Grant, *Digest of Educational Statistics* (Washington, D.C.: U.S. Government Printing Office, 1969), p. 56.

proved schools, the related issues of teachers' salaries, rising education costs, and the declining tax bases in many school districts, the problems of school finance are high priority items for both state and national concern.

HISTORICAL BACKGROUND OF SCHOOL FINANCE

The Southern colonies generally supported the concept of private education. The responsibility for schooling was accepted by the individual rather than the political unit. Schools in the Middle Colonies were established and supported by religious groups. As the nation grew and expanded in the first half of the nineteenth century, the demands for an educated electorate spurred development of free, public, nonsectarian school systems.

The notion that schooling is a public responsibility reaches far back into our heritage; the Massachusetts laws of 1642, 1647, and 1648 illustrate the New England attitude toward education as a public, rather than a private charge.[2] Crucial to the rise of public education was the belief that the benefits of schooling extended beyond the pupil, his family, and his community. The benefit was public and was properly a public responsibility, assigned by the new state constitutions to the legislative bodies.

FEDERAL ROLE IN SCHOOL FINANCE

As we have seen, the federal Constitution does not mention education; indeed, the Tenth Amendment provides that "The powers not delegated to the United States by the Constitution; nor prohibited by it to the States, are reserved to the State respectively, or to the people." The constitutional silence about education, coupled with the Tenth Amendment, places the primary responsibility for public schools on the state governments. Federal legislation, how-

[2] David B. Tyack, *Turning Points in American Educational History* (Waltham, Mass: Blaisdell Publishing Company, 1967), pp. 14–17.

ever, has played an active role in establishing and supporting public schools.

The Land Ordinance of 1785, the Northwest Ordinance of 1787, and the Morrill Act of 1862, are but three examples of federal interest in public education. Subsequent legislation includes the Smith-Hughes Act (1917), the G.I. Bill of Rights (1944), Titles IV and VI of the Civil Rights Act (1964), and the Elementary and Secondary Education Act (1965). These federal acts, implemented through such agencies as the National Science Foundation, National Institute of Health, and the U.S. Office of Education, have pumped billions of dollars into research, training, and development programs directly and indirectly benefiting public schools.

Federal aid to education continues, however, to be a controversial issue in this country. Widespread fears of federal "control" of state school systems trigger much suspicion· and spirited debate among state legislators and citizens alike. The proper relationship between Church and State generates another set of fears and arguments. The First Amendment [3] to the federal Constitution is at the heart of the issue of federal and state support to parochial schools. These and other problems related to federal aid to education act as deterrents to increased direct financial support for public schools by the federal government. Despite the legal and political problems surrounding the issue of federal aid, though, direct financial support of public schools by the federal government continues to increase. The estimate of federal support to elementary-secondary education for fiscal 1969 was $3.4 billion,[4] up from $554.4 million in 1962. In 1969 the federal dollar input for public elementary and secondary schools amounted to approximately 7.6 percent of the total national revenue for such schools. All federal support, it should be noted, is categorical rather than general; that is, the money can be used only for the purposes authorized by statute rather than for the general educational needs of the school district.

[3] "Congress shall make no law respecting an establishment of religion, of prohibiting the free exercise thereof . . ." First Amendment, *United States Constitution.*

[4] *Statistical Abstract of the United States, 1969,* p. 133.

SOURCES OF SCHOOL FUNDS

Public school funds flow from one principal source—the taxpayers—and through three channels: (1) federal grants, (2) local taxes, and (3) state grants. The legal responsibility for financing schools rests on the state legislatures. Each state has more or less similar machinery to levy, collect, and distribute tax monies to the schools. The states vary widely in the amount of contributions for public schools from local and federal sources. For the nation, in the 1966–67 school year, the relative percentage contributions to the public elementary and secondary schools were federal, 8 percent; state, 39.9 percent; and local, 52.1 percent. This means that of every $1.00 revenue to the schools, 8 cents came from federal grants, 39.9 cents came from state sources, and 52.1 cents came from local taxes and other sources. As one might expect, states varied widely in the proportions received from these sources. For example, in 1967–68 Alaska received 29.5 percent of school revenue from federal sources, 40.4 percent from state sources, and 30.2 percent from local sources. New York, on the other hand, received only 4.4 percent of its public school revenue from the federal government, 45.8 percent from the state, and 49.9 percent from local sources. The state-local ratio of support ranged from a high of 84.4 percent state-5.1 percent local (Hawaii) to a low of 3.9 percent state-87.5 percent local (Nebraska). Table 12 below summarizes the relative percentages of federal, state, and local revenue for public elementary and secondary schools during the eleven year period from 1957–68.

Table 12 indicates two significant developments: (1) a dramatic increase in school revenue from federal sources between 1964 and 1967, and (2) a relatively stable percentage of state revenue for schools. The state and local sources carry the major burden for school support, a fact which presents problems for the future of school finance. As schools increase their spending and the burden of local taxes spirals upward, greater taxpayer resistance can be expected. This resistance, sometimes called

TABLE 12. PERCENT OF REVENUE RECEIVED FROM FEDERAL, STATE,
AND LOCAL SOURCES FOR PUBLIC ELEMENTARY AND SECONDARY SCHOOLS

School year	Federal sources	State sources	Local sources
1	2	3	4
1957–58	4.0%	39.4%	56.6%
1959–60	4.4	39.1	56.5
1961–62	4.3	38.7	56.9
1963–64	4.4	39.3	56.4
1964–65 *	3.8	39.7	56.5
1965–66 *	7.7	39.2	53.1
1966–67 *	7.9	39.1	53.0
1967–68 *	7.7	40.3	52.0

SOURCES: U.S. Department of Health, Education, and Welfare, Office of Education. *Statistics of State School Systems, 1963–64* (Washington, D.C.: Government Printing Office, 1967), p. 11.

National Education Association, Research Division. *Estimates of School Statistics, 1967–68.* Research Report 1967–R19 (Washington, D.C.: the Association, 1967), p. 18.

* NEA Research Division estimates.

From Committee on Educational Finance, *Financial Status of the Public Schools* (Washington, D.C.: National Education Association, 1967), p. 48.

"the taxpayers' revolt," promises to be an increasing obstacle to school finance. From the maze of figures and projections, one thing seems clear: local taxpayers have become less and less willing to add substantial amounts to their tax bills for schools. A review of the legal and political structures, procedures, and machinery relevant to school revenue and school expenditures may clarify the emergent problems in school finance.

SCHOOL REVENUE

From a financial viewpoint, schools are similar to business enterprises. The goods, services, and facilities necessary for school operations must be planned, purchased, and paid for. The money available to purchase these materials, supplies, services, and facilities can be called receipts. Technically, receipts consist of two types: (1) revenue receipts and (2) nonrevenue receipts. Revenue receipts are tax monies for which there is no obligation to repay and which do not represent exchange of property for money. Local school tax funds and legislative appropriations exemplify revenue. In neither instance does the school district promise to repay the money granted or sell school property for the money. Nonrevenue receipts have one of two effects: (1) They may incur an obligation that must be met in the future (e.g., school bonds which are sold to raise money and which must be redeemed or "paid off" in the future), or (2) they may change the form of an asset from property to cash and therefore decrease the amount and value of school property (e.g., sale of surplus school real estate or the sale of surplus equipment). The vast majority of school funds are revenue receipts.[5]

School receipts can be used only for legitimate school purposes. Such purposes include the purchase of school supplies and equipment, salaries of professional and nonprofessional employees, services legally authorized by the school board (such as medical, legal, and other professional services, building construction, and plant maintenance). The legal guidelines for the use of school funds will be outlined in a subsequent section of this chapter. At this point, suffice it to say that school funds must be used for those purposes authorized under the law and in accordance with proper fiscal procedures.

SOURCES OF SCHOOL TAXES

The public schools are financed primarily by public tax funds; very small amounts come from private gifts, donations, and the like. As noted above, the tax monies come through three principal channels: (1) federal agencies, (2) state taxes appropriated to local district use, and (3) school taxes collected at the local level (usually the school district). Federal income taxes (individual and corporate) are the principal sources of federal funds for local schools. Congressional appropriations direct federal tax funds to national agencies (such as the Department of Health, Educa-

[5] For 1967–68, $29.4 billion of the total income ($32.4 billion) was revenue receipts. See Simon and Grant, *op. cit.* (above, n. 1), p. 53.

tion and Welfare, National Institute of Health, and the National Science Foundation) or state agencies (e.g., state departments of education), which distribute the funds to local districts. Federal taxes support specific projects proposed by the school district. These projects must comply with guidelines prepared by the specific federal or state agency. As categorical grants, federal funds are carefully audited to ensure their proper use for legislatively authorized purposes only.

Both the local and state school receipts are properly considered to be state taxes—the only difference lies in the source, mode of collection, and mechanics of allocation to the local school district. State laws vary widely in the provisions for assessment, collection, and distribution of tax funds for schools. The policies in Illinois may illustrate the mechanics and procedures in obtaining school revenue.

STATE SCHOOL TAX SOURCES

The states draw the authority and responsibility for public schools from the state constitution. The Illinois Constitution,[6] for example, provides that: "The General Assembly shall provide a thorough and efficient system of free schools, whereby all children of this State may receive a good common school education." This mandate, in conjunction with various statutes, legal decisions, and common law principles, provides the legal base and fiscal procedures for school finance. As pressures mount to increase tax support for schools, most states must not only increase the amounts from existing tax sources but also tap new ones. With some exceptions, the other states tend to produce tax revenue from similar sources.[7] The states rely heavily on taxation of sales, gross receipts, personal and corporate income, and licenses for revenue. In 1967, 38 of the 50 states taxed personal income and all 50 states taxed the other principal objects. The total state taxes col-

[6] Section 1, Article 8, *Illinois Constitution of 1870.*
[7] For a detailed breakdown on principal sources of state tax revenue, see *State Taxes in 1967,* Research Monograph, January 1969, National Education Association.

lected ($31.9 billion) in 1967 consisted of: (1) sales and gross receipts ($18.5 billion, 58.1%), (2) income, personal and corporate ($7.1 billion, 22.4%), and (3) licenses ($3.6 billion, 11.4%). The balance of $2.6 billion (8.1% of the total) came from such objects as property tax, death and gift tax, severance tax, poll tax, document and stock transfer tax, and a wide variety of state taxes. The national state average of tax collections in 1967 was up 8.7 percent over 1966. Only Rhode Island showed a decline in tax collections in 1967 (.5%); and Massachusetts, New Jersey, and Virginia led the country in percent of increase (21.9%, 41.6%, and 20%, respectively) from 1966 to 1967.

When Illinois enacted personal income tax laws in 1969, eleven states remained with no such tax. The personal income tax is regarded as an underused tax resource and states turn to it as a reliable tax base. The Advisory Commission on Intergovernmental Relations, for instance, made the following observation:

> The personal income tax represents the last under-utilized major revenue source for many states. One-third of the states, including some in the most industrialized high-income section of the country, do not tax personal incomes at all and another third tax them at relatively low effective rates.[8]

The federal experience with personal income tax collections supports the view that it represents a reliable and fruitful source of tax revenue. It seems evident that real estate (land and buildings), although once the major index of wealth in an agricultural economy, no longer constitutes the principal tax base in our industrialized nation. Despite constitutional problems involved in income taxes, the pressures to fund additional tax sources will undoubtedly force most states toward more extensive and productive income tax measures.

TAX STRUCTURE IN ILLINOIS

In examining the Illinois tax structure and the legal and fiscal machinery for school finance, the relative school burdens carried

[8] Advisory Commission on Intergovernmental Relations, *1967 State Legislative Program* (M33) (Washington, D.C.: The Commission, September 1966), p. 6.

by federal, state, and local agencies come into focus. The 1967–
68 school dollar in Illinois consisted of 5.8 cents federal money,
22.7 cents state money, and 71.5 cents local money. The local
tax funds come from two principal sources: (1) real estate taxes
and (2) personal property taxes. Real estate is simply defined as
land and permanent structures attached to the land. Personal
property is all property other than real estate. Examples of personal property are automobiles, bank accounts, and corporate
stocks.

The state school funds are appropriated by the Illinois General
Assembly (the legislature) to the *common school fund* from the
state's *general tax fund*. The state general fund comes from a variety of sources: (1) sales and use taxes (60%), (2) public utilities
taxes (9%), (3) liquor taxes (8%), (4) inheritance taxes (6%), (5)
cigarette taxes (5%), and (6) miscellaneous taxes (6%). The legislature draws upon the general state funds to meet its obligations to
the common school fund, which, in turn, supports two kinds of
school aid: (1) general aid (the flat grant) to each *recognized* [9]
school district on the basis of $47 per student in average daily at-
tendance (ADA), and (2) a special grant (equalization) to districts
on a formula basis. The latter grant aims to insure a measure of
equality of educational opportunity among pupils in the several
school districts in the state. Without going into detail, the equalization grants serve both as incentives and rewards for local district
effort.

To qualify for the equalization grant from the state, the local
district must assess its property at a minimum qualifying rate, the
details and procedures for which are treated below. If the tax
produced by the qualifying rate, plus the general aid, fail to equal
a legislatively determined foundation level (presently $520 per
year) for each pupil in ADA, the state grants the difference to the
local district.

The local school funds consist of taxes on property in the local
district, imposed and collected under state laws. These taxes
finance such school costs as instruction, supplies, equipment, and
other current, noncapital expenses. Capital outlay, usually for new

[9] A technical term signifying the district's compliance with state rules
and regulations pertaining to the quality of education.

construction, generally comes from school bonds, issued after voter approval through a school referendum. In school districts with rapid growth in school-age population, the demands for additional classrooms and school facilities force districts to "borrow" money for construction, issue bonds (long-term promises to repay), and increase the tax rate to provide additional school funds to repay the bonded indebtedness. In Illinois, as in many of the states, the local school tax rate includes an amount necessary to redeem, or pay off, the bonds issued to finance school construction, renovation, and similar capital outlay. The additional tax burden quite often falls on the same taxable property (principally, real estate) as the regular, annual school tax. Local taxation, then, provides both the operating funds and the capital funds.

FACTORS IN LOCAL TAX FUNDS

Two principal factors determine the total funds raised for school use by local taxation: (1) the assessed valuation and (2) the tax rate. The basic formula for determining tax yield is *assessed valuation × rate = tax yield*. There are other variables such as effectiveness of tax collections, delinquent tax redemptions, costs of administering the tax laws, etc.; but for our purposes here, the basic formula is adequate.

Assessed valuation is the dollar value placed on taxable property for the purpose of determining the amount of tax imposed. The term may refer to the value of a single parcel of taxable property or the collective value of all property subject to a particular tax. The assessed valuation of a particular piece of property is not the same as its market value (the price it would bring in a fair, voluntary sale) but rather is a fraction of the market value. Not all property in the school district is subject to taxation. Public lands and buildings (such as parks, forest preserves, and city buildings), property owned by charitable organizations (e.g., churches, service clubs), and other real estate may be legally exempt from taxes.

The assessment of taxable property is a state function delegated to the county assessor, an elected county official. Assisted by township assessors, the county assessor determines the valuation of all taxable property and periodically reassesses (revalues) the property. Buildings and land are valued separately. Building valuation depends on such factors as replacement cost, current value based on market transactions, income (rental) value, age, obsolescence, and depreciation. Assessment and valuation procedures for personal property are generally the same as for real property; the difficult problem is to find the personal property. Recording the ownership and location of taxable real estate is far simpler than maintaining systematic knowledge of taxable personal property. Substantial amounts of personal property are never taxed because the owners choose not to report their ownership (since the risk of detection is small and the penalty for nonreporting is less than the tax burden). Thus, in some states, including Illinois, the taxation of personal property presents difficult problems and constitutes, unfortunately, an underused tax source. In Illinois, furthermore, the tax assessor determines neither the amount of tax revenue which various governmental agencies, including school districts, spend, nor the tax rate; and he does not collect the taxes. He determines only the assessed valuation, and the various taxing bodies (government agencies such as city governments, school districts, park districts, etc.) determine their budget needs for the fiscal year.

TAX COMPUTATION AND COLLECTION

After all taxable property has been valued, the county clerk computes the tax rate (expressed in mills, or tenths of a cent, per dollar), based on revenue needed and on the value of taxable property. For example, if the total value of the taxable property is $100 million and the school needs $2 million for noncapital operation, the tax rate would be 20 mills per dollar or $2 per $100 of assessed valuation. For a taxpayer owning a house worth $40,000 on the market, assessed at 50 percent, the school tax bill would total $400 per year. The school tax would constitute only a part of the direct tax on the property. Other taxing bodies such as city government, park districts, sanitary districts, etc., add their revenue needs to the single tax bill. This simplistic example may illustrate one aspect of the school finance crisis: in school districts with high ratio of residential property to nonresidential property, taxes on real estate simply do not produce adequate revenue to operate the schools. A $400 school tax on a typical residence is not enough to pay for one child's education. If the home sends two or three children to the schools, the financial problems are compounded.

The tax bills are prepared and presented to the property owners some time in advance of the tax-due date. Upon collection of the taxes, school tax funds are transmitted to the appropriate government officer. Thereafter the school fiscal officer can draw upon the funds to pay operating expenses. When current tax receipts are inadequate to meet operating expenses, the district may sell part of its future tax claims to obtain additional revenue. These claims, called tax anticipation warrants, represent taxes not yet due. Districts must pay interest on such "borrowed money" and this, of course, reduces the district income for the next operating year. The sale of future tax claims has come to be a frequent mode of financing many school districts. This places the district in an awkward position; living on future income restricts the district's options for future educational planning.

Revenue receipts for schools, then, come primarily from local taxation (on real and personal property) and from general state tax funds distributed to the schools in a variety of ways. Nationally, the local taxes rest heavily on real estate, and the pressure grows to expand the tax base to include such taxable objects as income, business operations, and intangible personal property. Most states impose ceilings on school tax rates and provide referendum (election) machinery to raise the school tax rate periodically. Thus, the maximum revenue for schools is a function of assessed valuation, maximum legal rate, and the relative efficiency of the tax assessment and collection machinery.

SCHOOL BONDS

Nonrevenue receipts, principally proceeds from the sale of school bonds, are used for capital expenses specifically approved by referendum. Building construction and major remodeling of school facilities require voter approval in most states. The nonrevenue receipts from school bonds are restricted to the purposes outlined in the referendum. For example, money raised by a bond issue to build a new school cannot be used to increase teachers' salaries or buy school supplies. Most states limit districts' authority to issue bonds to a percentage of the district's assessed valuation. Illinois, for instance, limits the district's bonding power to 5 percent of the valuation, and thus a district with an assessed valuation of $100 million can issue school bonds up to $5 million. As bonds are paid off, additional bonds can be issued by a subsequent referendum.

School bonds are redeemed by money raised through additional taxes imposed on the district's taxable property. The bonds represent a future obligation on property; and the repayment generally is scheduled over a ten, fifteen, or twenty-year time period. Such installment payment systems moderate the additional tax burden in a given year. Publicity for school referenda usually emphasize this "nominal" tax increase in an effort to enlist voter support. School districts with rapidly expanding enrollments and building needs normally experience difficulty in obtaining voter approval for increased operating revenue and substantial bond issues. Voter resistance to tax increases and bond referenda for schools has intensified the schools' financial crisis in many states. Sharply increased taxes for local, state, and national government services add to the taxpayer's burden. In many states, school tax and bond referenda are the only opportunities for a taxpayer's direct response to tax measures; therefore, a negative vote may be a vote against taxes in general rather than a rejection of the schools' needs.

SCHOOL EXPENDITURES

School receipts reflect laws, government, tax burdens, and the mechanics of educational finance; school expenditures describe the schools' objectives and priorities. Total expenditures for secondary and elementary education in 1967–68 were an estimated $31.5

billion.[10] These totals were divided among three broad categories: (1) current expenditures ($26.4 billion), (2) capital outlay ($4.2 billion), and (3) interest on school debt ($.9 billion). The percentage distribution of school expenditures for 1965–66 is given in Table 13.

TABLE 13. PERCENTAGE DISTRIBUTION OF EXPENDITURES FOR PUBLIC ELEMENTARY AND SECONDARY EDUCATION BY PURPOSE

Purpose		Percentage distribution
Current expenditures		82.8
Public elementary and secondary schools		80.3
Administration	3.6	
Instruction	55.1	
Plant operation	6.7	
Plant maintenance	2.4	
Fixed charges	6.5	
Other school services	6.0	
Summer schools		.3
Adult education		.5
Community colleges		1.2
Community services		.6
Capital outlay		14.3
Interest on school debt		2.9
Total		100.0

NOTE: Because of rounding, detail may not add to totals.

Adapted from Kenneth A. Simon and W. Vance Grant, *Digest of Educational Statistics* (Washington, D.C.: U.S. Government Printing Office, 1968), p. 58.

The principal current expense for schools is instructional costs. Salaries for teachers, specialists, and teaching materials constitute the single greatest expense in any school district. Recent salary increases have forced many districts to use up to 90 percent of their educational fund budgets for teachers' salaries. The increased allocation of school funds for salaries indicates still another dimension

[10] Kenneth A. Simon and W. Vance Grant, *Digest of Educational Statistics* (Washington, D.C.: U.S. Government Printing Office, 1968), p. 57.

of the schools' financial plight: with relatively fixed revenue, the increased instructional costs take a larger share of the school revenue. Figure 8 illustrates school expenses in the nation's fifteen largest cities for the school year 1966–67.

TEACHERS' SALARIES

Teachers' salaries constitute a major (and sensitive) component in educational costs. Public awareness of salary demands and total instructional costs stems from the increased publicity given teacher-board conflict in many school districts. Recent data from annual salary and education cost surveys indicate that salary gains for teachers over the past decade, although substantial, were less

FIGURE 8. SCHOOL EXPENSES IN THE NATION'S FIFTEEN LARGEST CITIES, 1966–67

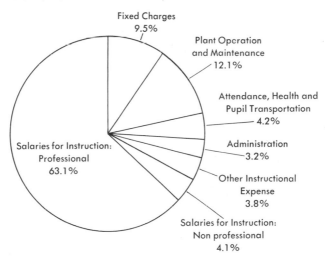

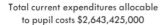

SOURCE: Statistics of Local Public School Systems: Fall 1967 Pupils/Schools /Staff, 1966–67 Expenditures (U.S. Department of Health, Education, and Welfare, Office of Education).

From *American Education*, IV (November 1968), back cover.

than increases in business and industry.[11] Indeed, they were less in terms of both beginning and potential earnings for men and women holding bachelor's degrees. Faced with stable revenues and increased competition for trained personnel, school districts have been forced to spend a greater proportion of school revenue for salaries to obtain teachers.

The financial plight of school districts and its relation to salary costs is illustrated by Table 14 below. The recent data compiled by the Bureau of Labor Statistics given in this table indicates the cost to a family of four of maintaining a low, a modest but adequate, and a relatively high standard of living in selected cities across the nation. When these costs are compared with the mean annual salary for classroom teachers in the same cities, the economic pressure on school districts comes into sharper focus.

TABLE 14. MEAN SALARY OF CLASSROOM TEACHERS AND THE COST OF LIVING IN SELECTED URBAN DISTRICTS, 1966–67

City	Standard of Living			Teacher's Salary
	Low	Moderate	High	
1. New York, N.Y.	$6,021	$9,977	$14,868	$8,966
2. Chicago, Ill.	6,104	9,334	13,325	8,221
3. Los Angeles, Calif.	6,305	9,326	13,645	9,050
4. Houston, Tex.	5,542	8,301	11,897	6,098
5. Pittsburgh, Pa.	5,841	8,764	12,551	7,597
6. Washington, D.C.	6,133	9,273	13,419	7,723

SOURCE: Prepared from data in *Financial Status of the Public Schools, 1968* (Washington, D.C.: Committee on Educational Finance, National Education Association, 1968), p. 32, and *Newsweek,* March 31, 1969, p. 58.

These data suggest that average salaries for teachers sustain a standard of living just above respectable poverty. Obtaining qualified teachers and the problems of recruitment in local school districts take on less mystery when viewed in an economic light.

[11] Frank Endicott, *Trends in Employment of College and University Graduates in Business and Industry, 1970,* 24th Annual Report (published privately by Frank S. Endicott).

OTHER CURRENT EXPENDITURES

In addition to instructional costs, schools must provide a variety of goods and services for adequate educational programs. Plant maintenance and operation take about 9.3 cents of every school dollar. Practically everything the schools buy costs more each year as the national inflationary trend continues. This per-unit cost increase of goods and services, coupled with increased educational services for greater numbers of pupils, creates growing pressures for increased school receipts. Total expenditures for public elementary and secondary schools have more than doubled in the period 1957–68 (from $13.5 billion to $31.0 billion).[12] In the same period, per-pupil current expenditures increased less rapidly ($341 in 1957–58 to $619 in 1967–68). Per-pupil expenditures vary widely among the states. Expressed in dollar amounts and as a percent of the United States average for 1967–68 ($619), the following data point up the variation: (1) New York, $982 (158.6%); (2) Wyoming, $670 (108.2%); (3) Illinois, $621 (100.3%); (4) Florida, $554 (89.5%); (5) Texas, $492 (79.5%); and (6) Mississippi, $346 (55.9%).

Unless some states have found a substitute for money in purchasing the needful components in education, the evidence seems clear that substantial variations, if not inequality of opportunity, do exist among schools across the nation. Until some standard unit of education is devised, the obvious fiscal variations can be rationalized away. Even today, in the face of urgent financial needs in most school districts, easy solutions to complex problems abound. Although these solutions vary in rhetoric, their common denominator is an admonition for a return to some "good old days" when education cost little and demanded less of our financial resources. Such anachronistic responses do not meet the need for effective education; they do divert attention from unsolved school problems. The massive problems in urban education will not be solved

[12] *Financial Status of the Public Schools, 1968* (Washington, D.C.: Committee on Educational Finance, National Education Association, Washington, D.C., 1968), p. 40.

by ignoring the realities of declining tax bases and increasing educational costs in urban schools.

CAPITAL EXPENDITURES

Land and construction costs constitute the basic elements in capital expenditures. The total capital outlay in education for 1967–68 was an estimated $4.2 billion, up 7.8 percent from the previous year (and 38.4 percent in the previous ten years).[13] In the same period (1957–67), construction costs increased 28 percent. These higher construction costs explain most of the composite increase. Interest rates on school bonds also show a steady increase, reflecting the national trend toward a higher cost of borrowing. Interest on school bonds amounted to a total of $965,933.00 in 1967–68, up 182.5 percent from the level of ten years earlier. The interest on debt is paid from current school revenues and represents a significant tax burden in most school districts.

CURRENT ISSUES
IN SCHOOL FINANCE

Unless some economic miracles occur, school expenditures will continue their upward trend. More, not less, educational services, facilities, and expectations must be translated into revenue and expenditures. While technological advances may reduce the shortage of trained teachers, the hardware and software will be expensive. Better use of professional and paraprofessional employees can result in more efficient use of available instructional dollars, but lowering standards of preparation or spreading the professionals thinner do not offer any real solution to our educational needs.

The prevailing social mood of the 1970's seems to demand extensive public spending for human needs. Whether the schools will get their needful tax support will depend, however, on their successful competition with a host of other social demands. School

[13] *Ibid.*, p. 52–53.

taxes are just one of the many tax burdens undertaken by citizens. Social, welfare, and government services compete with the schools for tax money. Massive amounts of tax money for housing, transportation, antipollution measures, and environmental improvements are high-priority demands. Federal resources will be allocated to these objectives, but the burden likely will rest primarily on the states.

Students of school finance realize that present support structures are hopelessly inadequate for current and future needs. Local property tax burdens are dangerously high; broader tax bases must be tapped in most states. In a time of national prosperity, school districts across the nation teeter on the edge of bankruptcy. The competing demands for the tax dollar from national and state governments push school needs aside in far too many legislative chambers. The crisis in urban education deepens as patchwork and makeshift alternatives are tried out in run-down schools. Good education is expensive, but poor quality schools are an extravagance no state or community can afford.

NEEDED IMPROVEMENTS IN SCHOOL FINANCE

At a 1968 workshop sponsored by the National School Boards Association,[14] some crucial elements in state school-support laws were examined in an effort to improve the school finance structure. The problems of raising revenue included a review of local reliance on the property tax for basic school revenues. In light of changing patterns of wealth distribution, real property no longer represents the best or most equitable tax base for schools. Income taxes and sales taxes may represent a far better tax base for schools than the property tax. Improved systems of tax revenue allocation are needed to match local and state school needs more closely with available tax resources. The present school-support system in many states promotes substantial variance in school

[14] National School Boards Association, *State School Finance Laws Handbook,* Proceedings of the 1968 Workshop, Detroit, Michigan, March 28 and 31, 1968.

quality; local school resources depend on assessed valuation rather than need. Thus, to end school "poverty" areas in the states, tax jurisdictions must be expanded. Not surprisingly, school tax reform is a politically sensitive issue in many states; the implicit response of many citizens to new school tax schemes is "what's in it for our district?"

Improvement in financial support for public schools will require some basic revisions in tax laws, support structures, and school district organizations. Local school districts, as presently defined geographically, do not represent an equitable balance between tax resources and educational needs. The quality of schools and the degree of educational opportunity are too often accidents of local resources rather than reflections of local needs. Antiquated tax laws enacted in an era when land represented the principal wealth of the nation must be changed to place tax obligations on forms of property presently outside the school tax jurisdiction. Income, personal property—particularly intangible personal property—and business transactions are contemporary property forms largely untapped for school support.

Local school districts may not represent the only viable school management units; larger units may be designed for financial, if not administrative, purposes. If local control of schools is favored, the tax structure could be statewide, and the policy and government of schools left at the local district level. Federal support of schools need not stay at present levels or follow current principles. Categorical aid seems to reflect a view that school districts lack the wisdom to shape and implement acceptable educational goals; somehow the congressional "categories" of aid represent superior wisdom.

Certainly, national goals and objectives can be realized through schools, but the system of competitive federal aid grants too often rewards proposal rhetoric rather than supports local or state school needs. Equalization of school resources to promote more equitable educational opportunity should be a high-priority concern for legislators, school people, and citizens alike. If our schools are to realize the purposes prescribed in our national conscience, the structures for school finance must promote a balance between resources and needs.

SUMMARY

From a financial standpoint, schools share the same problems as any business enterprise: human and material resources are needed and these resources require money. The funds for school support come from public tax monies raised and distributed at the national, state, and local levels. Nontax support for public schools (e.g., gifts, private grants, etc.) are inconsequential, and any improvement in school finance must come from tax sources. Nationally, the great bulk of school funds comes from local taxes with state and federal tax funds ranking second and third as sources.

The concept of local support of schools is under fire; the local tax bases are inadequate to provide the kinds of schooling demanded by large segments of our society. Land taxes constitute the bulk of the local tax base, and the urgent need to broaden this base is painfully evident in most local school districts. The financial resources for schools vary widely among states and the districts within states. Equality of educational opportunity is hollow piety unless equitable resource allocations reduce the gap between rich and poor school districts.

With limited income, schools face two simple economic choices: live within their income or borrow additional money. Even with clever use of limited income, there comes a time when school services must be limited. Improved teacher efficiency, careful program planning, budgeting, and critical evaluation can help school boards make better spending decisions. Unless additional resources can be found, the financial crises in urban schools will further impair their effectiveness. Financial demands of rapidly expanding government services in health, housing, transportation, and welfare render the schools' financial future most uncertain. Schools compete with a host of municipal, state, and national priorities for available tax funds. Increased school enrollments, spiraling costs, and stable or shrinking tax bases push many districts to the edge of bankruptcy. Unless the schools get the needed resources, the questions of innovation, effective teachers, and relevant curricula are pointless.

SUGGESTED READINGS

American Association of School Administrators, *Education Is Good Business*. Washington, D.C.: The Association, 1966.

American Association of School Administrators, *The Federal Government and Public Schools*. Washington, D.C.: The Association, 1965.

Burkhead, Jesse, *State and Local Taxes for Public Education*. Syracuse, New York: Syracuse University Press, 1963.

Burkhead, Jesse, *Public School Finance: Economics and Politics*. Syracuse, New York: Syracuse University Press, 1964.

Clark, Harold S., *Cost and Quality in Public Education*. Syracuse, New York: Syracuse University Press, 1963.

Daly, Charles, ed., *The Quality of Inequality: Urban and Suburban Public Schools*. Chicago: University of Chicago Press, 1968.

Gauerke, Warren E., and Jack R. Childress, eds., *The Theory and Practice of School Finance*. Chicago: Rand McNally & Company, 1967.

James, H. Thomas, James A. Kelly, and Walter I. Garms, *Determinants of Education Expenditures in Large Cities of the United States*. Stanford: Stanford University School of Education, 1966.

Johns, Roe L., and Edgar L. Morphet, *The Economics and Financing of Education*, 2d ed. Englewood Cliffs, N.J.: Prentice-Hall, Inc., 1969.

National Education Association, Special Project on School Finance, *Financing the Public Schools, 1960–70*. Washington, D.C.: N.E.A., 1962.

National Education Association, Committee on Educational Finance, *Financial Status of the Public Schools—1968*. Washington, D.C.: N.E.A., 1968.

Wise, Arthur E., *Rich Schools, Poor Schools: The Promise of Equal Educational Opportunity*. Chicago: University of Chicago Press, 1967.

138

WHO SHOULD TEACH?

IF IT is true that teaching is one of the most important professions, it follows that only the best should teach. The teaching profession should attract the brightest minds, the finest personalities, and the most committed young people. In electing this life of service, prospective teachers can look forward not only to finding personal fulfillment, but also interest and excitement in working with the minds and talents of others.

Those who choose teaching as a career should be aware of the importance of their decision. Teaching is a complex and demanding profession. Certain qualities are essential for successful teaching. It is important that those who have chosen teaching or who are considering teaching as a career evaluate themselves carefully and candidly. Results of such a self-analysis should be validated through the use of objective aids and with the help of others.

Persons who select the occupation that is right for them take a significant step toward a productive and happy life. Effective and happy teachers are prerequisite to continued advancement in all fields—social, economic, religious, and scientific. Society, then, is influenced greatly by those who choose to teach.

DEMANDS OF TEACHING

Throughout the world, teaching is recognized as hard work and a job of vital importance. The London *Times* recently remarked that "teaching must be constantly publicized as the demanding, complex and exceedingly skillful job it is, a job about which the practicing teacher never ceases to learn. The teacher in the classroom must be seen as the foundation of the whole vast edifice of education and not as a rather expensive and possible outmoded embellishment of the structure." [1]

Teaching is both a science and an art. The nature of the work of the teacher demands that he study human beings and understand the laws of human action. Some of the knowledge he needs can be obtained from the various sciences. Biological sciences provide information about human growth and development. From psychology, principles of mental change and development are derived. The social sciences provide knowledge of man's institutions and his social behavior. The term *behavioral sciences* is used to designate the fields which provide the knowledge about human development and learning that is the basis for the professional practice of teaching.

The process of teaching, itself, involves providing or withholding stimuli with the objective of producing certain responses in the pupil. This procedure requires the teacher to apply scientific principles in dealing with both group and individual instruction. Teaching, therefore, is based upon scientific knowledge; yet the practical application of such knowledge in specific situations becomes largely an artistic process.

Science provides knowledge; art provides the ability to apply it. A person may possess comprehensive knowledge of paints, their composition, use, and effects; yet he may not be an artist. He may not actually be able to paint. Similarly, a person may know his subject, understand appropriate behavioral sciences, and yet not be a teacher. The scientific foundations of education must be activated through the skill and insight of the artist-teacher.

QUALITIES ESSENTIAL FOR SUCCESSFUL TEACHING

What intellectual and scholastic abilities are required of teachers? What personal attributes are necessary? What interest patterns characterize good teachers? Fred H. Stocking, a scholar at

[1] *The* (London) *Times Educational Supplement,* November 26, 1965, p. 1143.

Williams College, has furnished an excellent and colorful commentary on what is a good teacher:

A good teacher can tell his students a lot of answers to a lot of questions. But the best teacher can play dumb while helping his students think out the answers for themselves.

A good teacher is an eager and enthusiastic talker. But the best teacher knows how to be quiet and patient while his students struggle to formulate their own thoughts in their own words.

A good teacher is humble: he naturally feels that the accumulated wisdom of his subject is far more important than himself. But the best teacher is even humbler: for he respects the feeling of young people that they are naturally far more important than a silly old subject.

A good teacher knows that his students ought to be responsible, honest, and good citizens. But the best teacher knows that responsibility, honesty, and good citizenship cannot be "taught" in a course because such qualities are communicated through daily actions, not daily lectures.

A good teacher strives to keep his class under control. But the best teacher knows that he must first be able to control himself.

A good teacher earns his salary many times over. But the best teacher also earns a deep and secret satisfaction which would be ruined if he tried to talk about it in public or convert it into cash.

The students of a good teacher pass their courses, graduate, and settle down with good jobs. But the students of the best teacher go on receiving rewards every day of their lives: for they have discovered that the life of the inquiring mind is exciting.[2]

Despite hundreds of studies on what constitutes good teaching, it is virtually impossible to find these characteristics precisely and neatly identified. Many studies of student perceptions of excellent teachers and countless other measuring instruments have not scientifically isolated the components of successful pedagogy. However, one of the most recent reviews of what research says about characteristics of good teachers is fairly optimistic about continuing efforts to identify good teachers. This writer indicates that "even though there is no single best or worst kind of teacher there are clearly distinguishable characteristics associated with

[2] "Who Is the Best Teacher?", *The Bennington Banner,* Bennington, Vermont, November 14, 1963, p. 4.

'good' and 'bad' teachers. There is no one *best* kind of teacher because there is no *one kind* of student." [3]

Undoubtedly, intellectual ability and a high quality of scholarship are important adjuncts to successful teaching. Knowledge of subject matter, professional practices and techniques, and scholarship or grade-point average correlate positively with teaching efficiency in many studies.

Recent research also shows that teacher personality plays an important role in establishing the learning climate in the classroom. Contrasting classroom climates and associated attitudes are listed in Table 15. The research results indicate that the integrative teacher-pupil contacts establish better pupil attitudes and superior patterns of work.

TABLE 15. INTEGRATIVE-DOMINATIVE TEACHING PATTERNS

The Integrative Pattern	*The Dominative Pattern*
a. accepts, clarifies, and supports the ideas and feelings of pupils	a. expresses or lectures about own ideas or knowledge
b. praises and encourages	b. gives directions or orders
c. asks questions to stimulate pupil participation in decision-making	c. criticizes or deprecates pupil behavior with intent to change it
d. asks questions to orient pupils to school work	d. justifies his own position or authority

Associated Attitudes of Teacher

outgoing	trustful	antisocial	hostile
good-natured	patient	surly	impatient
friendly	self-effacing	spiteful	self-centered
cheerful	self-submissive	dour	self-assertive
	responsive		aloof

SOURCE: Adapted from Ned A. Flanders, "Teacher Influence in the Classroom," in Arno A. Bellack, ed., *Theory and Research in Teaching* (New York: Teachers College, Columbia University, 1963), p. 41.

[3] Don Hamachek, "Characteristics of Good Teachers and Implications for Teacher Education," *Phi Delta Kappan,* L (February 1969), 341–345.

Just as innate intellectual potential is subject to the influence of the environment, so most of the traits which combine to form what is called personality can be cultivated within limits for each individual. Improvement in personal traits depends, first of all, upon the degree to which the individual is motivated. Equally important is the objectivity of self-analysis achieved in identifying strengths and weaknesses. Definition of goals, and development of a systematic plan of activities and practice to refine particular traits, are other steps toward such improvement. In some cases—as, for example, with emotional problems, lack of drive or buoyancy, or unattractive personal bearing—the individual may need professional help. Often such assistance can play a vital role in helping develop personal qualities needed for successful teaching.

INTEREST PATTERNS

A person who is considering teaching as a career should identify his own interest patterns with insight, candor, and accuracy. He should be fully aware that the soundness of his motives in his choice of teaching are vital in determining his success or failure in the profession. After an individual has carefully and honestly identified his own interest patterns, he should check them against those of others who have prepared to teach. Research reports may help to facilitate such checking.

In a survey which evaluated the attitudes of more than two hundred students at the University of Montana who were taking their first course in the School of Education during the 1964–65 term, Charles E. Hood asked for opinions concerning the advantages and disadvantages of a teaching career. The results, listed in Table 16, provide an interesting and realistic representation.

SUMMARY OF QUALITIES DEMANDED FOR SUCCESSFUL TEACHING

The foregoing consideration of the personal qualities and reasons for choosing teaching that have been found fairly typical of outstanding teachers and others planning to enter the profession

TABLE 16. ADVANTAGES AND DISADVANTAGES OF TEACHING AS A
CAREER (UNIVERSITY OF MONTANA SCHOOL OF EDUCATION SOPHOMORES,
1964–65)

Advantages	Score
1. Teacher Performs Valuable Service to Society	768
2. Teacher Works with Young People	615
3. Teaching Can Lead to Other Careers	549
4. General Teacher Shortage	315
5. Develops Character of Teacher	262
6. Pleasant Working Environment	258
7. Opportunity for Leadership	211
8. Long Summer Vacation	174
9. Opportunities for Advancement	133
10. Job Security	106
11. Acquisition of Culture	95
12. High Prestige	88

Disadvantages	Score
1. Personal Freedom Restricted	724
2. Low Salaries	484
3. Imbalance in Supply and Demand in Some Fields	410
4. Freedom to Teach Is Restricted	393
5. Teachers Are Overworked	301
6. Certification Requirements Are Unrealistic	279
7. Oversupply of Teachers in Desirable Locations	201
8. Low Prestige	194
9. Many Disciplinary Problems	120
10. Job Insecurity	97

From Charles E. Hood, "Why 226 University Students Selected Teaching
as a Career," *The Clearing House*, XL (December 1965), 228. Reprinted by
permission of *The Clearing House*, Fairleigh Dickinson University.

suggests that successful teachers (1) are above average in intelligence as compared with other college students; (2) are better-
than-average college students; (3) like and seek to understand people; (4) are able to communicate ideas effectively to others; (5)
enjoy good health, both mental and physical; (6) like to study and
are intellectually curious; (7) are socially and emotionally mature;
(8) believe in the worth of teaching; (9) enjoy associating with
young people; and (10) possess personality characteristics that enable them to work with people.

VERIFICATION OF CHOICE
OF TEACHING

Two major sources of information are available to help a person ascertain whether or not he is qualified to prepare for a career in teaching. First, a candid and searching self-appraisal enables him to catalogue his strengths and weaknesses and to compare his interests, goals, and abilities with those required for successful teaching. Check lists are available to those who wish to engage in serious self-analysis. The second source of information available to students might be referred to as objective aids—health examinations, speech tests, vocational interest inventories, personality adjustment scales, and general intelligence as we:l as achievement tests.

SELF-ANALYSIS

A person's philosophy influences and directs his rational behavior more than any other single force. The prospective teacher should be thoroughly acquainted, therefore, with his own value system and with those that motivate teachers. He should be cognizant of the fact that teaching is seldom a rapid approach to fame, social prominence, or economic abundance. Although financial rewards for teaching have been rising steadily in recent years, especially in larger school districts, the income of teachers is still below that of most professionals. Salaries improved greatly for elementary and secondary teachers during the decade of the 1960's. Indeed, in some areas many experienced public school instructors competed favorably with college professors in pay schedules. Tables 17, 18, and 19 will give the prospective teacher an idea of how salaries have progressed in recent years. In all probability, the time is not far distant when material security will combine with the inner satisfaction of service and interest to make teaching a much more sought-after career.

On the nonmaterial side, the value system of a teacher in the United States should commit him to the cause of democracy as a

TABLE 17. ESTIMATED AVERAGE ANNUAL SALARY OF CLASSROOM
TEACHERS IN ELEMENTARY AND SECONDARY SCHOOLS: UNITED STATES
1958–59 TO 1968–69

| School year | Average annual salaries of classroom teachers, 1958–59 to 1968–69 | | |
	Elementary	Secondary	Total
1958–59	$4,607	$5,113	$4,797
1959–60	4,815	5,276	4,995
1960–61	5,075	5,543	5,275
1961–62	5,340	5,775	5,515
1962–63	5,560	5,980	5,732
1963–64	5,805	6,266	5,995
1964–65	5,985	6,451	6,195
1965–66	6,279	6,761	6,485
1966–67	6,622	7,109	6,830
1967–68	7,208	7,692	7,423
1968–69	7,676	8,160	7,908

From *Estimate of School Statistics 1968–1969*. Research Report 1968—
R16 (Washington, D.C.: Research Division, National Education Association), pp. 15–16.

form of government and personal freedom and respect as goals of
human institutions. The teacher should stand unyieldingly against
the forces that tend to restrict or limit human rights or arbitrarily
deny opportunity to individuals or groups. He should protect the
ideals and form of democratic self-government against any form of
authoritarianism. He should believe in (1) the dignity of man,
without exceptions; (2) the brotherhood of man as a characteristic
of civilization; (3) constitutional freedoms and democratic processes, as the surest avenues to justice and sound government; (4)
the obligations of man to "walk in dignity and decency" as an individual and to accept fully his responsibilities as a citizen; (5) the
essential capacity for good possessed by all men, implemented by
the strength of spiritual values; and (6) the perpetuation of freedom of mankind through knowledge and its wise application. "As
we look upon life, so we teach."

Identification of interests is another way for the individual to

TABLE 18. PERCENTAGE DISTRIBUTION OF ESTIMATED ANNUAL SALARIES
PAID CLASSROOM TEACHERS IN PUBLIC ELEMENTARY AND SECONDARY
SCHOOLS: UNITED STATES 1958–59 TO 1968–69

School year	Percent of classroom teachers paid:							
	Below $4,500	$4,500– 5,499	$5,500– 6,499	$6,500– 7,499	$7,500– 8,499	$8,500– 9,499	$9,500– 10,499	$10,500 and over
1958–59	48.7%	26.7%	15.7%	8.9%[a]	...	...	...	...
1959–60	42.5	28.2	17.4	11.9[a]	...	...	...	...
1960–61	35.2	27.2	19.3	10.9	7.4%[a]	...	...	...
1961–62	26.6	28.9	22.6	12.9	9.0[a]	...	...	...
1962–63	22.0	28.0	23.4	14.5	8.1	4.0%[a]	...	...
1963–64	16.9	28.6	24.2	15.1	9.0	6.3[a]	...	...
1964–65	13.5	27.0	24.7	16.6	10.1	5.5	2.6%[a]	...
1965–66	8.8	22.7	26.8	19.1	11.5	6.6	4.5[a]	...
1966–67	4.4	19.7	26.7	19.8	13.2	8.6	4.5	3.1%
1967–68	2.1	11.5	25.5	22.0	15.3	10.5	6.6	6.5
1968–69	1.1	7.0	19.9	22.5	18.5	13.6	9.2	8.3

[a] Detailed breakdown not available beyond last salary range shown.

From *Estimate of School Statistics 1968–1969*. Research Report 1968—R16 (Washington, D.C.: Research Division, National Education Association), pp. 15–16.

TABLE 19. AVERAGE ANNUAL SALARY OF INSTRUCTIONAL STAFF [1] IN FULL-TIME PUBLIC ELEMENTARY AND SECONDARY DAY SCHOOLS, BY STATE: 1929–30 TO 1968–69

State	Unadjusted dollars						Adjusted dollars (1968–69 purchasing power) [2]					
1	1929–30	1939–40	1949–50	1959–60	1965–66	1968–69 [3]	1929–30	1939–40	1949–50	1959–60	1965–66	1968–69 [3]
	2	3	4	5	6	7	8	9	10	11	12	13
United States [4]	$1,420	$1,441	$3,010	$5,174	$6,935	$8,200	$2,955	$3,675	$4,529	$6,275	$7,739	$8,200
Alabama	792	744	2,111	4,002	5,450	5,050	1,648	1,897	3,176	4,853	6,082	6,050
Alaska	1,728	(5)	(5)	6,859	8,520	10,887	3,596	(5)	(5)	8,318	9,507	10,887
Arizona	1,637	1,544	3,556	5,590	7,498	7,819	3,407	3,937	5,350	6,779	8,367	7,819
Arkansas	673	584	1,801	3,295	4,676	6,291	1,401	1,489	2,710	3,996	5,218	6,291
California	2,123	2,351	(5)	6,600 [6]	8,817	9,700	4,418	5,995	(5)	8,004 [6]	9,839	9,700
Colorado	1,453	1,393	2,821	4,997	6,640	7,425	3,024	3,552	4,244	6,060	7,410	7,425
Connecticut	1,812	1,861	3,558	6,008	7,826	8,800	3,771	4,746	5,353	7,286	8,733	8,800
Delaware	1,570	1,684	3,273	5,800 [6]	7,864	8,400	3,267	4,294	4,925	7,034 [6]	8,775	8,400
District of Columbia	2,269	2,350	3,920	6,280	(5)	(5)	4,722	5,992	5,898	7,616	(5)	(5)
Florida	876	1,012	2,958	5,080	6,639	8,600	1,823	2,581	4,451	6,161	7,408	8,600
Georgia	684	770	1,963	3,904 [7]	5,619	7,200	1,424	1,964	2,954	4,734 [7]	6,270	7,200
Hawaii	1,812	(5)	(5)	5,390	7,169	8,300	3,771	(5)	(5)	6,536	8,000	8,300
Idaho	1,200	1,057	2,481	4,216	5,565	6,219	2,497	2,695	3,733	5,113	6,210	6,219
Illinois	1,630	1,700	3,458	5,814 [8]	7,408	9,300	3,392	4,335	5,203	7,051 [8]	8,267	9,300
Indiana	1,466	1,433	3,401	5,542	7,495	8,350	3,051	3,654	5,117	6,721	8,364	8,350
Iowa	1,094	1,017	2,420	4,030 [6]	6,100 [6]	8,167	2,277	2,593	3,641	4,887 [6]	6,807 [6]	8,167
Kansas	1,159	1,014	2,628	4,450 [6]	6,221 [9]	7,215	2,412	2,586	3,954	5,397 [6]	6,942 [9]	7,215
Kentucky	896	826	1,936	3,327	5,453	6,750	1,865	2,106	2,913	4,035	6,085	6,750
Louisiana	941	1,006	2,983	4,978	5,985	7,200	1,958	2,565	4,488	6,037	6,679	7,200
Maine	942	894	2,115	3,694	5,451	7,288	1,960	2,280	3,182	4,480	6,083	7,288
Maryland	1,518	1,642	3,594	5,557	7,238	9,185	3,159	4,187	5,408	6,739	8,077	9,185
Massachusetts	1,875	2,037	3,338	5,545 [10]	7,932	8,350	3,902	5,194	5,022	6,724 [10]	8,851	8,350
Michigan	1,534	1,576	3,420	5,654	7,445	9,492	3,193	4,019	5,146	6,857	8,308	9,492
Minnesota	1,251	1,276	3,013	5,275	6,995	8,788	2,604	3,254	4,533	6,397	7,806	8,788
Mississippi	620	559	1,416	3,314	4,410	5,912	1,290	1,425	2,131	4,019	4,921	5,912
Missouri	1,235	1,159	2,581	4,536	6,113 [9]	7,372	2,570	2,955	3,883	5,501	6,821 [9]	7,372
Montana	1,215	1,184	2,962	4,425 [6]	5,908	7,200	2,529	3,019	4,457	5,366 [6]	6,593	7,200
Nebraska	1,077	829	2,292	3,876	5,528	6,700	2,241	2,114	3,449	4,700	6,169	6,700
Nevada	1,483	1,557	3,209	5,693	7,375	8,739	3,086	3,970	4,828	6,904	8,230	8,739

	1	2	3	4	5	6	7	8	9	10	11	12
New Mexico	1,113	1,144	3,213	3,362	6,957	7,331	2,316	2,977	4,837	6,322	7,741	7,331
New York	2,493	2,604	3,706	6,537	8,475	9,400	5,188	6,640	5,576	7,927	9,457	9,400
North Carolina	873	946	2,688	4,178	5,661	7,041	1,817	2,412	4,044	5,067	6,317	7,041
North Dakota	900	745	2,324	3,695	5,402	6,300	1,873	1,900	3,497	4,481	6,028	6,300
Ohio	1,665	1,587	3,088	5,124	7,034	8,050	3,465	4,047	4,646	6,214	7,849	8,050
Oklahoma	1,070	1,014	2,736	4,659	5,824	6,853	2,227	2,586	4,117	5,650	6,499	6,853
Oregon	1,612	1,333	3,323	5,535	7,168	8,317	3,355	3,399	5,000	6,712	7,999	8,317
Pennsylvania	1,620	1,640	3,006	5,308	7,314	8,133	3,372	4,182	4,523	6,437	8,162	8,133
Rhode Island	1,437	1,809	3,294	11 5,499	11 6,999	8,178	2,991	4,613	4,956	6,669	7,810	8,178
South Carolina	788	743	1,891	3,450	4,963	6,025	1,640	1,895	2,845	4,184	5,538	6,025
South Dakota	956	807	2,064	3,725	5,136	6,200	1,990	2,058	3,105	4,517	5,731	6,200
Tennessee	902	862	2,302	3,929	5,318	6,520	1,877	2,198	3,464	4,765	5,934	6,520
Texas	924	1,079	3,122	4,708	6,330	6,794	1,923	2,751	4,697	5,709	7,064	6,794
Utah	1,330	1,394	3,103	5,096	6,569	7,400	2,768	3,555	4,669	6,180	7,330	7,400
Vermont	963	981	2,348	4,466	5,848	6,700	2,004	2,502	3,533	5,416	6,526	6,700
Virginia	861	899	2,328	4,312	5,717	7,550	1,792	2,292	3,503	5,229	6,380	7,550
Washington	1,556	1,706	3,487	11 5,643	11 7,605	8,858	3,238	4,350	5,247	11 6,843	8,486	8,858
West Virginia	1,023	1,170	2,425	3,952	5,433	6,900	2,129	2,984	3,649	4,793	6,063	6,900
Wisconsin	1,399	1,379	3,007	9 4,870	9 6,190	8,350	2,912	3,516	4,524	9 5,906	9 6,907	8,350
Wyoming	1,239	1,169	2,798	4,937	6,431	7,786	2,579	2,981	4,210	5,987	7,176	7,786
Outlying areas:												
American Samoa	(5)	(5)	(5)	852	(5)	(5)	(5)	(5)	(5)	(5)	(5)	(5)
Canal Zone	(5)	(5)	(5)	6,034	7,940	10,400	(5)	(5)	(5)	(5)	(5)	(5)
Guam	(5)	(5)	(5)	4,107	(5)	7,240	(5)	(5)	(5)	(5)	(5)	(5)
Puerto Rico	(5)	(5)	(5)	6 2,360	3,669	4,450	(5)	(5)	(5)	(5)	(5)	(5)
Virgin Islands	(5)	(5)	(5)	3,407	5,498	(5)	(5)	(5)	(5)	(5)	(5)	(5)

1 Includes supervisors, principals, classroom teachers, and other instructional staff.

2 Based on Consumer Price Index published by the Bureau of Labor Statistics, U.S. Department of Labor.

3 Estimated.

4 Beginning in 1959–60, includes Alaska and Hawaii.

5 Data not available.

6 Partly estimated by the Office of Education.

7 Excludes kindergarten teachers.

8 Includes administrators.

9 Excludes vocational schools not operated as part of the regular public school system.

10 Includes clerical assistants to instructional personnel.

11 Includes attendance personnel.

SOURCE: U.S. Department of Health, Education, and Welfare, Office of Education, "Statistics of State School Systems"; and "Fall 1968 Statistics of Public Schools."

From *Digest of Educational Statistics* (U.S. Dept. of Health, Education and Welfare, Office of Education, 1969), 38.

analyze his commitment to teaching. He may begin by selecting the school subjects he prefers to study; he may then identify the hobbies or extracurricular activities which interest him most, study his reading preferences, and examine the other kinds of work or recreational activities which have greatest appeal for him. In teaching, interest must be closely associated with the field to be taught; with scholarly, intellectual, or possibly creative endeavors; and with self-development projects that extend over substantial periods of time.

Self-analysis should also include examination of one's skill in human relations with classmates. College students work with each other in clubs, fraternities, classes, and religious organizations as well as in various other groups and associations. The extent to which a person is successful as an active and participating member in college activities is a good indication of how well he will work with his fellow teachers, administrators, service clubs, members of Parent-Teacher Associations, or church organizations.

OBJECTIVE AIDS

Objective aids are available to assist in the verification of choice of teaching. These aids—health examinations, speech tests, vocational interest inventories, personality adjustment scales, and achievement and mental ability tests—furnish objective data that may enhance the reliability of self-analysis.[4] The final result of self-analysis, then, should be a composite of a large number of estimates.

HEALTH EXAMINATIONS. Medical examinations can identify chronic diseases and physical disabilities which might bar an individual from certification for teaching. They also will reveal existing patterns of deficiency in energy or physical vigor which may work against success in an occupation as demanding of physical and nervous energy as teaching.

The problem of discovering weaknesses in mental health is more difficult. Here, too, professional help is available to aid the

---

[4] Ned A. Flanders, "Teacher Effectiveness," in *Encyclopedia of Educational Research,* ed. Robert L. Ebel, 4th ed. (New York: The Macmillan Company, 1969), pp. 1423–1437.

individual in discovering problems of mental health that need attention. Certain tests of personal adjustment—such as the *Minnesota Multiphasic Personality Inventory,* the *Rorschach Tests,* and the *Thematic Apperception Test*—can help to uncover deep emotional and mental stability problems. Psychiatric analysis and counseling are also available on some college campuses to assist students in verifying their mental health fitness.

Each individual will, of course, have some insight relative to the general status of both his physical and mental health. If his habits of health practice have included regular checkup examinations by his family physician, he will be conscious of his health pattern and sensitive to any significant changes that may occur in it. Regarding his mental health, the intelligent college student will, typically, be able to ascertain to some extent such factors as self-acceptance; emotional stability as opposed to rigidity; capacity for self-discipline; adaptability; existence of wholesome attitudes toward work, other human beings, and life in general; and capacity to organize life activities so that wholesome balance is maintained.

SPEECH TESTS. Many studies indicate a significant positive correlation between speaking ability and success in teaching. Better programs in the preservice education of teachers recognize the importance of speech skills for teaching by requiring either speech tests or a minimum amount of course work in the field. Prospective teachers should take appropriate tests from recognized speech clinics or departments of speech in college or universities.

VOCATIONAL INTEREST INVENTORIES. Standardized interest inventories are used to assist people to ascertain their vocational inclinations. It may seem strange that a person has to find out what his own interests are, but counseling authorities indicate that many college students cannot identify their own vocational interests.

Occupational counselors have recognized both the values and limitations of interest inventories. On the positive side, each individual needs to be aware of the fact that through directed effort and use of his ability he may gain more satisfaction from one activity than from another. Thus, one occupation holds more promise of satisfaction and success than another. On the negative side, what is often expressed as interest is nothing more than preference. Motivation is not likely to accompany preferences to the same extent that it goes with interests. It is a matter of degree, but still an important difference.

Several standardized vocational interest inventories are available. Among the more widely used are the *Kuder Preference Record* and the *Strong Vocational Interest Blank.*

PERSONALITY ADJUSTMENT SCALES. Why is it that pupils are happier and learn more with some teachers than with others having apparently equal qualifications? Most pupils would answer "Personality of the teacher." Personality measurement is a well-established means of describing teacher effectiveness, according to modern researchers.[5]

Numerous personality scales and tests are available. *The Bell Adjustment Inventory, Bernreuter Personality Inventory, California Personality Inventory, Rorschach Test, Thurstone Personality Schedule,* and *Willoughby Emotional Maturity Scale* are among the better known ones.

ACHIEVEMENT AND MENTAL ABILITY TESTS. Teaching requires above-average mental ability as compared to other professions. And scholastic attainment above the ordinary usually accompanies superior intellectual ability, if the student is serious about his work.

Standardized test results make it possible for a person to compare his mental ability and scholastic achievement with those of other students. Among the better-known tests of mental ability are the *American Council on Education Psychological Examination* (ACE), the *College Entrance Examination Board,* and the *Otis Self-Administering Test of Mental Ability.* Widely used achievement tests include the *California Achievement Tests* and the *Co-operative General Achievement Test.*

PERSONAL SOURCES OF HELP FOR MAKING CHOICE

Furnished with a still-life tableau of the career of the teacher, a prospective member of the profession may find it difficult to

[5] A. S. Barr, *Wisconsin Studies of the Measurement and Prediction of Teacher Effectiveness* (Madison, Wis.: Dembar Publications, 1961), pp. 99–106.

project himself into such a role and to consider his qualifications for teaching. Realistic self-evaluation is demanded, but as a single basis for making the decision to enter teaching, this procedure is rather tenuous. Also, to consider only a list of qualities, traits, and characteristics of the successful teacher—such as those presented in this chapter—would be to overlook certain important intangible factors basic to so important a judgment. Such approaches are analogous to looking through a microscope at the cell structure of a flower and becoming so involved with the mechanics that one forgets the form of the blossom.

Empirical evidence and research studies indicate that individuals seek and receive personal help in selecting their occupation from three major sources: parents and friends, teachers, and professional counselors.

As students select their occupations, teachers are able to be of assistance to them for several reasons. First, teachers are intimately associated with students at the time that many are choosing their occupations. (A surprisingly large number of students who decide to enter teaching do so at an early age, at the seventh or eighth grade. As many as 44 percent of those who choose teaching do so while in the early years of high school.) Teachers know their students, and they also are familiar with requirements for success in various occupations. Their skill in helping students analyze their potentialities is likely to be an invaluable aid, as is the wisdom of their advice.

Guidance counselors can be of inestimable value. Many colleges or universities have a guidance and counseling center. Smaller colleges often make available faculty members who have specialized in counseling to administer tests and to consult with students. Even if such a center is not available in a student's own school, it is likely that services of this type can be obtained at some institution nearby. Trained personnel in guidance and counseling centers can administer tests, conduct interviews, and in many other ways assist individuals in the selection of an occupation. Each individual should validate his self-evaluation and his choice of the teaching profession by utilizing the assistance of specialists in guidance and counseling.

SUMMARY

The best should teach. The profession of teaching is a demanding one. Successful teaching requires "the brightest minds, the finest personalities, ... the soundest moral and spiritual commitments," and good health. Further, good teachers put service to humanity above self.

The selection of an occupation is of enduring importance to the individual. A person's work influences his family living, social relationships, recreational activities, and health. The occupation he chooses should provide ample opportunities for self-realization, wholesome interpersonal relationships, self-respect, and personal satisfaction.

As a general rule, successful teachers possess certain specific intellectual and personal qualities. Among these are a broad cultural background, including sound scholarship, good work habits, skill in oral and written language, and adeptness in the solution of intellectual and social problems; a high level of general intelligence, represented by above-average scores on mental capacity tests as compared to other college students; intense specialization in the subjects taught; knowledge of the structure and processes of education, including learning, child development, and the organization and purposes of schools; knowledge of the techniques of instruction and functional skill in teaching; and an overall synthesis of personal traits that reflect a mature, well-adjusted, wholesome, well-balanced person. In addition, successful teachers have good physical and mental health, enjoy working with young people, and have highly developed commitments to social responsibilities.

Those who choose to teach usually have similar interest patterns. Typically, they go into the profession because of their desire to work with people, their interest in a subject field and desire to continue its study, and their commitment to values that place service to humanity ahead of personal goals.

Those who are considering teaching as a career should subject themselves to extensive self-analysis to verify the validity of such a choice. This process may well begin with an identification and appraisal of individual systems of values which give life its direction. Objective aids are available to supplement and complement the process of self-analysis. Medical examinations, speech tests, vocational interest inventories, and various other standardized evaluation instruments are available which can be valuable aids when administered and interpreted by professionally competent people.

Finally, after a person has carefully analyzed himself and collected objective evidence with regard to his suitability for the teaching profession, he may seek the counsel of parents, friends, teachers, and guidance specialists. Assistance of this type can be of inestimable value to the individual who is trying to validate his decision to become a teacher.

SUGGESTED READINGS

Bellack, Arno A., ed., *Theory and Research in Teaching.* New York: Teachers College Press, 1963.

Brembeck, Cole S., *The Discovery of Teaching.* Englewood Cliffs, N.J.: Prentice-Hall, Inc., 1962.

Broudy, H. S., "Can We Define Good Teaching?" *Education Digest,* Sept. 1969, pp. 20–23.

Burke, William J., *Not For Glory—Who Are Today's Great Teachers?* New York: Cowles Education Corp., 1967.

Colman, John E., *Master Teachers and the Art of Teaching.* New York: Pitman Corp., 1967.

Flanders, Ned A., "Teacher Effectiveness," in *Encyclopedia of Educational Research,* 4th ed., Robert W. Ebel, ed. New York: The Macmillan Co., 1969, pp. 1423–37.

Gelmas, Paul J., *So You Want to Be a Teacher?* New York: Harper and Row, Publishers, 1965.

Hamachek, Don, "Characteristics of Good Teachers and Implications for Teacher Education," *Phi Delta Kappan,* February 1969, pp. 341–45.

Henjum, Arnold, "A Study of the Significance of Student Teachers' Personality Characteristics," *The Journal of Teacher Education,* Summer 1969, pp. 143–47.

Highet, Gilbert, *The Art of Teaching.* New York: Vintage Books, 1962.

Johnson, James A. and Byron F. Radebaugh, "Excellent Teachers—

What Makes Them Outstanding?" *Clearing House,* November 1969, pp. 152–56.

MacCurdy, Robert D., "One Hundred Great Teachers," *Education,* February–March 1969, pp. 236–40.

Richey, Robert W., *Planning for Teaching.* New York: McGraw-Hill Book Co., 1968, pp. 133–145.

Shumsky, Abraham, *In Search of Teaching Style.* New York: Appleton-Century-Crofts, 1968.

Simpson, Ray H., *Teacher Self-Evaluation.* New York: The Macmillan Co., 1966.

Wagner, Guy, "What Schools Are Doing: Identifying Components of Good Teaching," *Education,* February–March 1969, pp. 280–85.

Weisse, Edward B., "Competition: Agent for Educational Change," *Educational Forum,* January 1970, pp. 247–50.

9.

PREPARATION FOR TEACHING

COMTE'S formula *Voir pour prévoir: prévoir pour pouvoir*—
"To see in order to foresee; to foresee in order to gain power"—
is sound advice to prospective teachers. Not only should the student be familiar with the qualities essential for successful teaching considered in Chapter 8, he should know the type of program of studies as well as the certification requirements established for admission to the profession.

The preservice preparation of teachers rests upon the trilogy of liberal education, specialized subject matter, and professional education. The essential foundation for preparation for teaching is a liberal education. The teacher must also possess deep and broad knowledge of his teaching field and adequate preparation in the processes and practice of education. Certification provisions in the various states embody minimum requirements for teaching licenses. Such legal regulations usually specify in quantitative terms the amount of liberal education, specialized subject matter, and professional education necessary for admission to practice.

THE LIBERAL ARTS–PROFESSIONAL EDUCATION CONTROVERSY

All educators agree that the preparation of good teachers rests upon a broad liberal education, specialization in the subject or fields to be taught, and professional knowledge and skills. However, the relative emphasis that each area should receive provokes strong disagreements among educators. The lack of agreement usually revolves around the question: "How much time should a student devote to courses in (1) his teaching field, (2) general education, and (3) professional education?"

The more radical opponents of professional education maintain that teaching ability is innate, that "teachers are born, rather than developed." Naturally, they insist, the study of pedagogy is a waste of time. They eagerly quote individual students who have criticized courses in education to prove their point. Counteraccusations, usually made by professors of education, have held that many liberal arts professors are unprepared professionally, know little about adapting their instruction to individual differences, and typically ignore sound principles of learning and teaching. Criticisms of education courses, professors of education contend, are often defensive devices used by college teachers to protect themselves from ever being required to learn anything about teaching.

Any disagreement between liberal arts and education professors is rooted in a larger, long-standing disagreement over the manner in which liberal and professional education should be provided. The latter half of the nineteenth century saw the appearance of a crusade to professionalize teaching, led by Horace Mann, Calvin Stowe, James G. Carter, and Edmund Dwight. These pioneers of the common school movement recognized that the new democratic school system being developed required teachers professionally prepared for their mission. However, efforts to introduce pedagogical courses into liberal arts colleges were resisted bitterly by administrators and faculties of such institutions, who were already entrenched against the expanding inroads of applied fields. Antagonisms against professional and technical programs—which originally had been generated against medicine and law but were literally fanned to intense proportions by the battle against agricultural and mechanical courses—were unleashed full blast against the new proposals to develop professional preparation for teachers.

So bitter was the resistance of liberal arts colleges, yet so strong was the determination of the American people to provide better training for teachers, that state legislatures established, as they were forced to do in the field of agriculture, separate institutions to provide professional preparation for teaching. Consequently, the normal school which later became the teachers college was created; and the schism and isolation of organization between liberal arts and professional education was perpetuated for a century, to the detriment of both the liberal arts and teacher education.

AREAS OF AGREEMENT ARE INCREASING. No one has been more influential than James B. Conant in recent years in reducing fruitless bickering between the various education interests. In his highly influential study, *The Education of American Teachers,* Conant made clear that no one type of institution was providing the superior educational program.[1]

Nothing revealed by a close study of institutions designated as "teachers college," as compared to those designated as "liberal arts" colleges, justifies a sweeping assertion that one *type* of institution consistently gives the student a better education than the other. The belief that "liberal arts" colleges provide more "breadth and depth" than teachers colleges rests essentially on the notion that courses in education in teachers colleges displace general requirement, subject specialization, or both. My investigations have convinced me that this is simply not the case. The time devoted to education courses in teachers colleges, and in teacher-preparation programs in multipurpose institutions, is not taken away from academic requirements; rather, the courses that are displaced are electives, and such elective courses also give way in a "liberal arts" college that prepares students for certification. Thus one would be quite mistaken to believe that a student necessarily gets a better academic education in one or another type of institution.

A significant widening in areas of agreement has occurred in recent years among those who are responsible for the education of teachers. Many, perhaps most, faculty members in teacher-preparing institutions now agree with liberal arts professors that prospective teachers need a broad liberal education and an adequate knowledge of teaching fields, as well as an understanding of the processes of education and skill in teaching. All favor, too, sufficient electives to enable students to develop special talents and interests and to correct deficiencies.

PROGRESS TOWARD ACHIEVING AN ACCEPTABLE BALANCE BE-

[1] James Bryant Conant, *The Education of American Teachers* (New York: McGraw-Hill Book Company, 1963) p. 77.

TWEEN LIBERAL AND PROFESSIONAL STUDIES. Despite the conflict which continues with vigor on some college campuses, substantial progress has been made toward achieving agreement between professors of liberal arts and education relative to a balance between courses in their respective fields that is desirable and acceptable to each group. Such agreements have reduced the overemphasis on pedagogy that prevailed in early normal schools and in teachers colleges, and increased the emphasis on liberal education. Similarly, the amounts of work required for general education purposes and for the subject field of the individual's specialization have been increased in teacher-education programs. Many institutions have also increased the number of semester hours required for graduation from teacher-education curriculums. It is apparent that the professional phase of teacher education has been added in many instances without reducing materially the amount of time devoted to liberal education or specialization in subject fields.

Only about 15 percent, in fact, of the work required for legal certification for high school teachers is devoted to the study of pedagogy and the practice, under supervision, of teaching. The median for state certification for elementary teachers is 20 percent. Individual teacher-education institutions, however, often have requirements that are higher than those set forth in certification regulations. The allocation is reasonably satisfactory to both professors of liberal arts and education—except to those who deny that the coexistence of these two aspects of the program of teacher education should be encouraged at all.

While areas of agreement are increasing among faculty personnel who help to prepare teachers, it should not be inferred that the "right" and final way to prepare teachers has been found. Nor should one assume that complete agreement exists as to the relative emphasis to be placed upon the various facets of preservice education for teachers. This same statement may well apply for years to come. In the meantime, the wise student will make the most of his opportunities to learn, whether they are under the aegis of a liberal arts professor or a professor of education. The dichotomy between liberal and professional education, real or imagined, is to be decried by all who are sincerely interested in helping prospective teachers gain the best possible education. The preparation of tomorrow's teachers is too important an assignment to be impeded by internal conflicts between professors; this task demands the maximum efforts of all members of faculties in colleges and universities. Prospective teachers have a right to insist that both professors of liberal arts and education cooperate to provide a complete, balanced, and high-quality preparation for teaching.

DESIRABLE ALLOCATION OF COLLEGE HOURS TO THE TRILOGY OF LIBERAL EDUCATION, SPECIALIZED SUBJECT MATTER, AND PROFESSIONAL EDUCATION. The typical proportionate allocation of the college program to the areas of the trilogy is shown in Figure 9. The work in liberal education usually is scheduled during the first two years, with concentration on the teaching fields in the last two. Professional education may be distributed throughout the four-

FIGURE 9. PROPORTIONATE ALLOCATION OF COLLEGE PROGRAM TO TRILOGY AREAS

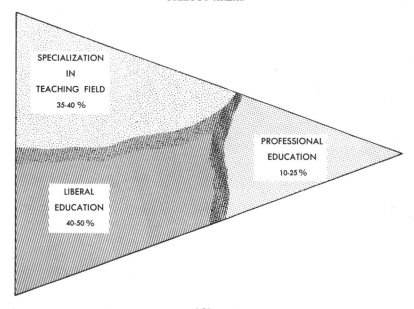

SPECIALIZATION IN TEACHING FIELD 35-40 %

PROFESSIONAL EDUCATION 10-25 %

LIBERAL EDUCATION 40-50 %

year program, thus paralleling both liberal arts and specialization, or it may be concentrated, along with the student's major and minor concentrations, in the junior and senior years. A few institutions place all of the professional work, and sometimes some of the subject-field courses, in the fifth year.

While distinctions between fields may be necessary for administrative purposes, it is well for both students and faculty members to keep in mind that the values of education must be assimilated and synthesized to produce effective teachers. Students should seek relationships between various subjects they study with the awareness that ultimately professional strength will depend on the quality of their total preparation and their ability to harmonize knowledge intended for separate purposes.

LIBERAL EDUCATION

The meaning of the word "liberal," as applied to education, has undergone an evolutionary process. In Greek and Roman education, liberal studies were those suitable for the aristocrat. The seven liberal arts of the Middle Ages, likewise, were for gentlemen. Indeed, until fairly recently, higher education was reserved for the privileged social classes, the elite. The development of modern democracies has, however, been accompanied by a steady expansion of opportunities for all young people, irrespective of class status, to go to college. Today, in various countries, and particularly in the United States, colleges and graduate schools are open to all who can meet scholastic and character requirements. Thus, liberal studies, once reserved for the economically and socially privileged few, are now available to all qualified citizens.

WHAT IS THE PURPOSE OF LIBERAL EDUCATION? Responsibility as a citizen of a complicated modern society and personal development of basic humanity is fostered by true involvement in liberal studies, since the purposes of these studies are to free the mind from ignorance and superstition and to stimulate the individual to search for truth. The aim of liberal education is, essentially, to produce men and women who have integrity and disciplined intelligence, who possess knowledge of self and culture, and who have a system of values worthy of citizens in a free society. Furthermore, liberal education is not only important for teacher education, but also for pursuance of the good life.[2]

A mere acquaintance with the liberal studies will not liberate the mind. As Bergen Evans has noted: "A liberal education . . . must be fundamentally self-motivated. . . . A liberal education can't be administered. The student must abstract and absorb it from everything around him—theaters, magazines, newspapers, concerts, museums, television, and conversation."[3] The student must interpret, synthesize, and apply facts and ideas gathered. He must be an active and interested participant in the learning process. His learning will be enhanced in every course he takes, regardless of the instructor's preparation and ability, because he has assumed some responsibility for his own education. Such an individual is on the way to becoming an educated person.

WHAT DOES LIBERAL EDUCATION INCLUDE? A modern, innovative program of teacher education at Northwestern University, The Tutorial and Clinical Program, offers an example of what a well-conceived liberal arts curriculum for teacher candidates includes. The following description indicates how professional and liberal education are brought together:

The study of the school in its social context requires knowledge of the social sciences such as political science, sociology, and anthropology. Study of value theory and history in education draws heavily upon the humanities, particularly philosophy and history. The teacher as a serious student of education must be knowledgeable in the social sciences and humanities as an academic base for the study of education.[4]

Specific attention to the art of communication, both oral and written, and concern with health and personal development, round out

[2] Harry S. Broudy, "Role of the Liberal Arts in Professional Study," *Journal of General Education,* XVIII (April 1966), 50–67.

[3] Bergen Evans, "Liberal Education Can't Wait for College," *The National Parent-Teacher,* LIV, No. 7 (March 1960), 13.

[4] William R. Hazard, *The Tutorial and Clinical Program of Teacher Education* (Evanston, Ill.: The Northwestern University Press, 1967), pp. 23–25.

growth of professional competency of the new breed of teachers emerging from such forward-looking programs.

EDUCATION DEMANDS ACTIVE INVOLVEMENT OF THE STUDENT

At least three attitudes toward education are prevalent among college students. Some students look upon learning as something to be accomplished with a minimum of effort and without reference to its value and meaning, simply because going to college is the fashion. A meal ticket from either a job or matrimony, or respectability in a particular social set, is more their goal than the achievement of an education. Unfortunately, some such students do graduate in spite of their superficial objectives and often cynical attitudes toward intellectual development. Yet with their degrees, they remain uneducated. A second group have the hoarding concept of education. They collect and store facts and ideas, repeat them to professors upon appropriate occasions, but never become personally involved in the educational process. Their knowledge is of the inert variety. The third attitude, characteristic of real students, is that education is a never-ending process motivated by an insatiable curiosity, requiring a personal love of truth and problem-solving approach to various situations encountered in life. Those with this attitude are personally involved in the educational process and take a share of the responsibility for their own learning. They know that education is not something that happens to them through the efforts of other people.

In no recent decade has this been so obvious as in the 1960's, with its student involvement and activism. Not only were national political questions such as the Vietnam War and the draft targets of student protest, but also in many high schools and colleges quality of teaching, relevancy of curriculum, and administrative policies occupied the attention of thousands of students. Future teachers were part of this corps of young people whose involvement extended from the classroom—where academic preparation had furnished points of departure for critical appraisal of their troubled society.[5]

For a student to be an intelligent activist he must be able to interpret, synthesize, and apply facts and ideas. He must be a vitally interested participant in the learning process. The learning of such a student will be enhanced in every course he takes because of his personal input, regardless of the instructor's preparation and ability. He has assumed major responsibility for his own education and is on his way to becoming a truly educated person.

SPECIALIZATION IN TEACHING FIELDS

The effective teacher must have reserves of knowledge far in excess of any demands placed upon him in regular classroom teaching. To acquire the necessary breadth and depth of preparation in his chosen teaching field, the prospective teacher specializes in one or more subjects. In most colleges and universities, this phase of the program is typically described as "majoring or minoring" in various subjects. For example, a person may major in history and minor in English. In some institutions, however, the emphasis may be placed upon the study of a cluster of subjects related to the organization of elementary or secondary school courses, for example, the social studies, language arts, mathematics and physics, or fine arts. The distributive major—that is, equal amounts of work in three or four subject fields—is a new type of development for the specialization of elementary, and some secondary, school teachers.

Why does the teacher need extended scholarly knowledge of the subject taught? The reasons are many and varied. Teachers must know enough to analyze and evaluate textbooks and other instructional materials: in many schools, teachers play an important role in the selection of books and related instructional materials. The teacher must also have a thorough understanding of his teaching

[5] See "Campus Unrest," *Today's Education,* LVIII, No. 8 (November 1969), 25–33.

field if he is to see it in proper relationship to all areas in the curriculum. If he is to avoid being merely a dealer in information gathered by others, he must help press the search for new knowledge. Successful research demands scholarly knowledge about the subject under study. The teacher must know enough to synthesize and use knowledge and to select the most important and appropriate content for an age level. Depth of knowledge is necessary if the teacher is to gain and maintain the respect of students. Finally, the teacher needs to experience the satisfaction that is derived from a high level of achievement in the academic world.

The need for specialization in subject matter applies to both high school and elementary school teachers. In practice, however, a difference is often encountered in the subject-matter specialization for these two levels of teaching.

SUBJECT-MATTER SPECIALIZATION FOR HIGH SCHOOL TEACHERS

Whereas elementary teachers are responsible for practically all subject fields, secondary teachers are typically certified in one or more subject areas. For this reason, secondary teachers usually take a greater amount of advanced work in one or two fields than do elementary teachers.

Before planning a final program of course work, the future secondary school teacher would do well (1) to study certification requirements in the state or states in which he desires to teach; (2) to examine supply-and-demand statistics in various teaching fields; and (3) to study major and minor requirements in the teaching fields in which he is interested. Certification requirements vary from state to state. The student may find descriptions of certification requirements in the various states in appropriate publications.[6] Teacher supply and demand statistics may be obtained

[6] W. Earl Armstrong and T. M. Stinnett, *A Manual on Certification Requirements for School Personnel in the United States* (Washington, D.C.: National Education Association, revised biennially); Robert C. Woellner and M. Aurilla Wood, *Requirements for Certification of Teachers, Counselors, Librarians, and Administrators for Elementary Schools, Secondary Schools, and Junior Colleges* (Chicago: University of Chicago Press, issued annually).

from the National Education Association. It would also be a good idea to discuss the employment outlook with the teacher placement officer.

The student is advised to study major and minor requirements for the teaching fields in which he is interested because it may be possible to have a double major with a small amount of additional work. In some states secondary teachers must qualify in two or more subject fields because in the small high schools in which many obtain their first positions they are required to teach in several fields, as, for example, in English and speech, history and government, or mathematics and science.

SUBJECT-MATTER SPECIALIZATION FOR ELEMENTARY TEACHERS

Elementary teachers are responsible for teaching most or, in many cases, all basic subject fields. Special teachers are provided in such areas as music, art, physical education, foreign language, and sometimes science. Even when such help is available, the regular classroom teacher works closely with special teachers to help with the instruction in such subjects. Clearly, the elementary teacher needs a broad background that includes all skills and subject fields common to the grade level taught.

Breadth of background is usually easier for the elementary teacher to achieve than is depth of understanding of the many subjects taught. The commonplace practice of permitting students to major in elementary education frequently results in the prospective teacher's failing to achieve depth in any subject-matter area. In fact, in many preservice programs future elementary teachers do not pursue course work in any of the subject fields beyond the sophomore level. In such instances, the student takes two or three courses in each of several fields.

The elementary teacher needs the broad-field type of specialization because of the demands of teaching at this level. In addition, the confidence and intellectual satisfaction that can be derived only from the development of scholarly knowledge in an academic field is essential to complete professional maturity; an understanding of methods of investigation and skills needed for research, for example, may be acquired only through specialization in subject fields. As a practical matter, if elementary teachers have achieved depth in a particular field, they can assist each other with teaching problems. This kind of cooperation is especially useful in the newer types of instructional teams that are being used experimentally in some school systems. The team approach, in fact, forecasts a demand for teachers who are specialists in particular subject fields as well as in the basic skills taught in elementary schools.

Assuming that the teacher has a good liberal education and adequate knowledge of his teaching field, is he prepared to teach? No, he still must know *how* to teach. The study of educational processes and the development of skill in teaching are the concern of professional education.

WHAT IS PROFESSIONAL EDUCATION?

Study of "the art and science of teaching" is commonly referred to today as "professional education," but such terms lack exactness in meaning. The term "professional education," for example, has an inaccurate connotation. Its implication is that only professors of education can prepare the student to teach. Liberal arts professors and various specialists in subject fields also play important roles as teacher-educators. Their work, as indicated throughout this chapter, contributes to the professional preparation of teachers. From them, teachers receive their subject-matter courses and their preparation in general education. Furthermore, liberal arts professors, by example, teach students their concepts of teaching.

"Professional education" is used to refer to that part of the college curriculum that is designed specifically for those who share the occupational goal of teaching in elementary and secondary schools. More specifically it refers to the courses labeled "education" in most institutions, whose objective is to provide the student professional orientation and training. The distinction between professional education, as used here, and liberal studies and specialized subjects should be clear. Typical liberal arts courses will enroll students with varied and diverse occupational goals. For example, a physics class may include future research physicists, college teachers, high school and elementary teachers, physicians, housewives, and chemists. Likewise, those who are majoring in a given field will differ considerably in occupational aspirations. English majors, for example, may include those who aspire to be college teachers, high school and elementary teachers, novelists, newspaper reporters, editors, playwrights, housewives, physicians, and lawyers. In professional education courses, on the other hand, one may expect to find only those who share the occupational goal of a career in education.

The course in professional education attempts to provide knowledge of education as a process, and skill in the art of teaching. Obtaining knowledge of education as a process requires study of such areas as history of education, philosophy of education, learning, human development, the organization and function of the school system, and the roles as well as responsibilities of teachers as members of a profession.

Skill in the art of teaching requires knowledge of the methods and materials necessary to teach a given grade level or subject, as well as ability to instruct. Frequently prospective teachers are provided laboratory experiences, prior to student teaching, which permit them to observe and analyze the work of schools and the learning of boys and girls, and perhaps to serve as assistant teachers. These may be related to, or required in, other education courses; or they may be organized separately or required as independent participation by students. Student teaching, the formal course in which supervised practice is provided, is usually scheduled in the senior year. This latter course is persistently rated by experienced teachers as the most valuable preparation for teaching of all college courses.

DO FUTURE TEACHERS NEED TO STUDY PROFESSIONAL EDUCATION?

Over the years empirical evidence and research findings in the field of education have accumulated. Significant research has been carried out in such areas as the learning process, individual differences, child development, instruction, audiovisual aids, evaluation of pupil progress, curriculum, and the objectives of various school subjects. Consequently, today a substantial body of specialized knowledge, skills, and techniques is available to reinforce the professional strength of the teacher.

Could not the specialized knowledge and skills needed by the teacher be learned best on the job? One might as well ask, could not the specialized knowledge and skill of the physician be learned best on the job? The answer to both questions is no, obviously. Such learning is too expensive and time-consuming, and represents too great a danger to clients. Children suffer at the hands of the unprepared teacher who is "learning on the job" just as patients would under trial-and-error learning by the physician. For both the teacher and the physician, the slow, unguided accumulation of experience on the job is an unreliable and unsatisfactory means of professional preparation when needed knowledge and skill can be acquired in a disciplined way through specialized formal education.

No less an authority than Alfred North Whitehead, a trained mathematician who became a professor of philosophy of education, attests to the need for formal study of professional education. He notes that: "We are only just realizing that the art and science of education require a study and genius of their own; and that this genius and this science are more than a bare knowledge of some branch of science of literature." [7]

Rigorous and disciplined study of professional education is essential for the prospective teacher. The trilogy of liberal education, specialized subject matter, and professional education has endured because it is a sound approach to the preparation of teachers.

CRITICISMS
OF PROFESSIONAL EDUCATION

Two major criticisms are often made of courses in professional education: first, that they deal with untested and contradictory

[7] Alfred North Whitehead, *The Aims of Education* (New York: Mentor Books, 1949), p. 16.

theories, and second, that they are not discretely organized, showing too much overlapping and duplication of material. Sometimes the teaching is also criticized as poor, uninspiring, superficial, and dogmatic.

Another type of criticism of professional education courses is sometimes heard. Some students complain that too much work is required, standards of the course are too high, too much reading is required, they are expected to do too much thinking and too much independent work. Chances are, however, that the courses that draw such criticisms are providing serious and able students with outstanding learning experiences.

Some of the negative criticism of courses in professional education is justified in certain situations. Proliferation of courses is a serious problem—in all fields of higher education. Some classes are monotonous and uninspiring. Meaningless verbalizations do characterize some and are an ever present danger in all courses because students have had so little experience with the ideas and concepts dealt with in professional education. Students have too little opportunity to gain firsthand professionally-oriented experience with children and youth; they therefore have little opportunity to test and apply theory in practical situations.

From the point of view of the conscientious student who does not expect to be spoon-fed, no course will be a waste of time. He will see to it that it isn't. He will bring a positive attitude to class and will recognize that he will receive from any course no more than he contributes. Furthermore, the thinking student will not stereotype any field. He knows there are good and poor courses, good and poor teaching in all fields. The real student takes a responsibility, along with the instructor, for making any course a success.

CERTIFICATION OF TEACHERS

In order to practice, teachers like lawyers, physicians, and other professionals, must hold valid certificates or licenses issued by legal bodies. The regulations governing types of certificates issued to teachers and the qualification needed for each type—as well as the procedures for renewal or revocation of teaching certificates —are controlled by statutory law or state educational authority in every state.

Teacher-certification regulations and practices are important for several reasons. Minimum qualifications for teachers prescribed in certification regulations, in effect, establish professional standards. Renewal provisions can encourage the professional growth and development of teachers in service. Revocation provisions can contribute to the adoption and enforcement of professional ethics.

Certification regulations and practices vary from state to state. Considerable differences exist in certification requirements for course work in general education, subject specialization, and professional education. In view of such considerations, the prospective teacher should study the requirements for certification, particularly in states in which practice may be anticipated. While space does not permit more detailed descriptions of certification requirements, Table 20 contains a summary of minimum requirements for regular elementary and secondary teaching certificates as of 1970. Certification data are published periodically and in some detail under the title *A Manual on Certification Requirements for School Personnel in the United States* by the National Commission on Teacher Education and Professional Standards of the National Education Association.

Many states maintain detailed requirements for a certificate in addition to those summarized here. The number of semester hours needed to teach an academic subject varies with the fields as well as the state. Some states require a specific pattern of professional education and/or general education courses.

Nationwide efforts are under way to improve teacher education. They aim essentially toward making certification regulations and practices more useful aids to school systems in their efforts to achieve the highest possible level of personal and professional competency and service from each teacher.

Many important reforms are also taking place in the certification process. Only a few states today, for example, still require special courses such as state history, which discriminate against teachers prepared in other states. In the past ten years over thirty states have issued initial teaching certificates on an almost automatic basis to out-of-state applicants if they are graduates of college programs accredited by the National Council for Accreditation of Teacher Education (NCATE). A few states have modified their requirements in an imaginative manner to meet special situations—making provisions, for example, for returning Peace Corps volunteers who wish to teach. In general, the certification procedures have been simplified today to facilitate the entry of qualified teachers into the nation's classrooms.[8]

SUMMARY

Preparation for teaching is actually begun when a person decides to be a teacher. From the time such a decision is reached, a person relates courses and educational experiences to his occupational aspirations.

The preservice preparation of teachers rests upon the trilogy of liberal education, specialized subject matter, and professional education. These areas are interdependent. Each is necessary for proper education of the teacher.

Educators do not always agree upon the amount of time to be devoted by prospective teachers to each area of the trilogy. As a consequence, the liberal arts-education controversy has developed. The schism, real or imagined, between faculties of liberal arts and professional education, with its genesis in the general rejection of all professional work by liberal arts colleges, developed many years ago. In recent years, however, progress has been made toward the development of cooperative working relationships between all who are responsible for the education of teachers.

The differentiation of teacher education into liberal arts, subject-matter specialization, and professional education is artificial and fraught with some undesirable consequences. Liberal studies, the central core of the program, are what is normally thought of as offerings of the college of arts and sciences. The aim of liberal education is to produce men and women of integrity with disciplined intelligence, who possess knowledge of self and culture and have a system of values worthy of citizens in a free society.

[8] Don Davies, "Comments on Teacher Certification," *NEA Journal,* LV, No. 6 (September 1966), pp. 18–19.

TABLE 20. MINIMUM REQUIREMENTS FOR LOWEST REGULAR TEACHING CERTIFICATES *

	Elementary School			Secondary School		
State	Degree or Number of Semester Hours Required	Professional Education Required, Semester Hours (Total)	Directed Teaching Required, Semester Hours (Included in Column 3)	Degree or Number of Semester Hours Required	Professional Education Required, Semester Hours (Total)	Directed Teaching Required, Semester Hours (Included in Column 6)
1	2	3	4	5	6	7
Alabama	B	27	6	B	21	6
Alaska	B	24	C	B	18	C
Arizona	5 [a]	24	6	5 [a]	22	6
Arkansas	B	18	6	B	18	6
California	B [b]	AC [b]	AC [b]	B [b]	AC [b]	AC [b]
Colorado	B	AC	AC	B	AC	AC
Connecticut	B	30	6	B	18	6
Delaware	B	30	6	B	18	6
District of Col.	B [e]	15	C	5 [e]	15	C
Florida	B	20	6	B	20	6
Georgia	B	18	6	B	18	6
Hawaii	B	18	AC [d]	B	18	AC [d]
Idaho	B	24	6	B	20	6
Illinois	B	16	5	B	16	5
Indiana	B	27	8	B	18	6
Iowa	B	20	5	B	20	5
Kansas	B	24	5	B	20	5
Kentucky	B	24	8 [e]	B	17	8 [e]
Louisiana	B	24	4	B	18	4
Maine	B	30	6	B	18	6
Maryland	B	26	8	B	18	6
Massachusetts	B [f]	18	2	B [f]	12	2
Michigan	B	20	5 [g]	B	20	5 [g]
Minnesota	B	30	6	B	18	4

Mississippi	B	30	6	B	18	6
Missouri	B	18	6	B	18	5
Montana	B	AC	5	B	16	AC
Nebraska	60h	8	AC	AC	AC	AC
Nevada	B1	18j	3	B	20	6
New Hampshire	B	30	6	B	18	6
New Jersey	B	30	6	B	21	6k
New Mexico	B	24	6k	B	18	6
New York	B	24	6	B	12	C1
North Carolina	B	24	C1	B	18	6
North Dakota	B	16	6	B	16	3
Ohio	B	28	3	B	17	6
Oklahoma	B	21m	6	B	21m	6
Oregon	B	20	—n	Bo	14	—n
Pennsylvania	B	AC	6–12p	B	AC	6–12p
Puerto Rico	68q	53q	6q	Bq	29q	5q
Rhode Island	B	30	6	B	18	6
South Carolina	B	21	6	B	18	6
South Dakota	60r	15	3	B	20	6
Tennessee	B	24	4	B	24	4
Texas	B	18	6	B	18	6
Utah	B	26	8	B	21	8
Vermont	90	18	6	B	18	6
Virginia	B	18	6	B	15	6
Washington	Bs	AC	AC	Bs	AC	AC
West Virginia	B	20	6	B	20	6
Wisconsin	64t	26	5	B	18	5
Wyoming	B	23	C	B	20	C

LEGEND: —means not reported. AC means approved curriculum; B means a bachelor's degree of specified preparation; 5 means a bachelor's degree plus a fifth year of appropriate preparation, not necessarily completion of the master's degree; C means a course.

* Professional requirements listed are the basic requirements for degree or lowest regular certificates. Some variations from the professional requirements as stated in this table may be found in the requirements for specific certificates listed for the respective states in Chapter III [of volume cited].

a Standard certificates: master's degree or 30 s.h. of graduate credit. Temporary certificates: bachelor's degree and completion of an approved program; valid for five years only.

b Under the approved-program approach for elementary and secondary teacher certification. California will accept the number of semester hours for the major, minor, professional education, directed teaching, and general education as required by the preparing institution for the completion of its approved teacher education curriculum. However, professional education is not acceptable for a credential major or minor. Four years of preparation (bachelor's degree) is the minimum requirement for initial elementary or secondary certification; a fifth year is required for the permanent certificate.

c Bachelor's degree for elementary and junior high school; master's degree for senior and vocational high.

d Not included in Columns 3 and 6.

e A teacher who has taught successfully for four or more years is required to take only 4 s.h. of practice teaching or a seminar of 4. A teacher who has had two years of successful experience may take a seminar dealing with professional problems instead of the 8 s.h. in practice teaching.

f Completion of the bachelor's degree or graduation from an approved four-year normal school.

g Total of 8 s.h. of laboratory experiences, 5 of which must be student teaching.

h Provisional teaching certificates are issued for specifically endorsed grades, subjects, fields, and areas in designated classes of school districts upon evidence of partial completion of an approved teacher education program, generally at least 60 s.h., including specified amounts of general and professional education. Effective September 1, 1972, elementary teachers in accredited schools must hold a certificate based on degree preparation.

i A temporary certificate will be issued on completion of 96 hours in a program leading to the bachelor's degree.

j For a five-year nonrenewable certificate. The holder must establish eligibility for a regular five-year certificate, the requirement for which is 30.

k The practice-teaching requirement is 150 clock hours, 90 of which must be in actual classroom teaching.

l One year of paid full-time satisfactory teaching experience on the level for which certification is sought may be accepted in lieu of college supervised student teaching but only when such experience carries recommendation of the employing school district administrator.

m For the standard certificate; for the temporary certificate, the requirement is 12.

n Required, but there is no specific hours requirement.

o Provisional certificate only; for standard certification, a fifth year must be completed within five years after provisional certification.

p Minimum 6, maximum 12.

q Puerto Rico did not report for 1970. Requirements shown are carried over from the 1967 Edition.

r All teachers in independent school districts must have a certificate based on a bachelor's degree. The 60-hour certificate has very limited validity. It will seldom be used after July 1, 1970; none will be issued after July 1, 1972.

s Provisional certificate only; for standard certification, a fifth year must be completed within six years after provisional certification.

t Bachelor's degree must be completed within seven years. Such certificates apparently are issued only to graduates of two- or three-year programs in state or county colleges and will not be issued after 1971–72. Effective with the 1972–73 school year, the bachelor's degree will be the minimum requirement for initial certification.

Stinnett, T. M. *A Manual on Certification Requirements for School Personnel in the United States,* 1970 Edition (Washington, D.C.: National Commission on Teacher Education and Professional Standards, National Education Association, 1970), pp. 48–49.

The successful teacher must have reserves of learning far in excess of any demands placed upon him in regular classroom teaching. Such reserves of learning are built up by specializing in the subject to be taught. The need for specialization in subject matter applies to both high school and elementary school teachers. The real objective of specialization is depth of understanding and insight in the subjects taught, insight which will complement and supplement the broad liberal education of the teacher.

Professional education or "the art and science of teaching" completes the trilogy in teacher education. Professional education means the part of the curriculum which is so specialized that only those who are preparing for a career in education will ordinarily be enrolled.

Certification regulations, based upon preservice programs for teachers, specify minimum requirements for entry into the profession. Requirements for teaching certificates are determined by each state legislature. Consequently, requirements vary considerably from state to state. Prospective teachers should study the certification requirements in the various states to get some indication of the educational goals and the quality of education in each state.

Teacher certification needs to be improved by including qualitative controls in requirements. Certificates are issued now on the basis of semester hours of credit in specific, discrete courses. Those responsible for the education of teachers should work together to devise more adequate certification regulations.

SUGGESTED READINGS

Allen, Dwight W. and Peter Wagschal, "A New Look in Credentialing," *The Clearing House,* November 1969, pp. 137–40.

American Association of Colleges for Teacher Education, *Reality and Relevance: Today's Agenda for Teacher Education.* Washington, D.C.: Yearbook, 1969.

Giammatteo, Michael, "Systems Concepts Related to Teacher Training," *The Journal of Teacher Education,* Fall 1969, pp. 295–98.

Hazard, William R., ed., *The Clinical Professorship in Teacher Education.* Evanston, Ill.: Northwestern University Press, 1967.

King, Edgar A., "Can Professional Education Survive in the Traditional Liberal Arts College?", *The Journal of Teacher Education,* Spring 1969, pp. 15–16.

Pearl, Arthur, ed., "Teacher Education: White Racism and Inner City Schools," *The Journal of Teacher Education,* Winter 1969, pp. 405–34.

Richey, Robert W., *Planning for Teaching.* New York: McGraw-Hill Book Co., 1968, Chap. 2.

Robbins, Glaydon D., "The Impact of Current Educational Change Upon Teacher Education," *The Journal of Teacher Education,* Summer 1969, pp. 182–87.

Stinnett, T. M., *Professional Problems of Teachers.* New York: The Macmillan Co., 1968.

Tanruther, Edgar M., *Clinical Experiences in Teaching for the Student Teacher or Intern.* New York: Dodd, Mead & Company, 1968.

Verdun, John R., ed., *Conceptual Models in Teacher Education.* Washington, D.C.: The American Association of Colleges for Teacher Education, 1967.

THE WORK OF
THE TEACHER

THE well-known expression "A school is as good as its teachers" in no way exaggerates the importance of the work of those who teach. What do teachers actually do? If one chooses to teach, how varied and interesting will his professional responsibilities be? Why is it claimed that the work of the teacher is becoming increasingly complex? These and other questions deserve honest answers if one's commitment to preparation for teaching is to be sincere and dependable.

Essentially, the work of the teacher is of three types: (1) teaching, (2) professional study, and (3) supervision of activities related to the general work of the school.

TEACHING

To the uninitiated, teaching may seem to be only presiding over the work of pupils while they are in class; actually much behind-the-scenes effort is required for each class period taught. The teaching aspect of what goes on in a classroom is comparable to what happens on the stage of a theatrical production. What the pupils experience is the culmination of hours of intensive study, planning, organizing of materials, selection of particular procedures, and charting the direction and pace of the class learning activities. Specific aspects of the total process of teaching include selection and development of instructional units, planning individual lessons, organizing materials for instruction, designing the method to be used, classroom management, evaluation of pupil achievement, and reporting of pupil progress.

SELECTION AND DEVELOPMENT OF INSTRUCTIONAL UNITS. Even though the curriculum of the school is firmly established, as it usually is for all first-year teachers, numerous decisions have to be made relative to the particular units to be taught and their order and organization. In the past twenty years the unit approach to teaching has become widespread in both elementary and secondary divisions. Thus, in spite of the fact that textbooks may already have been chosen, the teacher has the responsibility of designing from the text, resource books, and other materials the manner in which the unit will be presented. In some situations, provisions for optional units necessitate choices which often are influenced by the characteristics of particular groups of children to be taught.

The development of an instructional unit requires such steps as definition of objectives, outlining of topics, choice of materials; ordering of supplies; identification of resources—human and material, verbal and pictorial, in school and out—that may be useful; visualizing possible learning activities; selection and development of evaluation procedures and instruments; and the assembling of plans into a syllabus which in pedagogical terms is called a "resource unit." All this work must take place prior to classroom teaching. The burden on the first-year teacher is obvious since he will have no carry-over units for use. The experienced teacher will typically reorganize units each year or develop new ones to take the place of those that do not fit a new class group.

PLANNING INDIVIDUAL LESSONS. From the resource unit, individual lessons must be planned. Usually these may cover one or more days of class work. This phase of teaching requires close attention to the characteristics of individual pupils as well as to the background of the entire class. The resource unit must be designed to capture and hold attention and to help each child make maximum use of class and study time.

A common pattern for lesson plans provides for a formal presentation by the teacher to introduce the material or learning activity, followed by a period of pupil study. The third stage involves some form of group treatment of the subject matter by pupils and the teacher, such as recitation, group discussion, blackboard work, reports by members of the class, or interviews with committees or resource persons. The final aspects of the lesson involves the appraisal of progress or achievement and remedial work to eliminate learning inadequacies.

ORGANIZING MATERIALS FOR INSTRUCTION. In good schools, the classroom has been converted into a learning laboratory with an abundance of visual, auditory, and electronic resources as well as various types of printed material to facilitate study and teaching. Pictures, maps, charts, graphs, films, mock-ups, records, tape recording equipment, teaching machines, laboratory materials, newspaper and magazine stories, references—all must be assembled to make possible maximum learning.

Teachers' summer months often are devoted to finding and organizing materials needed for teaching. During the school year, the provision of particular resources for given phases of instruction is a continuing task. With the increase in audiovisual materials made available to teachers, including radio and television presentations to supplement the classroom work and teaching machines which permit individual self-instruction, teachers will expect to devote even greater attention to this aspect of their professional assignments.

DESIGNING THE METHOD TO BE USED. A book by V. T. Thayer entitled *The Passing of the Recitation* (1929) forecast the end of centuries of complete dependence on teacher-directed recitations as the single or major method of instruction in elementary and secondary schools. For the process of instruction, itself, the well-prepared teacher today can select from a variety of methods including laboratory procedures, group discussion, simulations, independent and team study, teacher-student planning, and film presentations. Less emphasis is placed in democratic schools on methods of teaching that place the teacher in the center of the stage; instead, pupil-centered or cooperative group procedures are used to involve students more in their own learning and to encourage initiative, self-direction, and teamwork as well as self-evaluation.

Yet, with all the variety of instructional procedures that have been tested and made available, the good teacher rarely depends exclusively upon any one of them. Quality instruction requires the selection and adaptation of methods to fit particular goals in teaching and the uniqueness of a given group of pupils. More often than not, the teacher designs his own method; for teaching is an art, as well as a science, that calls for maximum use of imagination, creativity, and professional skill. For this reason, the teacher is ever involved in developing methods to fit his instructional plans and appraising the effectiveness of his creations. To aid in this endeavor, he will, of course, attempt to keep well informed about progress and research in the field of methods.

CLASSROOM MANAGEMENT. This is the phase of teaching the college student will most likely visualize when he thinks of becoming a teacher. It is the entire instructional process seen as a stage presentation. In it the teacher plays a leading role and manages the production at the same time. Action, drama, intellectual stimulation, tensions, and emotional responses may characterize its daily enactment. It is in this aspect of teaching that the professional person may achieve the heights of excitement and satisfaction as he experiences communicating a complex idea to an eager mind or observes a child win a battle with his emotions or conquer a deficiency in skill or knowledge. On the other hand, discouragement and disappointment may be daily companions as the teacher engages in classroom management.

The untrained observer will miss many of the supporting roles and less obvious processes that take place while a good teacher is in charge of the class. Discipline, for example, the Achilles heel of many beginning teachers, may be handled so subtly by an experienced teacher that no apparent problems ever develop. In truth, such a teacher has learned to create a climate of interest and activity that deters pupil maladjustment; he also has become an expert at sensing a trend in pupil response before it happens so that positive counteractive steps can be taken before negative, punitive action is necessary. Classroom routines such as checking attendance, making assignments, passing out materials, collecting papers, and arranging for group work are all easily recognized. Less obvious, however, will be steps taken by the teacher to develop and maintain high-quality group rapport, to help individual pupils find release from tensions that inhibit learning, and to guide the intellectual applications of boys and girls to bench marks never before attained.

EVALUATION OF PUPIL ACHIEVEMENT AND REPORTING PUPIL PROGRESS. The dual goals of evaluation include the ascertaining of the degree to which overall educational objectives are achieved and the analysis of strengths and weaknesses for the purpose of enhancing achievement by each student. The former goal is a teacher purpose, while the latter is a learning experience for the student. It follows that in most instances effective evaluation procedures involve both teacher and pupil.

Reporting of progress may be an administrative device to record and communicate pupil attainment. Essentially, the quality of reporting depends upon the professional competence of the teacher to measure accurately as well as to appraise precisely and objectively the growth in skills, knowledges, understandings, attitudes, and behavior of individual pupils. Evaluation and reporting of pupil progress makes rigorous demands upon the teacher for professional knowledge of measurement theory and practice, understanding of individual pupils, insight into the goals of education, and the objectives of the work taught.

PROFESSIONAL STUDY

Finalities in education are but illusions, dangerous mirages, that destroy creativeness and weaken intellectual activities while encouraging the acceptance of folklore and dogma as rationalizations for complacency. This is true whether the absolutes relate to aims of education, subject matter of the curriculum, methods of teaching, or preparation of teachers themselves. As long as knowledge expands, change is inevitable. Education is, itself, in a continual state of transition. The principle of parity, for example, which was taught in physics classes, is no longer accepted as true. Since the development of the Salk vaccine, students in health classes are no longer taught that man has no defense against polio. "Poor little Rhode Island, the smallest of the forty-eight," a refrain in a popular song, along with many statements in history and political science books, is now out of date. Einstein's theory of relativity is creeping into mathematics books, even those used in upper elementary school grades. Each year scholars uncover new facts and reorganize old ones that change the subject matter in all fields.

The teacher, because he is a professional person, is obligated to keep abreast of and contribute to developments in his field. This responsibility involves independent scholarship and participation in group study projects in one's subject field, as well as in study of the processes of education. It means the continuous investigation of unsolved problems to help extend the quality of professional practice of self and others. The oldest and perhaps most basic means of keeping informed is independent study. The teacher who is dedicated to scholarship must rely upon self-direction and individual initiative to stay informed about important findings in today's information explosion.

The most exciting recent development to assist teachers in keeping up with current scholarship in their fields of interest has been the NDEA summer institutes held at universities and colleges throughout the country. Supported by federal funds, the aim of the program is to bring experienced teachers back to the campus for a stimulating summer of "refresher" reading and course work. Free tuition, fellowships, and a dependency allowance are provided to encourage teachers who might otherwise have to seek summer employment outside education for financial reasons. Several hundred institutes operate each year, with over eighty in the field of history alone in the summer of 1967. Some universities, like Stanford and the State University of New York at Stony Brook, have sponsored summer institutes similar in purpose to the NDEA project. In addition to summer study, the federal government has established a full-year Experienced Teacher Fellowship program to encourage more extensive enrichment in university study.

RELATED RESPONSIBILITIES

Some of the other responsibilities teachers assume in the general work of the school are counseling, direction of extracurricular activities, and supervision of pupils in nonclass situations.

COUNSELING OF PUPILS. Although all but the smallest schools

are coming to employ specialists to counsel pupils, classroom teachers are still considered the primary agents for guidance services because of their close acquaintance and daily contact with boys and girls. Often the rapport between a pupil and teacher is such that guidance is a natural aspect of the teaching process itself. In other situations, special administrative arrangements are made to utilize the counseling resources of teachers either with groups or individuals.

The homeroom is the device most frequently used to provide guidance services to pupils in groups, with some teachers called upon to serve as homeroom sponsors. In this capacity they provide information, administer inventories and tests, interpret vocational opportunities and requirements, assist with the planning of high school and college programs, and generally help with the choices that students must make. In some junior and senior high schools, homeroom sponsors continue with the same group of pupils throughout their school membership. Such continuity provides for close acquaintance, a variety of associations, and often promotes warm relationships between pupils and teachers that even surpass those possible in instructional groups.

Teachers typically engage in individual counseling in relation to their fields of specialization, providing occupational information to interested students and helping to plan suitable educational programs leading to career objectives. As is true with respect to homeroom sponsorship, responsibilities for individual counseling usually follow competence. In a real sense, teacher-counselors are selected by students. Because of this fact, the teacher to whom students turn naturally, and willingly, for help may find it difficult to control the amount of time devoted to this service.

DIRECTION OF EXTRACURRICULAR ACTIVITIES. Opportunities to direct student extracurricular activities are usually open to teachers who have special interest and talents, particularly in smaller schools. Such projects may be closely related to the teachers' subject specialization—for example, science club, speech, music, or dramatic activities—or it may be of a recreational or avocational nature—in sports, hobby, or social areas. High school teachers typically have more opportunities to direct extracurricular projects than do those in elementary schools because of the characteristics of the age groups involved. The latter, however, find numerous chances to guide children in musical, dramatic, artistic, and hobby activities, either as a related phase of schoolwork or in connection with the presentation of programs to student and parent groups.

Direction of extracurricular activities may provide opportunities for highly effective teaching. Often student motivation and self-discipline are at their highest in these projects. Tensions and anxieties that sometimes develop in class work usually are at a minimum. Cooperative teacher-student sharing of responsibility can be high. Through this type of leadership teachers find rich and rewarding associations with children and young people. It affords some of the best opportunities to observe the development and adjustment of boys and girls in informal situations when their true characteristics are most likely to be apparent.

SUPERVISING NONCLASS SITUATIONS. Teachers may be called upon to supervise certain nonclass situations such as study halls, lunchrooms, halls and playgrounds, or social events. Some of these routine duties are assigned by rotation, with a teacher having responsibility for monitoring the lunchroom one noon a week, for example. Others, such as an assigned study hall, may involve daily attention. In elementary schools, the teacher typically has full and continuing responsibility for a group of pupils throughout the school day. This often means being with them on the playground and in lunchrooms daily.

One of the reasons why some school systems are currently experimenting with the use of instructional teams is to free classroom teachers from the routine duties involved in supervision of nonclass situations. A capable instructional aide, who may be a young high school graduate or a more mature parent, can relieve the teacher of such time-consuming operations in order to permit the devotion of his full attention to the important processes involved in teaching.

LEARNERS AND LEARNING

The focus of the schools is on the learner as well as on the organization of knowledge and the processes by which learning is facilitated. Teachers must be thoroughly familiar with these three components of education—learners, curriculum, and instruction. Understanding learners—how they respond as individuals and in groups—and insight into how learning takes place are paramount to successful teaching.

CHARACTERISTICS OF LEARNERS: ESSENTIAL PROFESSIONAL KNOWLEDGE OF TEACHERS

Without knowledge of learners, their differences, similarities, stages of growth, needs, interests, and values, teaching is substantially a trial-and-error process. For this reason, the professional preparation for teaching emphasizes the study of human development and the techniques by which teachers may observe, measure, analyze, and appraise the characteristics of both individual children and groups.

Throughout the program of professional preparation, the teacher's study of individual pupils centers first upon general features of development that characterize the various growth stages through which children pass, and, second, on the individual deviations or differences that are found to exist. Because of the complexity of individuality and the uniqueness of human personality, the impossibility of providing absolute guides and descriptions that may be applied to all boys and girls can readily be understood. This situation, however, is often frustrating to the beginner, who, quite understandably, is eager to discover definite, dependable knowledge that will be certain to fit the children he expects to teach. It is a fundamental task of the professional education of the teacher to help him to realize that each pupil, although like his classmates in many respects, actually is unique and requires individual study, diagnosis, and treatment.

Although the existence of individual differences has long been known, only in recent years have they been recognized as vital factors in the process of education. Formerly, schools were organized, and instruction was provided, as though all students of a given age were more or less identical in maturity, ability, interests, responsiveness, and motivation. Every prospective teacher will no doubt have had some acquaintance with instruction of this type.

Fuzzy thinking has led some teachers to contend that equality of opportunity and individual differences make competing and mutually exclusive demands upon the schools. Such a claim is indefensible because both require of each individual his best. This point was made in a lucid fashion by John W. Gardner: [1]

> In education, for example, if we ignore individual differences we end up treating everyone alike—and one result is that we do not demand enough of our ablest youngsters. That is precisely the error we have made in recent decades. But if we toughen up the program and still ignore individual differences we only do an injustice to the average youngster, who will have to drop by the wayside. The only solution is to admit that individuals differ and provide different treatment for different levels of ability. And never forget that we must do a good job at every level of ability. Our kind of society calls for the maximum development of individual potentialities at all levels.

NEEDS AND INTERESTS OF CHILDREN AND YOUTH. While young people differ with respect to various traits, patterns of development, and capacities, they possess many common characteristics. Were it not for this fact, group instruction in school would be difficult if not impossible.

Children and youth have common requirements, which sociologists and educators call "needs," and similar interests that are dictated both by their environment and their natural inclinations. Needs have been classified as physical, mental, social, and emotional. All pupils, for example, have the physical need for food, clothing, shelter, and good health; intellectually, they must learn to use a language, read and write, gather and interpret information, solve problems, and use the accumulated wisdom of their culture. Social requirements of pupils include the necessity of living in a society, self-discipline, and cooperation. Common emotional needs are thought to be affection, recognition, a sense of security, and reasonable self-assurance.

VALUES OF PUPILS. Each learner has a system of values. He first enters school with the value patterns that have been taught him by

[1] John W. Gardner, "Excellence and Equality," in Eli Ginzberg, ed., *The Nation's Children* (New York: Columbia University Press, 1960), II, 230.

his parents, church, and neighborhood. In school, the values and cultural standards of fellow students, and of the teacher, become important. Conflicts sometimes develop between the two influences on pupils, those in and out of school. Also, as a child matures, he may find his natural desire to develop his own value system thwarted by parental or other adult reluctance for their imposed standards to be modified.

The teacher has an opportunity to help children and young people to clarify their values and to resolve conflicts they experience. Such a responsibility requires a thorough understanding of the nature of values, their characteristics at various levels of pupil maturity, and their impact on learning.

GROUP FACTORS. Not only must the teacher know the general characteristics of maturity levels, longitudinal patterns of development, and individual differences, he must also recognize and understand the impact of the group in which learning takes place. Pupils in school are influenced by such group factors as the morale that prevails, the goals that are endorsed, and the behavior that is applauded, as well as by the crosscurrents of acceptance and rejection by and of individual members. To attempt to understand a child without insights into the group forces that impinge upon his adjustment and behavior, as well as his learning, is an invitation to error. In school, as out, the individual maintains relationships to his peers that must be taken into account when learning is under way.

Recent developments in pedagogy have emphasized the role of the group in shaping characteristics of individual learners. Techniques for studying group composition, internal patterns of association, and leadership are being refined. The field of sociology has contributed various sociometric devices that are useful in discovering the composite personality of given groups. By use of the sociogram, for instance, a teacher may discover how a pupil feels toward his associates and their attitudes toward him. Leaders, recognized by students, can be identified. Pressures may be uncovered. Such information is invaluable as an aid both to helping individuals and planning suitable learning experiences for the total class.

THE STUDY OF LEARNERS

Professional competence in identifying individual differences requires expertness by teachers in such procedures as observation of pupil behavior, measurement of traits, and analysis of information pertinent to stages of growth and individual adjustment. Such skills cannot be learned entirely from books; they require laboratory practice under expert supervision. For this reason, the preparation of teachers typically includes opportunities for the study of children and youth in both school and community situations. The object is to furnish firsthand examples for observation which illustrate the facts and principles to be learned. The trend in programs of teacher education is to increase the amount of laboratory work so that theory and results from research may be tested or observed in operation at each stage of the prospective teacher's professional orientation. Such study of learners is usually included as a part of the requirements of education courses which the student takes prior to student teaching. Some institutions now arrange for class situations or observations of individual pupils to be televised via closed circuit TV to large groups of prospective teachers, thus providing identical laboratory situations for exercises in analysis.

Like the study of medicine, preparation for teaching will provide few ironclad formulas for diagnosis and treatment of particular clients. Even when fairly specific knowledge of cause and effect is available, individuals differ so greatly that the practitioner must expertly ascertain the pertinent characteristics for a particular case. Only then will he be able to apply his total professional knowledge so as to insure accurate diagnosis from which treatment may be prescribed or administered. Such professional discipline requires sustained, objective study and practice. Essentially, it is the mark of the professional teacher.

THE LEARNING PROCESS

Basic to effective teaching is the application of sound principles of learning. With this premise, everyone agrees; but as yet there has been no general acceptance of a complete theory of learning. Nor do scholars concur on the relationships that should prevail between learning and teaching. It was George Bernard Shaw who observed, "If you teach a man anything, he will never learn." Implied in this observation is the basic premise that learning is something a person does for himself; it is not done for him. Yet the schools exist because of the belief that teachers promote learning by teaching.

Research on learning has been concerned with such problems as what learning is, what happens when learning takes place, what conditions motivate or inhibit learning, nature of transfer, values, and retention and differences in types of learning.

Definitions of learning range from the philosophical characterization by John Dewey that learning is the reconstruction of experience, to the belief that learning is a more prosaic act of acquiring habits and knowledge. In various ways learning has been conceived as both a process and an outcome, as growth itself, or as adjustment to environmental forces. Some simply say that learning is a change in behavior. Regardless of the definition favored, most authorities recognize that experience and behavior are involved and that learning itself is highly personalized.

Most scholars of human learning, in the absence of verified theory, take an eclectic position regarding process and aspects of learning. Perhaps failure to devise a universal theory of learning is due to the dearth of research in the specific field of human learning. Most of the experiments have been concerned with the learning of lower animals, of rats and apes, for example. The failure may be attributable, also, to the fact that research in the field of learning as a whole has been relatively limited as compared to some of the areas of medical science, for example.

Yet, despite lack of complete agreement about what learning is and how it takes place, the prospective teacher studying it will be introduced to exciting and highly useful hypotheses which offer operating principles with which the practice of teaching can go forward. He will find also a challenge to join the search for truth about learning and its relationship to the process of teaching. For the college student who is looking for absolutes, of course, the study of human learning will prove frustrating and theoretical. But here again, the function of professional education must be to inspire the prospective teacher to shun the ranks of the cynical critics who respect only established fields and to join the highly stimulating intellectual venture of helping to test theory by systematic practice. A person so positively motivated will find enjoyment, satisfaction, and worthwhile knowledge essential to his profession in the study of what is known and what is yet to be discovered about the mysteries of the human mind and how it works.

SUMMARY

Teaching and its related responsibilities involve a variety of tasks, such as the selection and development of instructional units, planning of lessons, organizing materials, and designing methods which take place behind the scenes of classroom management. The evaluation of pupil achievement requires the highest level of professional knowledge, wisdom, and maturity. Related assignments of teachers include counseling pupils, direction of extracurricular activities, the supervision of nonclass situations, and one self-imposed obligation—living the life of a professional person. Knowledge expands and changes; hence, to retain his status as an expert, the teacher must be a student. Continual study is required of the teacher if he is to keep abreast of developments. The promotion of learning is central to the work of the teacher. To accomplish this objective the characteristics of learners must be known. Knowledge of the general features of human development, and of variations in traits, needs, interests, and values of pupils, is essential for professional competence. In addition, the teacher must understand the impact of the group on individuals and the general facts as well as hypotheses about the process of learning itself.

SUGGESTED READINGS

Adams, Sam, and John L. Garrett, Jr., *To Be a Teacher: An Introduction to Education.* Englewood Cliffs, N.J.: Prentice-Hall, Inc., 1969.

Balaski, Sylvester J., *Focus on Teaching*. New York: The Odyssey Press, 1968.

Bhaerman, Robert, "Education's New Dualism," *Changing Education,* Fall 1969, pp. 3–7.

Dale, Edgar, "The Roles of the Teacher," *The Newsletter,* Ohio State University, December 1967.

Inlow, Gale, *Maturity in High School Teaching*. Englewood Cliffs, N.J.: Prentice-Hall, Inc., 1963.

Melby, Ernest O., *The Teacher and Learning*. Washington, D.C.: The Center for Applied Research in Education, Inc., 1963.

Pullias, Earl V., and James D. Young, *A Teacher Is Many Things*. Bloomington, Ind.: Indiana University Press, 1968.

Raths, James, John R. Pancella, and James S. Van Ness, eds., *Studying Teaching*. Englewood Cliffs, N.J.: Prentice-Hall, Inc., 1967.

Richey, Robert W., *Planning for Teaching*. New York: McGraw-Hill Book Co., 1968, Chaps. 5 and 6.

Smith, B. Othaniel, Saul B. Cohen, and Arthur Pearl, *Teachers for the Real World*. Washington, D.C.: The American Association of Colleges for Teacher Education, 1969.

Tompkins, Ellsworth, ed., *The Beginning Teacher*. Washington, D.C.: National Association of Secondary School Principals, Bulletin 330, October 1968.

11.

PROFESSIONAL OPPORTUNITIES IN TEACHING

FOR the intellectually able, the emotionally stable, and the socially sensitive and mature person, teaching literally is a wide-open field. Not only are good positions available in classroom teaching assignments in elementary and secondary schools, but also the experienced and successful teacher who prepares for leadership in education may advance rapidly to work in such specialities as guidance, supervision, administration, or teacher education. In addition, for the highly qualified and specialized, opportunities in research, preparation of instructional materials, remedial work, special education, or work as a school psychologist are numerous. Analyses of career patterns of those already in the profession will reveal that advancement in teaching is relatively rapid, variety of experience is easily obtainable, and security factors are maximum.

Although demand for teachers in certain subject areas has decreased since the critical days following World War II, there is still a shortage of qualified teachers in many areas of the United States. This deficit of competent personnel has several possible implications for the prospective teacher. In the first place, choice of locality and particular school system will probably remain open for especially qualified people in the decade of the 1970's. Secondly, advancement in the profession will be fairly rapid for the able, ambitious, and well-prepared teacher.

Teaching positions are of four major types: elementary, secondary, college, and business or other types of technical institutions. In addition, new experiments with instructional teams promise to differentiate teaching functions by type, level of competence, and, perhaps, in terms of remuneration.

TEACHING POSITIONS IN ELEMENTARY SCHOOLS

The number of elementary classroom teachers increased from 890,000 in 1957 to 1,193,000 in 1967. From 1968 to 1977 it is projected that 1.8 million new elementary teachers will be needed in the public schools.[1] The number of elementary school teachers being graduated each year may not prove adequate to meet national needs. One continuing problem of teacher preparation is the fact that a good percentage of those who complete teacher-education programs fail to enter the teaching field. The occupations entered by those who receive a bachelor's degree in elementary education in a typical year are estimated to be distributed as indicated in Figure 10.

FIGURE 10. ESTIMATED OCCUPATIONAL DISTRIBUTION OF B.A. DEGREE GRADUATES IN ELEMENTARY EDUCATION IN A TYPICAL YEAR

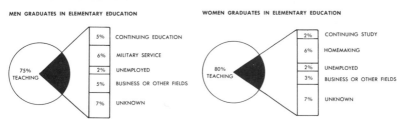

The dimensions of the shortage of elementary school teachers are further established by these facts: (1) The class size in many situations calls for additional teachers. It should be noted, however, that the Elementary and Secondary Education Act of 1965

[1] *Projections of Educational Statistics to 1977–78* (Washington, D.C.: U.S. Dept. of Health, Education, and Welfare, 1968), p. 41.

has helped to increase the number of elementary teachers by making federal funds available for reducing class size. (2) In many places, especially in large urban communities, temporary and provisional instructors who are now in service will eventually be replaced by adequately prepared and properly certified professionals. (3) More than 100,000 teachers leave teaching each year because of retirement, acceptance of jobs outside the profession, or to raise a family. As the nation moved into the 1970's, however, shortages in the elementary field became less pronounced.

Possibilities for employment in nursery schools and at the kindergarten level are extremely good for the years ahead. It is estimated that more than 1,000,000 children are now enrolled in public kindergartens alone, not counting those in private schools. Both kindergarten and nursery schools are likely to expand in the next decade or two, bringing about increased opportunities for teaching in these fields.

TEACHING POSITIONS IN SECONDARY SCHOOLS

Until recent years, the demand for high school teachers has remained fairly stable. Beginning about 1957–58 the post-World War II population increase began reaching secondary schools. The United States Department of Health, Education, and Welfare reports an increase in the number of secondary school teachers from 526,000 in 1957 to 902,000 in 1967. The projection is for 1,-096,000 by 1977. See Figure 11 for estimated occupational distribution of B.A. degree graduates in secondary education. The number of secondary school teachers seems to be increasing at a more rapid rate than those in elementary schools because of a larger enrollment rate increase and a lower pupil-teacher ratio in high schools. Also, many seventh and eighth graders are being moved from elementary to secondary schools.[2]

Prospective teachers should be aware that the distribution of those prepared for high school teaching does not match existing positions very well, with the number of positions available in

[2] *Ibid.,* pp. 41–42.

FIGURE 11. ESTIMATED OCCUPATIONAL DISTRIBUTION OF B.A. DEGREE
GRADUATES IN SECONDARY EDUCATION IN A TYPICAL YEAR

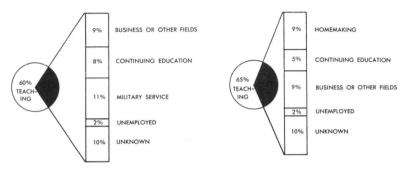

MEN GRADUATES IN SECONDARY EDUCATION

WOMEN GRADUATES IN SECONDARY EDUCATION

some fields greater than in others. Library science and general science teachers, for instance, have been in short supply for several years. Teachers for men's physical education, art, and speech are in greater supply than are teachers in other fields. While the data in Table 21 do not provide an infallible guide to the prospective high school teacher, they do serve as a reminder that one should study the relationship between supply and demand when he selects a teaching field in which to major. These indexes may not, of course, be applicable to a particular state or region; nor will they take into account the increasing demand for high school teachers to serve growing enrollments.

Additional insight into the relative opportunities open in high school teaching is provided by the information presented in Table 22 about the total number of students entering various fields.

The person preparing to teach in a secondary school should seek information about teacher supply-and-demand conditions in the locality where he would like to teach.[3] He should find out, in particular, which combinations of subjects are in greatest demand. For example, English and history, biology and physical education,

[3] No inference should be drawn that one should not prepare to teach in a field that is already adequately supplied. There is always room for outstanding teachers, whatever the field. The able and ambitious person can make a place for himself in any teaching field he chooses.

TABLE 21. SUMMARY OF ESTIMATED SUPPLY COMPARED WITH THE
ADJUSTED TREND CRITERION ESTIMATE OF DEMAND FOR BEGINNING
TEACHERS IN 1968, ELEMENTARY-SCHOOL AND SECONDARY-SCHOOL
SUBJECT AREAS, BY RANK

Assignment	Numerical difference in the estimated supply of beginning teachers and estimated demand based on		Percent of teacher education graduates entering the profession	Estimated additional supply if 70.0 percent of graduates entered	Additional demand if estimated re-entry rate is reduced by 10%	General condition
	Percent distribution in 1967	National estimate				
1	2	3	4	5	6	7
Mathematics	−2,977	−3,578	69.1%	93	−293	Critical shortage
Natural and physical sciences	−2,033	−2,367	63.1	780	−266	Critical shortage
Trade, industrial, vocational, technical	−1,489	−954	44.2	157	−51	Shortage
Special education						
Elementary	−743	+1,855	71.9	...	−161	Low supply
Secondary	−484	+734	71.9	...	−46	Low supply
Industrial arts	+789	+801	70.3	...	−65	Low supply
Elementary, regular instruction	+1,865	+4,438	78.1	...	−2,945	Low supply
English language arts	+35	−503	65.1	1,294	−498	Low supply
Distributive education	−174	...	51.6	87	−12	Low supply
Junior high-school subjects	−802	...	80.7	...	−41	Possible shortage [a]
Physical and health education						
Elementary	−1,258	−504	69.8	1	−72	Possible shortage [a]
Secondary (total)	+2,707	+5,033	67.6	349	−206	Adequate supply
Men	+2,329	...	63.5	583	−95	Adequate supply
Women	+378	...	74.2	...	−111	Low supply

198

Agriculture	+333	+459	57.2	262	−24	Near balance[a]
Home economics	+950	+1,491	63.4	447	−97	Near balance[a]
Art						
Elementary	−175	+469	67.5	21	−33	Near balance[a]
Secondary	+1,329	+2,017	66.2	220	−73	Near balance
Business education	+1,111	+1,592	63.5	585	−133	Near balance
Music						
Elementary	−1,042	−68	76.0	. . .	−72	Possible shortage[a]
Secondary	+1,129	+2,363	67.5	166	−97	Adequate supply
Foreign languages						
Elementary	+105	−2	75.6	. . .	−7	Near balance[a]
Secondary	+1,403	+1,907	64.7	478	−128	Adequate supply
Social studies	+4,995	+5,648	59.0	2,976	−317	Adequate supply

[a] Information is not sufficiently complete to allow an accurate estimate of the supply-demand condition.

From *Teacher Supply and Demand in Public Schools, 1968*, Report 1969–R4, Research Division (Washington, D.C., National Education Association), 48.

TABLE 22. PERCENTS OF TEACHER EDUCATION GRADUATES ENTERING CLASSROOMS IMMEDIATELY FOLLOWING GRADUATION, 1954–1967, BY SUBJECT AREAS

Subject or level	1954	1956	1958	1960	1962	1964	1966	1967
1	2	3	4	5	6	7	8	9
Elementary school, regular instruction	78.9%	80.8%	83.3%	82.2%	82.3%	81.2%	80.8%	78.1%
High-school subjects:								
Agriculture	41.0	50.6	47.3	47.5	56.2	52.7	45.5	57.2
Art [a]	62.6	66.5	70.5	70.5	70.1	66.8	67.2	66.4
Business education	58.1	56.2	59.8	60.7	63.3	62.7	65.4	63.5
English	67.9	68.4	73.1	73.5	74.7	70.9	71.8	66.3
Foreign languages [a]	56.0	62.1	68.9	69.6	72.4	70.0	69.4	64.9
Home economics	66.4	65.2	65.3	65.5	65.9	64.7	63.1	63.4
Industrial arts	57.1	61.5	68.9	68.6	72.2	73.9	72.8	70.3
Journalism	59.3	26.5	56.2	53.2	38.8	60.9	59.5	61.3
Library science	85.6	76.8	78.0	77.8	81.8	82.5	69.0	56.5
Mathematics	59.0	66.3	75.8	74.2	73.9	74.1	70.8	69.1
Music [a]	68.5	68.9	74.5	74.2	72.9	70.1	71.0	68.6
Physical education—Men [a]	47.1	60.2	66.1	64.3	69.1	65.7	65.4	63.8
Physical education—Women [a]	76.3	78.2	79.5	79.6	84.2	80.3	78.3	73.8
General science	52.0	64.2	73.5	71.0	73.5	67.4	69.9	65.0
Biology	45.4	58.5	65.0	66.2	68.3	66.7	67.6	64.3
Chemistry	36.1	54.3	65.3	64.4	65.0	61.8	60.5	60.6
Physics	51.5	47.3	69.6	62.1	66.7	60.1	61.4	58.8
Social studies	51.8	59.8	65.2	64.9	64.2	60.5	60.2	59.2
Speech	57.8	61.5	69.9	65.9	65.9	61.4	60.5	57.5
Total, high-school subjects [b]	55.7%	63.2%	67.8%	68.1%	69.2%	67.0%	66.7%	64.3%
Grand total [b]	65.8%	70.7%	73.7%	73.6%	74.4%	72.7%	72.2%	69.7%

[a] Includes persons prepared to teach the subject in elementary schools.
[b] Includes persons prepared for ungraded assignments such as special education, library science, and guidance counseling.
From *Teacher Supply and Demand in Public Schools, 1968*, Research Report 1969–R4, Research Division (Washington, National Education Association), p. 24.

and science and mathematics have been fairly popular combinations. The teacher-placement officer of the college or university and the faculty adviser are reliable sources of information about supply-and-demand conditions.

TEACHING POSITIONS IN COLLEGES OR UNIVERSITIES

The tidal wave of students that hit elementary schools about 1950, and high schools six to eight years later, has reached the colleges now. Statistics reveal that colleges and universities may be hard pressed to find an adequate number of instructors in the years ahead.

Consider these facts. About one-third of the college-age youth are now enrolled in institutions of higher learning. During the past thirty years the percentage of college-age youth who have actually gone on to higher education has increased each year. As Figure 12 indicates, approximately nine million students will be enrolled in institutions of higher learning at the undergraduate level by 1975. This number is nearly double the size of present enrollments. It follows that the need for teachers will also increase proportionately during the next ten to fifteen years. Again, the need differs according to subject areas, much the same as in secondary education.

Salaries for college teachers are improving. The best professors in the highest-paying institutions earn as much as $25,000 to $30,000 per year, in addition to royalties and consulting fees. Such high salaries go only to a few, however. And even though college teachers are now earning higher salaries, many of them continue to receive tempting offers from business and industry. Consequently, as is true in elementary and secondary schools, some college teachers leave classrooms each year for other employment, thus creating openings for personnel prepared to teach in colleges and universities. In addition, many new positions have opened up in the fast-growing junior college field.

Colleges and universities prefer that teaching-staff members have earned a doctorate, or at least a master's degree. Therefore, young people who wish to find their career in college teaching would do well to start graduate work as soon as possible after finishing the bachelor's degree. Graduate work is expensive and takes time. The earlier a future college teacher can begin his graduate work, the better for him, usually.

FIGURE 12. ENROLLMENT IN COLLEGES AND UNIVERSITIES: FALL 1955, 1965, AND 1975 (IN THOUSANDS)

Enrollment	1955	1965	1975
Total	2,660	5,526	9,012
Men	1,737	3,375	5,410
Women	923	2,152	3,602
Public institutions	1,484	3,624	6,146
Private institutions	1,177	1,902	2,866
First-time students	670	1,442	1,977
Men	416	829	1,084
Women	254	613	893
Public institutions	400	990	1,387
Private institutions	270	452	590

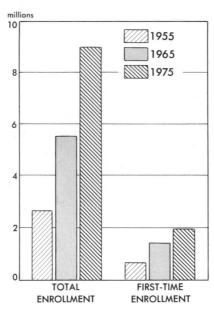

From *American Education,* II, No. 3 (March 1966), back cover.

SPECIALIZED TEACHING POSITIONS

The practice of arranging special classes, or even special schools, for exceptional children has increased during the past few years. Typical examples are classes for the mentally retarded, the physically handicapped, the emotionally disturbed, and the academically talented. These special classes demand teachers with preparation that differs somewhat from that of the regular classroom teacher.

Another type of specialization open to teachers in such fields as art, music, physical education, science, and foreign language is teaching or assisting classroom teachers with these subjects in the elementary school. Most larger schools employ such personnel, usually at higher rates of pay. Those so assigned typically work at various grade levels and often in different schools. In Hagerstown, Maryland, for example, specialists in art, music, and science supplement the work of regular classroom teachers with closed-circuit television presentations.

Other types of specialization for teachers include speech correctionist, occupational therapist, critic teacher in a college laboratory school or in a school system to which student teachers are assigned, correspondence teachers, visiting teachers, remedial-reading specialists, and evaluation specialists. In recent years, many teachers specializing in urban education have found challenging careers among educationally disadvantaged children and those speaking English as a second language.

TELEVISION TEACHING

Educational television has made much progress since 1953, when the Pittsburgh school system pioneered in experimenting with this medium. Today, hundreds of school districts are making use of televised instruction.

Figure 13 presents a sample composition of instructional teams at school, school system, and national levels. The scheme is now in use in a number of areas.

FIGURE 13. POSSIBLE PERSONNEL IN INSTRUCTIONAL TEAMS AT SCHOOL, SCHOOL SYSTEM, AND NATIONAL LEVELS

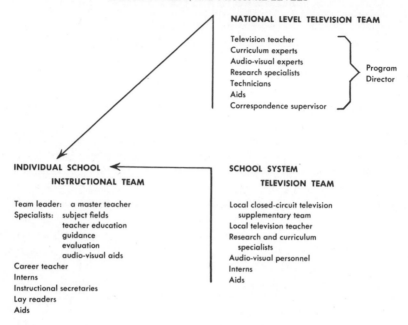

NATIONAL LEVEL TELEVISION TEAM

Television teacher
Curriculum experts
Audio-visual experts
Research specialists   Program
Technicians   Director
Aids
Correspondence supervisor

INDIVIDUAL SCHOOL
INSTRUCTIONAL TEAM

Team leader: a master teacher
Specialists: subject fields
               teacher education
               guidance
               evaluation
               audio-visual aids
Career teacher
Interns
Instructional secretaries
Lay readers
Aids

SCHOOL SYSTEM
TELEVISION TEAM

Local closed-circuit television
   supplementary team
Local television teacher
Research and curriculum
   specialists
Audio-visual personnel
Interns
Aids

Practical use of television and other electronic teaching aids will require innovations in the design of school buildings. Multipurpose classrooms are necessary. Provisions have to be made for the installation and effective use of television equipment, teaching machines, and other electronic educational aids. While research has not fully determined the value of television as a mode of educational instruction, this medium undoubtedly has its place in particular learning situations, furnishing a needed change of pace in teaching.

TEAM TEACHING

Newer developments in the utilization of instructional teams to teach large groups of students, with the objective of providing for a better employment of various types and levels of teacher competence, suggest opportunities for advancement in teaching that may become more generally available in the future. In addition, the variety of possible teaching assignments made possible by team teaching suggests that teaching is moving toward a type of differentiation of personnel that has been accomplished in the field of medicine and other professions.

A good example of a successful use of the instructional team approach is provided by Evanston, Illinois, Township High School. In Evanston High School teachers "team up" to share teaching responsibilities in English, social studies, mathematics, and other subjects. The instructional team approach is based upon the belief that differentiated teaching involving average, small, or large groups helps to create desired learning outcomes. In this school a modular system of scheduling also adds to flexibility, allowing class periods of varying lengths. It is likely that more and more elementary and secondary schools across the country will adopt these innovations. Some educators feel it is still too early to judge the general applicability of team teaching since a great deal depends on the quality of the teaching personnel involved. It is, however, a worthwhile example of experimentation and needed innovation.[4]

POSITIONS IN ADMINISTRATION AND SUPERVISION

Men and women with superior training, experience, and competencies serve in executive posts—such as superintendent of schools, principal, department head, supervisor, or consultant. Just as in other professions, opportunities are plentiful for those with advanced preparation who have the ability to lead others. Such positions typically pay higher salaries and permit the individual to exercise extensive responsibility for an educational program.

What kind of salaries do administrators and supervisors earn? They are surprisingly good ones even when compared to earnings

[4] J. Lloyd Trump and Delmas F. Miller, *Secondary School Curriculum Improvement* (Boston: Allyn and Bacon, 1968), pp. 307–325.

in other fields. Superintendents of schools in urban districts over 500,000 in population earn, on the average, well over $25,000 per year. Many school principals make in excess of $18,000 per year, and the top range for supervisors exceeds $15,000. Administrative salaries are attractive, as indicated in Table 23.

Good salaries, however, are not the only attractive features of work in educational administration and supervision. Such positions carry a high level of prestige and permit broad and extensive leadership in an important professional field. The work permits close association with community leaders and members of the teaching force. There are ample opportunities for creativeness, exercise of skill in human relations, guidance and development of teacher personnel, and influencing the direction of the program of education. In short, administration and supervision are prized fields of professional endeavor open to the capable teacher who prepares for them.

Capable people are being sought continually for administrative and supervisory positions. School systems compete vigorously for individuals who are prepared for leadership responsibilities.

POSITIONS IN STATE DEPARTMENTS OF EDUCATION

Each state maintains a state department of education which is ordinarily staffed with former teachers, administrators, and supervisors. Salaries for positions in state departments of education vary from state to state. Usually state department personnel make slightly more than the better-paid teachers in the state.

RESEARCH, WRITING, LECTURING, AND CONSULTING OPPORTUNITIES

Opportunities in the educational field include research, writing, lecturing, and consulting. These opportunities may be in school systems; in business or industrial concerns; or in other organizations, such as civic or fraternal associations. Also, highly talented individuals sometimes go into one or more of these activities on a

TABLE 23. MEAN MAXIMUM SCHEDULED SALARIES,[a] TEACHER AND
ADMINISTRATIVE PERSONNEL, 1962-63 TO 1969-70
(Reporting systems with enrollments of 25,000 or more)

Position	School year							
	1962-63	1963-64	1964-65	1965-66	1966-67	1967-68	1968-69	1969-70
CLASSROOM TEACHERS (systems reporting schedules for administrators).	$ 7,819	$ 8,213	$ 8,611	$ 9,025	$ 9,788	$10,530	$11,254	$12,274
SUPERVISORY PERSONNEL ASSIGNED TO INDIVIDUAL BUILDINGS								
Supervising principals								
Elementary	10,597	11,345	11,732	12,499	13,295	14,378	15,428	16,657
Junior high	11,297	11,981	12,301	13,115	14,058	15,120	16,289	17,521
Senior high	12,064	12,682	13,236	14,062	14,973	16,188	17,408	18,735
Assistant principals								
Elementary	9,882	10,129	10,649	11,316	12,027	12,825	13,596	14,742
Junior high	10,186	10,419	10,820	11,460	12,120	13,207	14,128	14,988
Senior high	10,298	10,770	11,298	11,889	12,656	13,776	14,766	15,806
Counselors	9,094	9,183	9,421	10,314	10,960	11,844	12,525	13,484
CENTRAL-OFFICE ADMINISTRATORS								
Supervisors	11,040	12,286	11,756	12,469	13,572	14,492	15,716	16,684
Consultants and/or coordinators	...	...			13,938	15,094	16,140	17,523
Directors	13,043	13,520	14,184	14,853	16,011	17,061	18,252	19,581
Assistant superintendents	15,990	16,669	17,675	18,415	19,246	20,466	21,746	22,929

[a] Highest salaries scheduled, exclusive of long-service increments or special supplements.
From *Research Bulletin*, XXVIII, No 1 (Washington, D.C.: National Education Association), 8.

free-lance or entrepreneur basis. Successful experience as a professional educator is an aid to success in any of these fields.

LIST OF EDUCATIONAL POSITIONS

The positions that have been discussed in the foregoing pages account for perhaps 90 to 95 percent of the career opportunities in the profession of teaching. There are additional opportunities which should be mentioned, however. The following list, which is extensive but by no means complete, gives an idea of the number and variety of opportunities for teachers.

I. Elementary schools—including nursery and kindergarten
  A. Classroom teacher
  B. Teacher of special subjects, such as music or art
  C. Teacher of a subject in a departmentalized school
  D. Teacher of exceptional children
  E. Critic teacher in a laboratory school
  F. Visiting teacher
  G. Supervisor
  H. Consultant
  I. Director of research
  J. Hearing therapist
  K. Librarian
  L. Speech correctionist
  M. School psychologist
  N. Assistant principal
  O. Principal

II. Secondary schools
  A. Teacher of subject such as social studies or English
  B. Department head
  C. Guidance director
  D. Athletic coach
  E. Supervisor
  F. Librarian

    G. Visiting teacher

    H. Consultant

    I. Critic teacher in laboratory school

    J. Assistant principal

    K. Principal

III. Administrative and general services

    A. Superintendent of schools

    B. Assistant superintendent

    C. Director of research

    D. School psychologist

    E. Attendance officer

    F. Director, special fields such as public relations or audiovisual material

    G. Vocational counselor

IV. College or university

    A. Teacher

    B. Critic teacher in laboratory school

    C. Head of department

    D. Principal of laboratory school

    E. Dean of men

    F. Dean of women

    G. Business manager

    H. Registrar

    I. Director, special functions such as placement, public relations, and development

    J. Dean of a college

    K. Director of research

    L. Assistant dean

    M. Field worker in admissions

    N. Alumni secretary

    O. Vice President

    P. President

V. State Departments of Education and U.S. Office of Education

    A. Supervisor, special fields such as secondary education

    B. Director of division

    C. Assistant state superintendent

    D. Superintendent of public instruction
    E. Assistant commissioner of education
    F. Commissioner of Education of the United States
    G. Consultant to foreign governments

VI. Professional associations, such as state education associations and NEA
    A. Field worker
    B. Staff member
    C. Research worker and writer
    D. Director of division
    E. Executive secretary

VII. Educational director or consultant to noneducational organizations
    A. Business or industrial firms
    B. Chambers of commerce
    C. Service agencies, such as heart fund
    D. Religious organizations
    E. Director of recreation
    F. Camping sponsored by various agencies
    G. Youth groups—YMCA, YWCA
    H. Instructor in a hospital
    I. UNESCO
    J. Boy and Girl Scouts
    K. Labor organizations

VIII. Other opportunities
    A. Free-lance writer
    B. Member of educational consulting firm
    C. Research worker
    D. Employee of foundation
    E. Teacher in adult education program
    F. Free-lance lecturer
    G. Teacher in church or Bible school

One conclusion stands out at this point: preparation for the teaching profession qualifies an individual for many and diverse opportunities. A corollary is that positions exist in education that pay well and provide highly satisfactory work. Success in the educational field awaits those who have intelligence, personality, health, and the will to work hard.

CAREER PATTERNS OF TEACHERS

The phenomenon of career patterns of teachers has not been completely understood by educators. Consequently, this subject has not yet been dealt with very realistically. For example, teacher recruitment efforts and discussions of the possible teacher shortages have been predicated upon what "ought" to be rather than upon what is. An examination of the career pattern concept and types of career patterns will illustrate the point.

Some authorities contend that the term "career pattern" does not have a single, precise meaning. As employed here, however, it is intended to mean "the sequence of occupations in which a person engages throughout his lifetime." Within this definition a person may change assignments while remaining in the same position. Similarly, he may retain his professional assignment but change positions. To illustrate, an individual may change from third-grade teacher to second-grade teacher (change of assignment) and still remain in his position in the same school (as a teacher). Or a teacher of third grade may move from one school to another, thus changing positions but not changing his professional assignment.

The two types of career patterns common to teaching are the double-track and the interrupted. In the double-track pattern, for instance, the married woman serves as a teacher and at the same time as a housewife. The interrupted career is also common in teaching. The married woman teacher takes time out from her teaching career to raise a family, and when her children reach school age she resumes her work as a teacher.

The major reason career patterns in teaching have not yet been clearly defined stems from the fact that about three-fourths of all teachers in the United States are women, over half of whom are, or have been, married. The increase in married women has been rapid since the depression days of the 1930's, when single status was required for women teachers by most school boards. In 1940, only 31 percent of women teachers were married, as compared to

80 percent at present.[5] Thus, education is becoming a promising field for women who wish to follow a double-track or interrupted career pattern. This characteristic gives teaching a distinct advantage over many other careers for women which are not adapted to such career plans. Increasingly, this fact is being recognized, not only by young women who are considering preparation for teaching, but also by the profession, which is becoming aware that women in teaching can, provided their attitudes toward their careers are healthy and their commitments sound, build a stronger profession.

FACTORS THAT WILL AFFECT PROFESSIONAL OPPORTUNITIES IN THE YEARS AHEAD

A promising future lies ahead for teachers, according to present indications. Some indications are (1) increasing population, (2) improving working conditions, and (3) increasing emphasis upon the importance of education.

INCREASING POPULATION. An increasing population means that additional teachers will be needed. Although a peak in the birth rate appears to have been reached in the mid-1960's since the tremendous rise after World War II, school enrollments will continue to grow.

IMPROVING WORKING CONDITIONS. Efforts are being made constantly to improve the working conditions of teachers. This trend will affect the profession in several ways; as welfare and working conditions improve, for example, more people will be attracted to teaching. Some of the improvements being made will necessitate additional teachers and specialists. One illustration of this factor is the trend toward the reduction of the number of pupils assigned to each teacher. The teacher-pupil ratio has declined significantly in recent years and is expected to continue to do so as all levels of government increase investments in education.

Teachers' salaries have been increasing annually at the rate of 5

[5] For a good survey of current socio-economic data on teachers, see Hazel Davis, "Profile of the American Public School Teacher, 1966," *NEA Journal,* LVI, No. 5 (March 1967), 12–15.

to 10 percent from the increments provided in adopted schedules. Although beginning salaries are still below those paid college graduates in fields such as engineering and business, when the working time is equated and the long-term increments calculated, the remuneration of teachers is more closely approaching salaries in other professions for similar amounts of preparation. It is unrealistic, for example, to compare salaries for teachers who have completed only four years of college with the income of members of the medical profession whose preparation required a minimum of eight to ten years. On the other hand, the number of working years of teachers, since their life expectancy is exceeded only by ministers, is considerably greater than those available to people in some other professions.

It is believed by many educators that substantial improvements will be made in the teaching profession itself in the years ahead. Standards for admission to the profession are being raised each year. Salaries are advancing at a steady pace. More men are becoming teachers each year. The profession is improving, thereby making teaching a more desirable career. One important reason for improvement of conditions is the fact that teachers are no longer accepting substandard environments and compensation in the same docile fashion they did in years gone by. Teacher militancy increased tremendously in the decade of the 1960's, and teacher organizations were able to gain substantial improvements in conditions of employment. In some instances, however, strike, or threat of strike, became an important weapon.

INCREASING EMPHASIS UPON THE IMPORTANCE OF EDUCATION. Even though education has always been regarded as important and necessary in a democracy such as that of the United States, a number of events has caused a reawakening of the American people to the critical importance of schools and the work of teachers. First of all, international developments have convinced thoughtful Americans that the real battlefield between democracy and communism is to be found in the schools, colleges, and universities. Because of the growing complexity of life, intellectuals, including teachers, are being accorded new stature. They are more highly regarded now than they have been in many years.

Economic conditions are lending a new importance to the contribution of schools. In an era of automation, education is absolutely essential. As machines become more complex, an increasing emphasis upon better education is imperative. Also, it is a well-recognized fact that the standard of living of a people and the educational level advance simultaneously. Great progress has been made in education in the last twenty-five years, and more achievements are predicted in the years ahead as Figure 14 shows.

FIGURE 14. EDUCATIONAL ATTAINMENT OF YOUNG ADULTS 25 TO 29 YEARS OF AGE: UNITED STATES, 1940 TO 1960, AND PROJECTIONS TO 1985

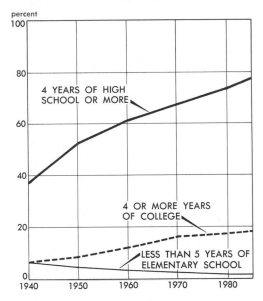

From *American Education,* I (June 1965), back cover.

Another reason education is receiving a new emphasis stems from social developments. The crisis suffered by the people of the United States during World War II and the cold war that followed, and the fact that America has been catapulted into leadership of the free world, have caused a reexamination of our system of values. There is renewed determination in the United States to come closer to realization of the ideal of equality of educational opportunity. Then, too, the value placed upon material things is being challenged by the new emphasis upon humanitarian objectives. Education is benefiting from the current reexamination of values. Consequently, the future for teachers is brighter than it has been for some time.

SUMMARY

The profession of teaching holds promising opportunities for capable young people who are *willing to work*. Good positions are available in classroom teaching, supervision, administration, research, and consulting.

The demand for competent classroom teachers remains a serious problem. Approximately 100,000 new elementary school teachers are needed each year, but only 50,000 students prepared for teaching are graduated each year. Of all the graduates prepared for elementary school teaching, a substantial proportion never enter the profession.

The supply-and-demand imbalance is not so pronounced in the secondary field as in elementary education. The problem at the secondary level is that balance is lacking between the number and types of existing positions and the distribution of individuals prepared for the various teaching fields.

Colleges and universities are diligently seeking additional faculty members. It is estimated that the demand for college teachers will increase in many fields and will remain fairly constant in others. Outstanding students who are willing and able to prepare themselves for college teaching will find many opportunities awaiting them.

In addition to regular classroom teaching positions, many opportunities are available for various types of specialists. Teachers with special preparation are needed to work with exceptional children, to serve as critic teacher, speech correctionist, occupational therapist, visiting teacher, department head, principal or superintendent, and as television or team teachers.

Certain conditions indicate a bright future for teachers. The population of the United States continues to increase. Working conditions of teachers are improving. The great reawakening of the American people to the critical importance of schools and the work of teachers that has occurred in the last decade augurs well for the future of talented and ambitious individuals who select teaching as their profession.

SUGGESTED READINGS

Calisch, R. W., "So You Want to Be a Teacher?", *Today's Education,* November 1969, pp. 49–51.

Campbell, Roald F., "Teaching and Teachers—Today and Tomorrow," *Education Digest,* November 1969, pp. 12–15.

Goodwin, Leonard, "The Academic World and the Business World: A Comparison of Occupational Goals," *Sociology of Education,* Spring 1969, pp. 170–87.

Hontz, Glenn, *Finding the Right Teaching Position.* Columbus, Ohio: Charles E. Merrill Books, Inc., 1965.

Inlow, Gail, *Education: Mirror and Agent of Change.* New York: Holt, Rinehart and Winston, 1970, Chap. 17.

Lieberman, Myron, *Education as a Profession.* Englewood Cliffs, N.J.: Prentice-Hall, Inc., 1956.

Pounds, Haskin R. and Michael L. Hawkins, "Adult Attitudes on Teaching As a Career," *The Journal of Teacher Education,* Fall 1969, pp. 339–42.

Richey, Robert W., *Planning for Teaching.* New York: McGraw-Hill Book Co., 1968, Chaps. 3 and 4.

Stinnett, T. M., *Professional Problems of Teachers.* New York: The Macmillan Co., 1968.

12.

TEACHERS' ORGANIZATIONS

THE past decade has witnessed a national reexamination of the quality and direction of American public education. The goal of equality and the ideal of excellence—long-cherished aims that have received new impetus in recent political, social, and economic developments that affect education—have made school administrators take a long look at traditional school organization and management.

An equally profound development under way today is the movement by classroom teachers to reevaluate their professional position and status within the educational system. In general, new relationships are developing among the teacher, the school administrator, and the school board. More than ever before, teachers are taking an active part in the decision-making process affecting such issues as curriculum, wages, and working conditions. John H. Fisher, president of Teachers College, Columbia University, has noted the great implications of this new development:

> Virtually every innovation in American schools during the coming decade will be influenced by the increasing insistence of teachers on the right to express their views on school policy questions.[1]

A basic assumption held by many teachers is that increased professional responsibility and influence will result in quality education. It is believed that highly qualified persons in much larger numbers will be attracted to a profession that is characterized by the

---

[1] Lowell McGinnis, "Another Look at Teacher Militancy," *Journal of Secondary Education,* XLII, No. 2 (February 1967), 78.

members' increased social and economic status and self-determination in their professional work.

The national teachers' organizations play a significant role in supporting the classroom instructor's demand for increased professional participation in the decision-making process. More than ever, teachers are looking to these organizations for assistance in implementing reforms on the local level.

The growth of teacher professionalism and the increased importance of the national teachers' associations in shaping new patterns of shared decision-making are among the most important developments in American education today. Both reflect the ferment of the times, and these complex trends will be analyzed in this chapter.

TEACHING AS A PROFESSION

Many different sets of criteria have been suggested which must be met in order to consider an occupational group professional.[2]

First, the profession must provide a unique and essential social service. It is assumed, also, that the professional is more concerned with service to be rendered than with economic advancement. The importance of the teacher has always been acknowledged, and the service he rendered considered essential. In this respect teaching has always been considered as a profession. However, the question persisted, especially in the 1960's, as to the actual decision-making role of the teacher. The traditional assumption that the teacher should passively submit to predetermined school policy and program is being seriously challenged.

The second qualification is that a professional must have had a prolonged education. He must have acquired extensive technical training and accumulated a body of theoretical knowledge to be used in the performance of his service. Education, like the other professions, has become increasingly rigorous in its requirements

[2] Criteria consolidated from Myron Lieberman, *Education as a Profession* (Englewood Cliffs, N.J.: Prentice-Hall, 1960), pp. 1–6; Paul Woodring, *Introduction to American Public Education* (New York: Harcourt, Brace & World, 1965), pp. 93–94; and William O. Stanley, "Issues in Professionalism," *Bulletin of the School of Education of Indiana University*, XL, No. 5 (September 1964), 4.

to maintain a high level of professional quality. Preparation requirements have become more specified. Those expecting to teach are now generally required to complete the equivalent of four years of college work in liberal arts and professional education courses. On the average, 50 hours of college courses are devoted to general education; 22 hours to professional education courses; 45 hours to academic teaching specialty and electives. In contrast to earlier times, when a general high school education or an unspecified number of years of additional education was sufficient, 91 percent of all teachers today have their bachelor's degree. Several states are considering making a fifth year of training mandatory, and eight states have already passed a law to that effect.

The final qualification is that of professional autonomy, the achievement of which is especially important to those involved in education. Lieberman defines professional autonomy as the range of decisions and behaviors which are left to the discretion of the professional group.[3] Any profession requires a comprehensive, autonomous organization of practitioners. The National Education Association (NEA) and the American Federation of Teachers (AFT) are the two most significant representative organizations today. Neither of the organizations, however, has control over matters considered to be vital to professional growth. Such issues as accreditation, licensing, and ethical conduct are beyond the scope and responsibility of these groups. However, both organizations are involved in the current struggle for increased teacher independence, influence, and professional status.

Although teaching appears to be a profession in several aspects, there are many obstacles preventing full professionalization. Teachers seem to take a narrow view of their potential as contributors to the educational enterprise. Too often the teacher defines himself and his co-workers as classroom operators only. This limited definition does not recognize the valid contribution the teacher can and should make in such related areas as curriculum, instructional organization, evaluation, and methodology. If teachers fail to take initiative in these areas their role will be a limited one and their function defined by other sources.

[3] Lieberman, *ibid.*, p. 89.

Other obstacles preventing full professionalization include the lack of a sufficient number of men in teaching, a source of instability to the profession. Although no significant personality or intelligence differences exist between the sexes, women tend to enter teaching on a temporary basis. Men, in general, consider it as a permanent career. There is some evidence, however, that the number of men entering the field is increasing. Finally, the status and salary of teachers is not always consistent with the service rendered. Status can be defined as the amount of prestige one is granted by other members of his society. It depends to a large extent on one's occupational role and economic level.

Lack of status among teachers is partly a result of the nature of American public educational development. As the system developed, an increased need, primarily for elementary teachers, but also for instructors at other levels, was apparent. This situation forced the acceptance of untrained, unqualified individuals into the profession. There has always been a certain percentage of unqualified teachers operating in our schools because of a continual teacher shortage. The unhappy circularity of the problem is evident: modest salaries and low status for teachers limits the number of qualified applicants, which in turn opens the jobs to unqualified and underqualified applicants, which creates salaries and working conditions commensurate with underqualified professionals, which renders the occupation unattractive, etc.

The financial rewards of teaching have also limited professional status and desirability. A great variation exists among teachers' salaries. Although federal aid to education increased in the 1960's, local school district taxing ability remains the primary determinant of teacher salary. As noted earlier, federal funds rarely are available for salaries. Obviously, salary and status are interrelated. In most cases, the initial stimulus for improving teachers' salaries will have to come from the teachers themselves.

The question most often asked is what decisions should be made by the practitioners to ensure the professionalization of education? T. M. Stinnett has stated that decisions relating to standards, certification, teachers' programs, professional growth, welfare, and the protection and discipline of members should be made by professional agencies. Such power is considered necessary, by many involved, for the achievement of professional autonomy.[4]

NATIONAL TEACHERS' ORGANIZATIONS

According to Myron Lieberman, the professional organization "Provides the machinery by which the members of an occupational group can do collectively what is impossible for them to do individually." [5] Two rival professional organizations, namely the National Education Association and the American Federation of Teachers, claim the membership of the majority of organized teachers. Each competes for recruitments and recognition. Although some observers believe that perpetuation of this division will result in the continued retardation of teacher professionalization, others see benefit to the profession from this competition.

The NEA, founded in 1857, is a complex, multifaceted organization involved in many areas of education and engaging in an endless variety of activity. It includes 33 departments, 25 commissions and committees, and 17 headquarter divisions. The Association of Classroom Teachers (ACT), totaling close to 800,000, is organized to strengthen the profession and "To help classroom teachers to improve their status and welfare and thereby upgrade the quality of service they provide for the children." [6] Other departments within the NEA complex include the AASA (American Association of School Administrators, established in 1865), the NASSP (National Association of Secondary School Principals, established in 1916), and DESP (Department of Elementary School Principals). The ATA (American Teachers Association), primarily representing black members of the profession, merged with the NEA in 1966. One index of the effect of this merger

[4] T. M. Stinnett, "Teacher Professionalization: Challenge and Promises," *Bulletin of the School of Education of Indiana University*, XL, No. 5 (September 1964), 12.

[5] Lieberman, *op. cit.* (above, n. 2), p. 257.

[6] *NEA Yearbook* (Washington, D.C.: National Education Association, 1965), pp. 134–135.

might be the election, in 1969, of Mrs. Elizabeth Koontz, a black teacher, as president of NEA.

The NEA offers a wide range of services to the profession. Various subject matter departments are engaged in research and publication. The Research Division, organized in 1922, conducts research studies concerned with teaching. Its major publication is the *NEA Research Bulletin.* This division offers extensive consulting services. Other publications of the organization include *NEA Journal, Personal Growth Leaflets,* and *The NEA Handbook.* A variety of workshops and conferences are sponsored by the National Education Association during the course of a year.

Current membership in the NEA totals over 1,115,000, most of whom are classroom teachers and other instructional personnel. The NEA, unlike the AFT, includes both teachers and administrators, although the 53 state and 8,827 local affiliated associations vary in their membership qualifications.[7] Over one-half of the American public school teachers are NEA members and over three-fourths (1,749,000) are members of affiliated state associations.[8] The NEA makes its strongest appeal in smaller towns and rural areas, but has recently moved into the urban systems with increasing success.

The AFT was formed in 1916. It is an affiliate of the AFL-CIO, and in most instances is open to classroom teachers only. The constitution of the AFT defines its objectives as follows:

(1) To bring associations of teachers into relations of mutual assistance and cooperation; (2) To obtain for them all the rights to which they are entitled; (3) To raise the standard of the teaching profession by securing the conditions essential to the best professional service; (4) To promote such a democratization of the schools as will enable them to equip their pupils to take their places in the industrial, social, and political life of the community; (5) To promote the welfare of the childhood of the nation by providing progressively better educational opportunities for all.[9]

[7] *The NEA Handbook* 1969–70, National Education Association (Washington, D.C.: The National Education Association, 1969), pp. 16–20.

[8] *Ibid.,* p. 417.

[9] *Constitution of the American Federation of Teachers,* Article II.

The total AFT membership exceeds 110,000, organized in some 450 locals concentrated in the large cities. The national governing body of the AFT is the Annual Convention, representing local affiliates according to a proportional formula. The Executive Council assumes the leadership between the annual conventions. Unlike the NEA, the AFT locals tend to be active organizational units— they are the seedbed of growing teacher militancy.

Although the AFT has not, in the past, been involved with research and publication to the extent of the NEA, the union currently is correcting this professional deficiency. AFT is now publishing various magazines, the most recent and scholarly of which is *Changing Education.* These organs are mostly concerned with professional growth, union activity, and teaching problems, very often as they relate to big city schools. Series devoted to specific problem areas are also sponsored by the AFT. "The Grassroots Research Project," financed by a federal grant to the AFT, deals with such problems as school dropouts and censorship. "The AFT Research Series" and "The Curricular Viewpoints Series" concentrate on a wider range of educational issues which relate to professional practices and vocational conditions.

NATIONAL TEACHERS' ORGANIZATIONS AND NEGOTIATION WITH SCHOOL BOARDS

A major problem confronting the NEA and AFT is the role of teachers in policy-making decisions about salary and working conditions. Traditionally, the NEA has not been as active as the AFT in programs aimed at implementing improved working conditions. However, the NEA convention in 1962 passed two significant resolutions that reflected a new attitude. The first recognized the right of teachers to negotiate with school boards regarding working conditions and salary. An increased interest in these areas reflects a new mood of the NEA. Second, the Association passed a resolution specifying the use of sanctions to settle impasses. Sanctions refer to a variety of actions initiated by state or local teacher associations to object to a specific policy. The types of sanctions which may be applied against a school district or a community and its official bodies, endorsed by the NEA as of 1966, are:

1. Censure through public notice including release of investigation report; articles in national and state journals; reports through various mass media of communication.
2. Notification to state department of education of findings concerning unsatisfactory conditions.
3. Notification to certification and placement services of unsatisfactory conditions of employment for educators.
4. Warnings to members that acceptance of employment as a new teacher in the school district would be considered unethical conduct and could lead to discharge from or future refusal of membership in the national professional association.
5. Advice to members presently employed that, if their private arrangements permit, they should seek employment elsewhere.[10]

Furthermore, the NEA's resolutions of 1966 maintain that collective negotiations between representative teacher organizations and policy-makers should be the primary mode of deliberation between the two agencies. In the late 1960's, NEA adopted the strike as a primary weapon in its organizational arsenal to deal with teacher-board impasses.

The AFT also believes in local negotiations, offering much active support for collective bargaining procedures. Until 1963 the AFT did not overtly support the strike. The National Convention of 1963, however, passed a resolution favoring the employment of the strike in certain instances and urged the AFL-CIO to support such actions.

The difference between the NEA's "professional holiday," by which a teaching group refuses to work for a specified number of days, and AFT's strike, is one of degree, frequency of use, and semantics. The difference between the NEA's "collective negotiation" and AFT's "collective bargaining" is questionable. There is no internal agreement as to the definition of each term. It appears therefore that the difference between the NEA and AFT is, in part, an ideological one stemming essentially from the former

---

[10] National Commission of Professional Rights and Responsibilities, *Guidelines for Professional Sanctions,* rev. ed. (Washington, D.C.: National Education Association, 1966), p. 9.

group's inclusion of administrators, and the latter group's affiliation with labor.

COLLECTIVE NEGOTIATION

"Collective negotiation" (a term which refers to the various negotiation processes used) came of age in the 1960's. Until recently, the teacher and his organizations had little power in their relations with the school administration on employment issues.

Federal legislation has been concerned with business and union activity. Of particular note are the Norris-LaGuardia Act (1932), which granted minimum rights to the union, and the NLRA (Wagner Act, 1935), which recognized the right of employees to organize and be protected. However, teachers and other public employees were excluded by the terms of these acts. Education is a function of the state. The state delegates much power to local boards, so these local agencies are, in fact, political subdivisions of the state. Because teachers are contracted by the local boards, they are public employees, and not affected by legislation pertaining to employees involved in private businesses.

However, two events mark the turning point in teachers' involvement in collective negotiation procedures. In 1961, public school teachers of New York City went on strike for improved conditions of employment. Following this action, the New York Board agreed to enter into a new type of relationship with its teachers, similar to the one commonly existing between labor and management. The agreement provided for the recognition of one professional organization to represent the teachers. The United Federation of Teachers (UFT) was elected to be the exclusive bargaining unit for the New York City teachers. Such agreement and recognition were acknowledged in a written form. The second development was the issuance of Executive Order #10988. Presented by President John F. Kennedy in January of 1962, the order gave federal employees the right to voice their concern regarding working conditions through a collective employee organization. Both developments stimulated the rise of purposeful employee organizations and the establishment of collective bargaining procedures.

The first legislation for teacher-board bargaining was enacted in 1959. By 1970, legislation authorizing or requiring collective negotiation was enacted in seventeen of the states. Alaska, California, Connecticut, Florida, Maryland, Massachusetts, Michigan, Minnesota, Nebraska, New Hampshire, New Jersey, New York, Oregon, Rhode Island, Texas, and Washington followed Wisconsin's lead, each passing laws providing for teacher-board collective negotiations in school districts. Most states, however, still have no statutory or judicial requirements regarding collective negotiations. Thus, most school districts are legally free to formulate their own policies regarding collective bargaining procedures between teachers and the board. The policies of these local agencies are tempered to a large extent by the attitudes of the community they represent.

Many problems surround the struggle for collective rights. There is much question as to the best means of representing teachers in collective negotiation procedures. Both the NEA and AFT favor exclusive representation—i.e., a single, elected organization to represent all teachers, regardless of affiliation, in a certain district. Other groups favor dual representation (both organizations would send delegates), and still others suggest an open election. A related question is: Who shall be represented? Perhaps even more basic is the question of what is negotiable. Teachers want collective bargaining opportunities for more than economic reasons alone. They are also concerned with participation in educational policy decisions and with the achievement of organizational security clauses.

The issue of method is central here. Collective bargaining agreements will give more bargaining power to the teacher organizations. If an impasse is reached, and neither board nor teacher representative will yield, the teachers can resort to coercive or semicoercive measures. Both the NEA and AFT have done so. In 1964, for example, the NEA instituted a two-day "professional holiday" in Utah to encourage an increased appropriation of funds for educational purposes. Teachers remained away from their classes during this time. The statewide NEA "strike" by Florida teachers in the late 1960's further illustrates organizational efforts to coerce education decisions. The AFT has sponsored various strikes, especially since 1963. Both organizational tactics result in a temporary withdrawal of the vital services of the teacher. As mentioned before, although both groups have this potential source of power, the AFT has resorted more often to its use. The decade ahead promises increased work stoppages, walkouts, strikes, and other militant activity by organized teachers. The frequency of these disruptions may be related to the success of workable alternatives. Collective negotiation agreements likely will become common. The implementation of these agreements through good faith bargaining, mediation, and arbitration is the key to labor peace in the schools.

SUMMARY

The issues of professionalism, organizational development, and collective negotiation all involve an increase of teacher power. If further professionalization is to occur, if the attainment of organizational autonomy is to be a fact, if teachers are to be granted some right of participation in policy, the traditional balance within the educational system will inevitably be altered. The monopoly of power held by local agencies will be undermined somewhat as unilateral decision-making gives way to bilateral negotiation. The hesitation of the public is to be expected, for such an alteration will give teachers a greater power than ever before. The welfare of the nation at large is dependent upon the wisdom with which this power is exerted.

Thus, a warning must be issued to future and present teachers alike. Social power will inevitably be used to advance professional and vocational ends. It is the teacher's professional duty, however, not to employ methods, nor define objectives, that are inconsistent with the public interest. Teachers deserve better working conditions, improved salaries, and more professional status; but occupational improvement must not be made at the expense of quality education. The primary obligation of the teaching profession, even while attempting vocational welfare and occupational recognition, is to the society which it serves.

SUGGESTED READINGS

Ackerly, Robert L., and S. Stanfield Johnson, *Critical Issues in Negotiations Legislation.* Professional Negotiations Pamphlet No. Three. National Association of Secondary School Principals, 1969.

Elam, Stanley, Myron Lieberman, and Michael Moskow, *Readings on Collective Negotiations in Public Education.* Chicago: Rand McNally and Co. 1967.

Epstein, Benjamin, *What is Negotiable?* Professional Negotiations Pamphlet Number One. Washington, D.C.: The National Association of Secondary School Principals, 1969.

Illinois Association of School Boards, *When Boards Negotiate or Bargain.* Springfield, Illinois: IASB, December, 1967.

Lieberman, Myron, and Michael Moskow, *Collective Negotiations for Teachers.* Chicago: Rand McNally and Co., 1966.

Rehmus, Charles M., and Evan Wilner, *The Economic Results of Teacher Bargaining: Michigan's First Two Years,* No. 6. The Research Papers. Institute of Labor and Industrial Relations, The University of Michigan, 1968.

Rosenthal, Allen, *Pedagogues and Power: Teacher Groups in School Politics.* Syracuse, New York: Syracuse University Press, 1966.

Rosenthal, Allen, *School Boards in an Era of Conflict.* Stanford University: Cubberly Conference Highlights, July 26–28, 1966.

West, Jonathan P., and William R. Hazard, *Perceptions in Teacher-Board Negotiations.* Beverly Hills, California: The Center for Study in Educational Personnel Policies, Inc., 1969.

13.

EDUCATION AND
THE FUTURE

THE decade of the 1960's undoubtedly will be recorded by future historians as a major turning point in American education. During no other period were the schools subjected to such close and critical examination. The entire educational establishment was exposed to the scrutiny of lay as well as professional critics; teaching and learning became subjects debated by all kinds of people. Somewhat sobering, but extremely useful, this general probing and dissecting resulted in unprecedented intervention by the federal government in sponsorship of projects for the improvement of education at all levels. At lower echelons, states and municipalities also contributed materially to new programs.

It will be for the historians to determine the effects of such spending on the nation's schools. It is clear that the 1960's saw only the beginning of a new era of heightened ideals and expectations. The road ahead has only been partially charted, and it will prove to be rocky a good part of the way. Major controversies and problems will inevitably arise as fundamental transformation of the educational system takes place. However, educators and laymen alike agree that education in the future must take bold and imaginative steps to meet rapidly changing conditions in modern America.

Thus, teachers will be part of a movement which promises to be one of the most exciting in the history of the United States. What changes can one look forward to in the next generation? What innovations, already begun or in the offing, will become standard procedures in the years ahead? How will institutions change, and how will the lives of teachers change? In this final chapter, a few basic developments which are bound to affect teaching will be examined. These are (1) new approaches to urban education, (2) increased use of technology in the classroom, (3) more research and development in education, (4) innovations in school administration, (5) closer school-community relations, and (6) growing importance of junior colleges.

NEW APPROACHES TO URBAN EDUCATION

The biggest challenge facing educators is the upgrading of urban schools where enormous demographic changes, deteriorated neighborhoods, and outmoded educational plant and equipment have combined to create a monumental problem. This is not to say that serious problems are absent from suburban schools, which, as a matter of fact, were beginning to experience some of the difficulties of the urban schools as the decade of the 1960's ended. The gravity and intensity of the problem, however, is far exceeded in city school systems.

The nature of the population entering the central, or inner city, following World War II, was radically different from the city dwellers, who for a long time had sent their children to urban public schools. The influx of large numbers of black, Puerto Rican, Mexican, and other minority peoples placed an obligation upon large city systems such as New York, Chicago, Los Angeles, and Detroit, to accommodate the children of these families and to help integrate them into the urban culture. Overenrollments and insufficient financial resources, alone, were not to blame for the chaotic conditions which developed. The sheer lack of teachers and administrative staff equipped to understand and handle the new school population accounted for a large portion of the difficulty. Title I of the Elementary and Secondary Education Act of 1965 was the first major attempt to provide assistance to schools serving low-income families. Private corporations and foundations have also lent support to projects aimed at upgrading education in the inner city. However, no major impact or dramatic change had resulted from the efforts of these agencies as the country entered the decade of the 1970's.

Thus, the problem of serving the minority children in the inner city continues and is especially critical where school population is predominantly black. It is important to note that educators are agreed that the ghetto environment must be altered to provide maximum educational opportunities for the children trapped in the pattern of existing slums.

But how can this objective be achieved? The influential "Coleman Report" [1] revealed how complex is the problem of attaining quality education in today's cities. Based on a 1965 survey of approximately a million students in 6,000 schools, the report showed that economic factors in the composition of a student body are more important than racial considerations in creating the best learning environment for the disadvantaged Negro. In other words, a lower-class Negro had a better chance of achievement in a school where there were substantial numbers of middle-class students—white or Negro—than a lower-class Negro attending a school with lower-class white students. Furthermore, according to the Coleman Report, the popular notions that black schools do not spend as much money per pupil, have larger classes than white schools, and employ inferior teachers, could not be supported. Socio-economic background, personal attitudes, and sense of worth, were cited by the report as important variables in educational accomplishment. The Coleman Report has been criticized on a number of counts, but it brought out useful information and interesting conclusions. [2]

The basic dilemma facing urban educators is that the Negro middle class is far too small to create the adequate balance suggested by Coleman and his team of researchers. Some educators see little hope for meaningful progress in improvement of ghetto schools until massive school integration takes place between in-

[1] James S. Coleman, *et al., Equality of Educational Opportunity* (Washington, D.C.: Office of Education, 1966).
[2] See Christopher Jencks, "A Reappraisal of the Most Controversial Educational Document of Our Time," New York *Times,* August 10, 1969, for a provocative evaluation.

ner-city students and middle-class white children. On the other hand, the recent campaigns by black militants to establish neighborhood control of schools has been considered by many Negroes to be a more realistic alternative.

A fundamental approach to urban school problems has been the reappraisal of the role of the school district in the city today. Many educators agree with the report of the U.S. Commission on Civil Rights [3] that the neighborhood school no longer fulfills its historic role in providing a democratic cross section of students from families with varied social and economic backgrounds. The population of school districts has become relatively homogeneous through the gradual process of compartmentalization by class and race.

Plans for abandoning traditional concepts of school districts have evolved in a number of cities. Such ideas include the "educational park," a complex of schools on a single site that can serve students from all over the city. Some of the projects like the New York City Plan combine elementary and secondary schools (see Figure 15; others are clusters of either elementary or high schools. The Syracuse Plan, for example, would close the present elementary schools and reassign all the children to four new educational parks built on the city's outskirts.

Other cities are considering modified programs such as the Evanston (Illinois) Plan, which eliminated the elementary school in the predominantly Negro school district and transferred the students to other schools according to a uniform and predetermined racial ratio.

One of the most innovative ideas for rearrangement of both school and student is the "school without walls." Still in its early stages of development, this plan, largely for high school students, eliminates dependence on fixed classrooms and conventional school buildings. The Parkway School in Philadelphia is an example of such a school operating in warehouses, factories, business establishments, museums, and other locations where small groups through informal contacts follow a flexible and action-oriented

[3] U.S. Commission on Civil Rights, *Racial Isolation in the Public Schools,* 2 vols. (Washington, D.C., 1967).

FIGURE 15. PLAN FOR NEW YORK'S NEW EDUCATIONAL PARK

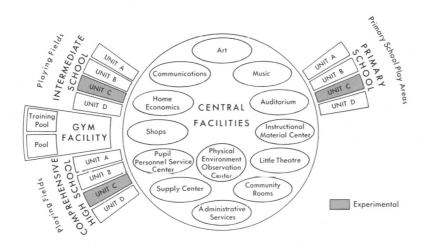

Plan for New York's new educational park provides for primary schools for 2,800 pupils, intermediate schools for 3,600, and a comprehensive high school for 4,000. Students will be grouped in units of 700 each in the primary schools, 900 in the intermediate schools, and 1,000 in the high school. The central unit will offer common facilities for all schools in the complex.

From "Schools Make News," *Saturday Review,* November 19, 1966, p. 93. Reprinted by permission.

curriculum.[4] The Chicago Public Schools have organized during 1970 the "Metro High School," in which randomly selected students from each of the city's secondary schools will make use of the city's cultural, business, athletic, and other facilities in a simi-

[4] "Philadelphia's School Without Walls," *American Teacher* (American Federation of Teachers), LIV, No. 5 (January 1970), 12–13.

lar program which promises to increase the retention powers of the urban high school system.[5]

INCREASED USE OF TECHNOLOGY IN THE CLASSROOM

Since the late 1950's, education has participated in the technological revolution.[6] In the coming decades we are certain to see an increased use of machines and programmed materials to enrich the learning environment and enable the teacher to guide more closely the progress of the individual student. It is clear also that the teacher of tomorrow will need more training in the teaching strategies as well as operation of the growing number of classroom devices.

The first extensive development in the use of technology for individualized instruction were the foreign-language laboratories, which grew from forty-six in 1958 to more than 7,000 by 1967. An increasing number of schools are using programmed materials that employ a computer to enable each student to advance at his own learning speed. In some colleges and universities like the University of Wisconsin, physical science experiments performed by the instructor are videotaped and later viewed by the student on his own television set as he, himself, performs the experiment in laboratory class. Here, too, technology allows the student to work at his own speed since he can stop or replay the tape if necessary.

In group instruction, educational television, sound tape recordings—and the less-recent teaching aids of films and records —have already demonstrated their value and are recognized as valuable devices in creating new approaches to learning. The teacher of tomorrow will be using technology in all its varied forms to extend the world of learning beyond the limits of the printed page and classroom walls.

[5] "For Chicago: A New Kind of High School," Chicago *Daily News*, October 15, 1969, p. 38.

[6] James E. Allen, Jr., "Technology and Educational Renewal," speech before annual convention of educational broadcasters, Washington, D.C., November 10, 1969 (mimeographed).

MORE RESEARCH AND DEVELOPMENT IN EDUCATION

Until recently the United States has shown little interest in investing money on basic research and the development of learning materials and technology—despite the fact that education is the country's largest "industry," spending approximately $40 billion dollars at all levels. Today the situation has changed greatly, and we can expect to see further advancements in this important area.

Research and development centers have been established at several universities through the assistance of the Office of Education to perform basic research in learning problems. At Harvard, for example, educators with the cooperation of the school systems in Boston, Cambridge, Newton, Concord, and Lexington, studied the psychological and cultural differences among school children. Curriculum centers, also funded in part by federal grants, are bringing together school and university educators in the development and experimentation of new learning materials.

Foundations and corporations are taking an active role in research and development. Educational Development Center in Cambridge, Massachusetts, a curriculum project receiving funds from the Ford Foundation, has been working with scholars like Harvard psychologist Jerome Bruner in research on the learning process and the development of new methods of instruction. Large corporations like Xerox and IBM are developing materials and equipment for classroom use as the implications of the new technology for educational purposes become increasingly apparent.

A successful program of research, development, and diffusion of the "packages and programs" is a lengthy and complex process. However, educators agree that more than ever basic research and experimentation in the learning process are necessary to meet the challenges of the decades ahead.

INNOVATIONS IN
SCHOOL ADMINSTRATION

The typical American school used to take a summer vacation along with its students. Today in many cities both the school and the students are on the job all year long. The trend is certain to continue as administrators experiment with ways to increase learning opportunities while using costly school plants with maximum efficiency.

Many schools are expanding their summer sessions for regular course work as well as for enrichment and remedial courses. Undoubtedly there will be a widespread acceptance at the elementary and secondary level of the four-quarter system that many colleges and universities already use. The years ahead will see many exciting innovations as educators reevaluate the traditional school-year calendar.

We are certain to see new ideas in other areas of school administration. More flexible personnel policies will be established to enable artists, writers, and composers to enrich the curriculum by teaching on a part-time basis. Greater use of teacher aides will become prevalent to relieve the teacher of routine administrative paperwork and allow him more time for research and lesson preparation.

CLOSER SCHOOL-COMMUNITY
RELATIONS

In the years ahead school administrators and local citizens will be working closely in developing new educational policies and programs. More than ever, the schools are attempting to meet the problems arising from economic and social conditions in the community. Head Start Programs for disadvantaged youngsters, for example, call for close cooperation between school and civic leaders. Reevaluation of school district lines, plans for educational parks, new proposals in curriculum and school-year scheduling, programs in adult vocational training—all of these educational issues and many others will require good working relationships between the school and the community to meet the challenges of contemporary America.

NEW IMPORTANCE OF THE JUNIOR OR COMMUNITY COLLEGES

One of the most dramatic developments in higher education, and one which should affect thousands of teachers in the future, is the great increase in enrollments at the junior-college level. Approximately 25 percent of students entering college today do so at a junior college. A good proportion of such institutions are of a public nature and are classified as community colleges.

Offering a two-year program which meets diverse needs, the junior college has had phenomenal growth since World War II. In the early 1920's fewer than 200 existed, with an enrollment of only 16,000. By 1950 the number had risen to more than 600, with approximately 466,000 students. At present there are more than 800 junior colleges, with a total enrollment exceeding 1.5 million students.

The community college plays an important role in making higher education more available for high school graduates. It is designed to offer a variety of programs to meet individual needs, often in the area of preparation for certain vocations. For many students the community college furnishes a stepping-stone for further work at a four-year institution, especially for marginal students whose academic records in high school bar them from entering colleges of their choice or who are uncertain about future plans. More and more junior college graduates who have "found" themselves in a two-year institution are being accepted by well-rated universities where they go on to attain degrees.

Teachers for junior colleges will be increasingly in demand in the decade of the 1970's. Estimated instructional staff in junior colleges, public and private, during 1967–68 was 76,000. By 1977–78 the projected number of instructors in such institutions is estimated at 133,000.[7] Especially those with master's degrees

[7] *Projections of Educational Statistics to 1977–1978* (Washington, D.C.: U.S. Dept. of Health, Education, and Welfare, 1968), pp. 60–61.

(and many with doctor's degrees) will be interested in this growing field. Experienced high school teachers undoubtedly will be recruited for two-year colleges, leaving openings for prospective secondary school instructors. The increased importance of the community college will also bring together college and high school teachers in attempts at needed articulation through curriculum planning in many areas.

SUMMARY

The 1960's marked an historic turning point in American education. New policies and programs have set higher than ever our country's educational ideals and expectations. In the years ahead it is clear that a basic transformation of American education will take place to meet the demands of changing economic and social conditions.

In urban education new programs to aid the disadvantaged are under way with public and private assistance. Plans for abandoning traditional concepts of school districts are evolving in many cities. Educational parks, for instance, are being developed to meet the problems of economic and racial segregation.

In classrooms everywhere advances in technology as well as in educational research and development will assist the teacher in providing quality instruction. Innovations in scheduling and school use will also take place as administrators experiment with ways to increase learning opportunities and maximize school plant efficiency.

In the community, closer relations between the school and citizens will develop as the educational system attempts to meet the problems of contemporary society.

In higher education the junior college will assume a role of new importance as greater numbers of students continue their education beyond high school.

All of these developments will closely affect teachers—members of a profession in one of its most exciting and innovative periods in history.

SUGGESTED READINGS

Anderson, Robert H., *Teaching in a World of Change*. New York: Harcourt, Brace and World, Inc., 1966.

Brown, B. Frank, *The Appropriate Placement School: A Sophisticated Nongraded Curriculum*. Englewood Cliffs, N.J.: Prentice-Hall, Inc., 1965.

Cuban, Larry, *To Make a Difference: Teaching in the Inner City*. New York: The Free Press, 1970.

Frost, Joe L., and G. Thomas Rowland, *Curricula for the Seventies*. Boston: Houghton Mifflin Co., 1969.

Gard, Robert R., "A Realistic Look at Flexible Scheduling," *The Clearing House*, March 1970, pp. 425–29.

Gleazer, Jr., Edmund, "The Community College Issue of the 1970's," *Educational Record*, Winter 1970, pp. 47–52.

Kelley, Win and Leslie Wilbur, "Junior College Development in the United States," *School and Society*, December 1969, pp. 485–98.

LeBaron, Walt, "Technological Forces and the Teacher's Changing Role," *The Journal of Teacher Education*, Winter 1969, pp. 451–64.

Palmer, Edward L., "Can Television Really Teach?", *American Education*, September 1969, pp. 2–6.

Polos, Nicholas C., "Flexible Scheduling—Advantages and Disadvantages," *Education*, April–May 1969, pp. 315–19.

Sargent, Cyril G., John B. Ward, and Allan R. Talbot, "The Concept of the Education Park," in *The Schoolhouse in the City*, Toffler, Alvin, ed. New York: Frederick A. Praeger, Publishers, 1968, pp. 186–99.

Shane, Harold G., and June G. Shane, "Forecast for the 70's," *Today's Education*, January 1969, pp. 29–32.

Skinner, B. F., *The Technology of Teaching*. New York: Appleton-Century-Crofts, 1968.

Smiley, Marjorie B., and Harry L. Miller, eds., *Policy Issues in Urban Education*. New York: The Free Press, 1968.

Wisniewski, Richard, *New Teachers in Urban Schools: An Inside View*. New York: Random House, 1961.

INDEX